Nation, State and Empire in English
Renaissance Literature

Nation, State and Empire in English Renaissance Literature

Shakespeare to Milton

Willy Maley
Department of English Literature
University of Glasgow

First published 2003 by
PALGRAVE MACMILLAN
Houndmills, Basingstoke, Hampshire RG21 6XS and
175 Fifth Avenue, New York, N.Y. 10010
Companies and representatives throughout the world.

PALGRAVE MACMILLAN is the global academic imprint of the Palgrave Macmillan division of St Martin's Press, LLC and of Palgrave Macmillan Ltd. Macmillan® is a registered trademark in the United States, United Kingdom and other countries. Palgrave is a registered trademark in the European Union and other countries.

ISBN 0–333–64077–2

This book is printed on paper suitable for recycling and made from fully managed and sustained forest sources.

A catalogue record for this book is available from the British Library.

Library of Congress Cataloging-in-Publication Data
Maley, Willy.
    Nation, state, and empire in English Renaissance literature: Shakespeare to Milton/Willy Maley.
        p. cm.
    Includes bibliographical references (p.) and index.
    ISBN 0–333–64077–2
        1. English literature – Early modern, 1500–1700 – History and criticism. 2. Nationalism and literature – Great Britain – History – 16th century. 3. Nationalism and literature – Great Britain – History – 17th century. 4. Shakespeare, William, 1564–1616 – Political and social views. 5. Milton, John, 1608–1674 – Political and social views. 6. Nationalism in literature. 7. Imperialism in literature. 8. State, The, in literature. 9. Renaissance – England. I. Title

PR428.N37 M35 2002
820.9'358–dc21
                                                                2002068341

10 9 8 7 6 5 4 3 2 1
12 11 10 09 08 07 06 05 04 03

Printed and bound in Great Britain by
Antony Rowe Ltd, Chippenham and Eastbourne

For Andrew Hadfield – friend, Roman, countryman and lender of ears.

Contents

Acknowledgements

Earlier versions of the named chapters appeared in the following publications, and the original editors and publishers are gratefully acknowledged.

Chapter 1 first appeared as '"This Sceptred Isle": Shakespeare and the British Problem', in John Joughin (ed.), *Shakespeare and National Culture* (Manchester University Press, 1997; reprinted with the permission of Manchester University Press).

Chapter 2 first appeared as 'Postcolonial Shakespeare: British Identity Formation and *Cymbeline*', in Jennifer Richards and James Knowles (eds), *Shakespeare's Late Plays: New Readings* (Edinburgh University Press, 1999; reprinted with the permission of Edinburgh University Press).

Chapter 3 was first published as 'Shakespeare, Holinshed and Ireland: Resources and Con-texts', in Mark Thornton Burnett and Ramona Wray (eds), *Shakespeare and Ireland: History, Politics, Culture* (Macmillan, 1997).

The first section of Chapter 4 appeared as 'Dialogue-wise: Some Notes on the Irish Context of Spenser's *View*', in *Connotations: A Journal for Critical Debate* 6, 1 (1996/97), pp. 67–77, and an earlier version of the second section will be published as '"This ripping of auncestors": The Ethnographic Present in Spenser's *A View of the State of Ireland*', in Philippa Berry and Margaret Tudeau-Clayton (eds), *The Texture of Renaissance Knowledge* (Manchester: Manchester University Press, 2003).

Chapter 5, '"Another Britain?": Bacon's *Certain Considerations Touching the Plantation in Ireland* (1606)', appeared in *Prose Studies: History, Theory, Criticism* 18, 1 (1995; reprinted with the permission of *Prose Studies* and Frank Cass).

Chapter 6 appeared as 'Fording the Nation: The Abridgement of the British Problem in *Perkin Warbeck* (1633)', in Andrew Murphy (ed.), special early modern issue of *Critical Survey* 9, 3 (1997; reprinted with the permission of *Critical Survey* and Berghahn Books) (an earlier version had appeared as 'The Incorporation of Identities in *Perkin Warbeck*: A Response to Lisa Hopkins', in *Connotations: A Journal for Critical Debate* 7, 1 (1997/98), pp. 105–15).

Chapter 7 first appeared as 'Milton and "the Complication of Interests" in Early Modern Ireland', in Balachandra Rajan and Elizabeth Sauer (eds), *Milton and the Imperial Vision* (Pittsburgh, PA: Duquesne University Press, 1999; reprinted with permission of Duquesne University Press).

A version of Chapters 5 and 7 appeared in 'The British Problem in Three Irish Tracts by Spenser, Bacon, and Milton', in Brendan Bradshaw and Peter Roberts (eds), *British Consciousness and Identity: The Making of Britain, 1533–1707* (Cambridge: Cambridge University Press, 1998; reprinted with permission of Cambridge University Press).

*

I would like to thank the two anonymous readers at Palgrave Macmillan who commented on successive drafts of this work. Due to pressures of time and space, I was able to respond more fully to the first than to the second, but that second reader can be sure that their stringent and sensitive suggestions will be taken on board for my next monograph. I owe heartfelt thanks to Becky Mashayekh at Palgrave Macmillan, who helped prise my fingers from the final typescript.

Foreword

John Kerrigan

Where is Willy Maley coming from? A quick way to answer that question is to look at his address. 'Department of English, The University of Glasgow' it starts, and the mix of Irish and Scottish themes in his work (his sense of how significantly they interact) makes a lot of sense in the context of the city where he was born, brought up and teaches. Now that the Scots have their own parliament as well as their own legal system, football team and liking for Irn-Bru, anyone writing to Maley would be wise to put 'Scotland' after 'Glasgow G12 8QQ'. But Scotland has not yet wriggled out from under the thumb of Westminster, so that line in the address feels both supplementary and incomplete. The postman might not need much more help. But if you're writing from Tucson or Tokyo, should you add 'Great Britain' or 'United Kingdom' or both?

Addresses do not just specify what estate agents call 'location, location, location'. The alternative endings to Maley's address each proposes a different relationship with England, Wales and the divided territory of Ireland. They are fraught with politics, and, in the ceaselessly interactive regions of the North Atlantic littoral, that means fraught with history. Indeed, those competing addresses have a chronological as well as a geographical order. 'Scotland' was forged out of different peoples into an independent kingdom in the high Middle Ages (the Declaration of Arbroath, 1320, is often picked out as a decisive event), though it did not secure its present boundaries until the fifteenth century. 'Great Britain' acquired a regal existence in 1603, when James VI of Scotland came to the English throne, but the new entity did not develop much of an apparatus of statehood or cultural infrastructure until after the Treaty of Anglo-Scottish Union in 1707. As for 'United Kingdom', England/Wales and Scotland were declared a united kingdom in 1707, but rebellious Ireland was added in 1801, only for twenty-six of its counties to break away in 1922, leaving a large proportion of the population of the remaining six counties bidding to do likewise after 1968.

In his research Maley has shed light on the confusions and contradictions generated by this process of geopolitical change by focusing on the literature and culture of a formative period: the late sixteenth and early seventeenth centuries. His first book – very much a precursor of the present work – was *Salvaging Spenser: Colonialism, Culture and Identity* (1997). With tremendous innovative brio, it broke away from the emphasis in Anglo-American scholarship on the moral allegory of *The Faerie Queene*, and brought out the importance of Ireland to a poet who left England and settled in Co. Cork. Before *Salvaging Spenser*, important work had been done by (chiefly Irish) historians on the nature of Elizabethan colonialism as it exploited both Munster and Virginia. As his subtitle suggests, Maley profited from this research. But he also triangulated Spenser between the three kingdoms of the early modern 'British Isles' and brought out the significance of Scotland to the poet's thinking about the English in Ireland.

This bold contribution to Spenser studies prepared Maley to make the link with the 'new British history' which underpins the present book. A few words of background are necessary. For generations, English historians had debated the causes of the civil wars of the 1640s. As Whig constitutional and Marxist economic explanations of the crisis were discredited, scholars began to look beyond England and to focus (in the late 1980s) on the so-called 'British problem': the difficulty of governing the three religiously and culturally heterogeneous kingdoms of the Stuart multiple monarchy in ways which did not generate concatenating instabilities. There were problems with 'the British problem', not least the fact that its exponents identified the Irish Rebellion of 1641 as a trigger of disaster but did not fit Ireland into their formulation. By not giving Ireland an address in the British problem, they failed adequately to address that problem. Whatever the drawbacks of the new British history, however, work on the early modern period has been galvanized by the changed agenda.

Willy Maley is only one of a number of scholars excited by the implications of this new British history for our understanding of Renaissance literature. Among those exploring the field are Andrew Hadfield, David Baker, Philip Schwyzer and myself. Journal articles and books are starting to fill the shelves. But Maley's Scottish–Irish axis makes him distinctively receptive to the new paradigm and alert to its limitations. When, in *Nation, State and Empire in English Renaissance Literature*, he looks at the British and Irish problematic as it develops from Spenser through Shakespeare to Ford and Milton, he does not just bring a fresh historical perspective to bear on familiar (and some strikingly unfamiliar) literary texts, but seeks to use the literature to correct the biases and blindspots of the historiography. True to his intellectual roots in the British Left (the Raymond Williams tradition), he brings out issues of class, violence and language, and is acutely self-aware about the implication of the new British history in devolutionary politics. He also concentrates on regions arguably under-analysed by cultural historians (though he in turn neglects Wales and matters Anglo-Welsh). Hence his attention to Ulster in the essays on Bacon and Milton. As a site where Scottishness, Irishness and Englishness met in the plantations of the early seventeenth century, this contested, bloodstained region became (as it has remained) a crucible of British identity formation.

Given Maley's interest in Ulster and colonialism in Ireland generally, it might seem strange for him to make so much use in this book of the language of postcolonial theory. How could Ireland be 'post-' something that was only just happening to it? As his vigilant, probing chapters on 'Shakespeare, Holinshed, and Ireland' and on Spenser's *View of the State of Ireland* bring out, the area around Dublin had been an Anglo-Norman colony since the thirteenth century, and a great deal of what was taken to be Irish by early modern English people had been brought to Ireland by their ancestors. Moreover, although the Old English descendants of the original colony remained attached to England and were regarded both by themselves and by many of the Gaelic Irish as culturally distinct, they were seen by the New English incomers of the Tudor period (neocolonialists in a postcolonial situation) as having 'degenerated' into Irish ways. So the Ireland described by Spenser's *View* resembles certain modern postcolonial societies in the sense that both the indigenous Irish and the Old English were busy hybridizing and imitating each other, developing modes of common existence under the shadow of an English polity that had culturally moved on.

If Willy Maley stopped there, this book would be less challenging. He also proposes, however, a postcolonial mentality in early modern England itself. When Henry VIII broke with the Roman Church, in the Act in Restraint of Appeals (1533), declaring 'this realm of England is an empire', he was initiating, Maley argues, an empire that 'copied (in true deconstructive fashion) the thing to which it was ostensibly opposed' (p. 35). To claim that the make-up of an expansionist Tudor England was 'copied' from the Roman empire of Julius Caesar and Augustus somehow transmitted through the medieval popes confounds too many variables, and it would be hard to substantiate from sixteenth-century sources. A clearer post-colonial moment might be found in the late thirteenth and early fourteenth centuries, when English writers chose to define their national identity against that of the Normans, who had invaded the country under William the Conqueror, at a time when English power was reaching into Ireland and Wales and claiming overlordship of Scotland. This quasi-postcolonial reaction against Norman occupation revived in the seventeenth century when those resisting arbitrary authority and exploitative law called it 'the Norman Yoke'.

But Maley has a gift for skating on thin ice. He would rather provoke an argument than put criticism to sleep. So even if he exaggerates when he says that Shakespeare's 'England was caught between empires, Roman and British, as Ireland was in James Joyce's day' (p. 4) – exaggerates not least because, at this date, England was almost wholly Protestant – the intervention is far from fruitless. It can make us think differently about such texts as Spenser's *Ruines of Time* (1591) – not a work that Maley discusses – which is set among the ruins of the Roman city of Verulamium, later St Albans. This poem has some sympathy with the ancient British queen Boudicca, who led an anti-colonialist rebellion against the occupying Romans, and it mounts a critique of the vanities of Rome as a site of empire and false religion which carries over into a complaint against the vices of late Elizabethan England. Spenser believes that the English reformation was incomplete, leaving both church and state impregnated with the bad characteristics of Roman Catholicism, but as the poem builds there are suggestions of a larger assault on the nature of empire itself – its westward migration from Rome to Britain – thoughts which go against the grain of Spenser's *View*.

As elsewhere with Maley, then, what looks like a polemical gesture turns out to change the way that we can read particular texts. But the example also points to a gap that can become an opportunity for other scholars. Although *Nation, State and Empire* notices how confessional allegiance figures in the conflicts in

Ireland, it does not make much of religion. An account of the Act in Restraint of Appeals that recognised the centrality of ecclesiastical politics to sixteenth-century history would better support the idea that Tudor England was like Joyce's Ireland. It is worth remembering that the British problem in its classic, mid-seventeenth-century incarnation caught fire in 1637 when the Scots rejected a prayerbook that they thought too 'papistical' as well as too English, and that the Irish Rebellion of 1641 was driven, in large measure, by a desire to win back rights for the Catholic religion. When Maley writes about Milton's attack on the Belfast presbyterians in his *Observations* of 1649, he is surely correct to make a connection with Anglo-Scottish politics, but the antagonism was more than political. Milton hated presbyterians because they wanted to deny liberty of worship to the independent sects in England.

In a rapidly developing new field, differences of emphasis are inevitable. And it is a genuine strength of this book that it makes you look for what it excludes. One way forward would be to devolve what it calls 'English Renaissance Literature'. Almost all the texts discussed in *Nation, State and Empire* were written within the sound of Bow Bells. It is time for poems, plays, romances and treatises produced in the English regions, including Cornwall, and from Scotland, Wales and Ireland, to be given fuller attention. The choice need not to be confined to those like Spenser, Barnabe Rich and Jeremy Taylor who went from England to the 'Celtic fringe'. There are plenty of significant figures born and bred outside England who have been either distortingly folded into Eng. Lit. or excluded from the category and left unread because their circumstances are relatively unfamiliar: William Drummond and Sir George Mackenzie (Lowland Scotland), Henry Vaughan (Breconshire), Richard Bellings (Leinster) and Roger Boyle, Earl of Orrery (Munster) to name but a few.

Then there is the question of the European context. *Nation, State and Empire* starts by discussing a revue that was staged in London in 1941 as a contribution to the war effort. Maley is struck by its opening speech, taken from Shakespeare's *King John*, which displays 'a siege mentality, England backed into a corner by Europe' (p. 8). It is true that, during Shakespeare's lifetime, many English people feared that the Catholic powers of Spain and France would use Ireland, Scotland and even Wales as badly guarded backdoors into England. But the isolationism can be overstated; and although Maley is right to say that the English lost a foothold on the continent when they ceded Calais in 1558, they soon became militarily involved in the Dutch rising against Spain in the Low Countries (where Elizabeth I was granted political rights). At the end of the period covered by this book, patriots like Cromwell were so sympathetic to the Dutch that a scheme for political union with England was put to the Netherlands in 1651. This initiative and its failure left its mark on the work of Milton and Marvell, as it did across the water on the Dutch and English poetry of Constantijn Huygens.

Yet although the centrifugal agenda of this book can stimulate the reader to go off at a tangent, its chief success is in being so direct and involving. Historically rich and trenchantly argued, it is also ebulliently verbal, seamed with irregular puns and riveted with punchy phrases. Few critics can match Willy Maley's combination of solid research and theoretical panache. Happy to explore an overdetermined work of the imagination such as *Cymbeline*, he is equally good (and this is rare) on political treatises. He shows how Bacon's 1609 *Considerations* and Milton's *Observations* grow in significance if we understand what authorities they were written for (king or commonwealth), the audiences they were aimed at (court élite or public), and the circumstances of their (instant or delayed) reception. Maley is alert to all sorts of unconsidered angles, but his attention is never merely local; he sets the stakes high, and brings the past and its sometimes obscure literature to life by making the reader recognise that we are caught in the same geopolitical flux as Spenser, Shakespeare, Ford, Bacon and Milton – that the present, like the early modern period, is a time of the breaking and making of nations.

Nation, State and Empire in English Renaissance Literature is an indispensable introduction to a topic whose moment has come. Its plentiful and hospitable footnotes give the reader a road-map of the scholarly resources available in the field, while its combative encounters with such luminaries as Stephen Greenblatt, Edward Said and Lawrence Stone put a clear line between inherited paradigms and the new British-Irish problematic. But the book is much more than a survey. Often highly original in its particular claims, it is written with a vitality that flows from Maley's understanding that to work in the field he has chosen is always a political act. This is so not just for those based in Britain and Ireland. Since we all have addresses, and are caught up in history and geopolitics, the implications of this book extend to Tucson and Tokyo. Maley makes his readers reflect on where they, as well as he, are coming from.

Liverpool, Cambridge, Co. Mayo

Introduction: Fostering Discussion – From the Irish Question to the British Problem by Way of the English Renaissance

Researching a PhD on Spenser and Ireland at Cambridge in the 1980s, I came across three essays by Roy Foster which had a profound and lasting effect on my thinking.[1] Foster was – is – a formidable and influential historian of modern Ireland. My own work as a literary critic had forced me to forage in the field of early modern Ireland, a field being parcelled out at the time by three Irish historians who, fortunately for me, were all interested in Spenser, though they did not quite see eye-to-eye on him, or much else for that matter.[2] There were many things that troubled me about Foster's work, but in a nutshell it struck me as untheoretical, anti-Marxist, anglocentric and elitist – and these were, to my mind, the Four Horsemen of the Apocalypse.[3] At the time, I lacked the critical discourse, the political nous and the historical awareness even to begin to challenge Foster's views. Over the years I have tried to develop arguments that foreground 'varieties of Englishness' to supplement his 'varieties of Irishness', and to press for the supplanting of the old Irish question with the new British Problem.[4] I have also tried where possible to introduce Scotland as a complicating factor in readings of Anglo-Irish history.[5] One of the three essays by Foster was titled '"We are all revisionists now"'. I suppose there must be some truth in that.[6] We are all of us compelled to revise our initial opinions based on deeper study.[7] Whatever influences are at play in my own work – Marxism, deconstruction, postcolonialism, the New Historicism – it has taken a revisionist turn in recent years.

At around the same time that Roy Foster was making me think harder about the shaping of modern Ireland, and Brendan

Bradshaw, Ciarán Brady and Nicholas Canny were making me rethink the role of Spenser in Ireland, I came across a body of work that was then quite new, but has since emerged as the new orthodoxy. The historiography of the 'British Problem', also known as Archipelagic history, three kingdoms history, and the new British history, identified a crisis of multiple monarchy in the 1630s and 1640s which precipitated what was hitherto known as the 'English Revolution' or 'English Civil War'.[8]

Every problem has more than one point of origin, and so it is with the British Problem. We can point to at least three sources for the new British history. The first, and arguably the most important, is John Pocock's plea almost three decades ago for a new subject: British studies.[9] The second is the significant body of work produced by historians of Scotland, Wales and Ireland, including Brendan Bradshaw, Nicholas Canny, Rees Davies, Steven Ellis, Jane Ohlmeyer, David Stevenson and Jenny Wormald.[10] The third is the shifting of ground by English historians, among them Conrad Russell and John Morrill, who, starting from a node of conflict in the mid-seventeenth century, have opened their own work up to an enlarged British context.[11] All three strands are intimately linked.

This historiographical shift has not yet been matched by a similar move in literary studies, yet it could be argued that documents of culture can offer much in the way of highlighting the tensions within the emerging British polity.[12] In particular, the English history play provides a useful starting-point in any attempt to map out the literary representation of British identity formation in the early modern period. It also subverts the short-term historical interpretations of the British Problem that confine it to the middle of the seventeenth century.

The British Problem has implications for postcolonial criticism, which too often relies on a naturalised version of the British state, because it tends to see in empire an image of modernity, thus conveniently forgetting the vicissitudes of early modern English colonialism. Rather than seeing the new British history as seeking to appropriate postcolonial theory in order to gain credibility and currency and thus become more 'sexy' or streetwise, it could be argued, conversely, that postcolonialism has been all too blind to the alternatives of British state formation, preferring to start with Empire in the eighteenth century and work its way forward, and that it has to be more attentive to national and colonial differences within the British state, as well as to earlier developments.[13]

The make-up and break-up of Britain may have been marked by a succession of failures, but the rise of English is an unqualified success story. The essays collected here fasten upon the texts, minor and major, of key figures in the English Renaissance. In their discussions of drama and prose written between 1590 and 1650, a crucial formative period in the history of the British state, these essays, taken collectively, signal a shift in studies of nation, state and empire in the early modern period. That shift is from a preoccupation with Ireland as the exemplary site of English colonial activity, towards a recognition of the complex ways in which a problematic British identity is worked out – rehearsed, resisted, revised – in the texts of some of the most influential writers of the sixteenth and seventeenth centuries.[14]

These major canonical authors are not merely reflecting on Britain as an emerging political reality. They are actively engaged in constructing – and deconstructing – its origin-myths, in blurring, as well as bolstering, its boundaries. Moreover, even as they forge a new British identity, Spenser, Shakespeare, Bacon, Ford and Milton are producing the very English culture that is threatened by this enlarged polity. The paradox at the heart of this book is that the precarious Britishness out of which these founding figures forge their colonial visions has been obscured by the emphasis, in literary criticism, on the supposedly peculiarly English culture to which they contributed.

My three opening chapters address themselves to Shakespeare, moving from the general to the particular. The first, '"This sceptred Isle": Shakespeare and the British Problem', offers an overview of the literary and historiographical concerns that motivate the collection as a whole, and may stand here as a fuller preface to the essays that follow than this short introduction can provide. In the conclusion to that first chapter, I refer to Shakespeare as 'the banished bard of Britain', precisely because of the ways in which a whole critical tradition has conspired to confine to England a playwright who plied his trade for half of his career under the auspices of a new British state. The second chapter, 'Postcolonial *Cymbeline*: Sovereignty and Succession from Roman to Renaissance Britain', picks up on the closing remarks in

Chapter 1, and focuses on a single dramatic work that can be seen to wrestle with notions of nationhood at a time when England was caught between empires, Roman and British, as Ireland was in James Joyce's day. Although it is essentially a local reading of a single text, my interpretation of this particular late play can stand here for an approach that endeavours to combine an awareness of the new British history with an understanding of postcolonial theory, within an early seventeenth-century milieu marked by union and plantation. The third chapter, 'Shakespeare, Holinshed, and Ireland: Resources and Con-texts', does something yet more specific. It takes two fragments from the Irish section of Holinshed's *Chronicles* and shows how they are adapted by Shakespeare and incorporated into two of his best-known histories, *Richard II* and *Henry V*. Taken together, these three essays constitute an attempt to make Shakespeare appear less English, and certainly less anglocentric, than his critics have hitherto allowed.

Chapter 4 is less the centrepiece of the book than its turning-point. I have been working on Spenser for more than 15 years, concentrating on mapping out a detailed Irish context for a poet who spent the majority of his working life in Ireland. 'Forms of Discrimination in Spenser's *A View of the State of Ireland* (1596; 1633): From Dialogue to Silence', is, with due acknowledgement to Roy Foster, a revisionist essay. It attempts a new reading of Spenser's *View* which is attentive to both its form as a dialogue and to its treatment of the Irish, and other (multi-)national cultures, including English. What emerges from this chapter is a Spenserian text which is at once more monological than it was previously thought to be, and more multivocal than conventional readings of it as an anti-Irish polemic would suggest.

The chapter on Spenser is followed by one on Francis Bacon – 'Another Britain?': Bacon's *Certain Considerations Touching the Plantation in Ireland* (1606; 1657)' – which breaks new ground, and in two ways. First, by bringing into the debate on the formation of a British identity an obscure and neglected treatise by Francis Bacon, and then by situating Bacon's views on the Ulster Plantation at the turn of the seventeenth century in terms of political union and unionist myth. Though less well known than Spenser's *View*, Bacon's *Considerations* is an elegant and persuasive piece of prose which takes a tack arguably unavailable to Spenser in the 1590s, using Anglo-Scottish union as a bridge between Ulster and Britain. The fifth chapter, 'Fording the Nation: Abridging History in *Perkin Warbeck* (1633)', marks a return to historical drama of the kind practised by Shakespeare. John Ford's playful tribute to the bard is barbed, though, and not just because he chooses a pretender to depict the reign of Henry VII. What makes *Perkin Warbeck* 'British' in a way that Shakespeare's English histories are not is Ford's subtle and varied use of the so-called Celtic fringe of a state that was sufficiently established by the 1630s to be feeling its first tremors, especially from Scotland, where key stages of its action unfold.

The essay on Ford leads nicely, both chronologically and conceptually, into the final chapter, 'Milton's *Observations* (1649) and "the complication of interests" in Early Modern Ireland'. At first glance, this looks like a return to the Irish question which the earlier chapters had sought to answer with a British problem. What this reading of Milton's brief and troubling tract uncovers, however, is not the anti-Irish diatribe which apologists and opponents of Milton alike have envisaged. Rather, the *Observations* do what they were asked to do, and expose the 'complication of interests' which feed political ferment in Ireland. In short, Milton's task in this text is a very British enterprise, namely to unravel and ultimately reconstitute the conflicting priorities of three warring kingdoms. As I say in the conclusion to that final chapter, England was – is – a colonising culture, and colonialism is a process that cuts both ways. Whether or not we see Milton as a poet against empire or an advocate of colonialism, like the 'sage and serious' Spenser whom he so admired, the fact remains that between the Irish question and the British problem, the undiscovered country is England – unrevolutionary England.[15]

These essays are interventions – tactical, probing, mobile, contingent – in the adjoining fields of early modern Irish history and the new British historiography. The emphasis throughout is on the shaping power of language and literature in creating and contesting national and colonial identities. Taken together, they offer a series of readings revolving around the vexed issues of identity, difference, and repetition implicit in the process of union, plantation, and conquest. English is a colonising culture, and its investment in empire is first and foremost bound up with the invention of Britain, a creative enterprise in which the writers whose work is examined here played a double part, as advocates and cross-examiners, witnesses for the defence and for the prosecution. It is for the reader to judge whether they should continue to be viewed as straightforwardly 'English' Renaissance writers, or whether they ought to be reinscribed, together with their contemporaries, within a problematic British context.

1
'This Sceptred Isle': Shakespeare and the British Problem

And some I see
That two-fold balls and treble sceptres carry
(*Macbeth* IV.i.119–20)

A scepter is one thing and a ladle another.[1]

This Shakespeared isle

In the summer of 1941, the eminent Shakespearean critic G. Wilson Knight staged a special Shakespeare revue entitled *This Sceptred Isle* at Westminster Theatre in London. Billed as a 'Dramatisation of Shakespeare's Call to Great Britain in Time of War', the performance was in three parts. The first, headed 'St. George for England', opened with Faulconbridge's lines from the conclusion of *King John*. This was followed by John of Gaunt's 'sceptred isle' oration from *Richard II*, Richard III's speech before the Battle of Bosworth against 'those bastard Britains', and Henry V's pronouncements before and during Agincourt. After a ten-minute interval, Part Two, 'Patriotism is Not Enough', comprised two soliloquies from *Hamlet*, Macbeth's vision of a line of British monarchs stretching out to 'the crack of doom', and three scenes from *Timon of Athens*, showing Timon's encounters with Alcibiades and his army, with the bandits, and with the Senators of Athens. A further interval of five minutes preceded the third and final Part, 'The Royal Phoenix', which consisted of two excerpts from *Henry VIII*, Buckingham's farewell and Cranmer's prophecy. The performance was rounded off with Queen Elizabeth's address to English troops at Tilbury before the Spanish Armada. A notice in *The Times* had reservations about Knight's acting, but praised the event and the vision of its organiser:

> the whole unusual production firmly establishes his conception of Shakespeare as the poet and prophet of a free and virile people united under a benevolent monarchy and determined to fight in themselves the evils of greed and corruption and to take up arms against tyranny and the lust for power in others.[2]

It was fitting that this call to arms should open with a bastard and end with a virgin. England was of uncertain parentage, but relied on a myth of purity of origins. It was also appropriate that the performance drew on material from a variety of genres, and that the series of dramatic monologues culminated in a 'historical' speech.

The closing speech from *King John* which opened the performance contains several recurring features of English nationalism: a siege mentality, England backed into a corner by Europe; the myth of an expatriate culture – specifically a monarchical culture – repatriated; a defiant claim to global power; and a sense of identity and a claim of right to self-determination that transcends unions and empires:

> This England never did, nor never shall,
> Lie at the proud foot of a conqueror.
> But when it first did help to wound itself.
> Now these her princes are come home again,
> Come the three corners of the world in arms,
> And we shall shock them. Naught shall make us rue,
> If England to itself do rest but true.
>
> (V.vii.112–18)

Reflecting, in the wake of the Falklands War, on this war-time production, Wilson Knight wrote:

> I have for long accepted the validity of our country's historic contribution, seeing the British Empire as a precursor, or prototype, of world-order.[3]

This Sceptred Isle summed up Wilson Knight's approach to Shakespeare's texts, which he saw as 'royal propaganda'. Out of that war-time production grew an essay of the same name on 'the British Crown' and 'Shakespeare and the nation'.[4] Remaining within the realm of Knight, this 'Shakespeared Isle' – the first British Empire – and the place of England's national bard within it, is the subject of this chapter.

There are three overlapping elements to the growing interest in the so-called 'first British empire', two of them author-based. The first is the little empire of activity that has grown up around Spenser and Ireland.[5] The second is the body of work that emerged around readings of Shakespeare's *The Tempest*, one of the best examples being Paul Brown's influential essay in Dollimore and Sinfield's *Political Shakespeare*.[6] The third is the theoretical investment in the other side of national identity, colonial Otherness, an area of interest pioneered by New Historicists, most famously Stephen Greenblatt (who has in fact touched base in all three areas).[7]

Shakespeare's corpus undergirds the Englishness of British literary culture, and his work is often enlisted in the service of a conservative English nationalism. Yet the bard was preoccupied with putting the problems of the state onto the stage. His representations of the history, formation and future of the British state are complex and heterogeneous. We find an elaboration of the British Problem in the plays of Shakespeare, works which, due to their position within the canon of *English*, are read historically as a contribution to the making of a national literature rather than the critique of a multinational state. Indeed Shakespeare's texts offer a much more fragmented picture of British politics than that adumbrated by some radical English critics. In the Foreword to *Political Shakespeare*, Jonathan Dollimore and Alan Sinfield set out the method by which 'cultural materialism' approaches a text:

> A play by Shakespeare is related to the contexts of its production – to the economic and political system of Elizabethan and Jacobean *England* and to the particular institutions of cultural production (the court, patronage, theatre, education, the church). Moreover, the relevant history is not just that of four hundred years ago, for culture is made continuously and Shakespeare's text is reconstructed, reappraised, reassigned all the time through diverse institutions in specific contexts.[8]

The history of four hundred years ago, history today and the history that informs Shakespeare's plays, from *Cymbeline* to *Henry VIII*, impinges upon parts of the British Isles other than England. Cultural materialism, which has a more palpable identity in English Renaissance studies than Scotland, 'registers its commitment to the transformation of a social order which exploits people on grounds of race, gender and class'.[9] But Britain, a site of contested identities in the early modern period, and in Shakespeare's plays, manifests itself in *Political Shakespeare* either as Elizabethan or Jacobean England, or as contemporary Britain. Paul Brown's essay on *The Tempest* and Irish colonial discourse is a notable exception, but then, as Dollimore and Sinfield remark elsewhere, 'Ireland was the great problem'.[10] I submit that Britain was the great problem. To naturalise Britain while retaining Ireland as a colonial or semi-colonial other is to reproduce the post-1603 ideological reification of political relations in the British Isles. In fact, it is to forget the origins of Partition, which lie in the Anglo-Scottish plantation alluded to in Brown's suggestive essay.[11] The four hundred years of history between Renaissance England and contemporary Britain are leapt over lightly in any critical discourse that can say of the 'state' with respect to *Henry V* that Ireland was, and remains, its bad conscience'.[12] The so-called National Curriculum in Britain covers England, Wales and Northern Ireland. It does not apply in Scotland. Yet Alan Sinfield's article on Shakespeare and education slips easily between 'English' and 'British'.[13] Ironically entitled 'Give an account of Shakespeare and education, showing why you think they are effective and what you appreciate about them. Support your comments with precise references', this essay answers the question it poses very successfully. Shakespeare is effective in the Englishing of the British state, and in protecting that state from constitutional interrogation, from a questioning that goes to its heart, excepting occasional references to Ireland.

Shakespeare, for half of his literary career, lived in a polity that consisted of England, Wales and – contested – Ireland. The royal house was of Welsh provenance, and the Irish wars were the most pressing contemporary political conflict. For the remainder, he wrote in the context of an enlarged state presided over by a Scottish king, a state whose most significant events, provoking successive crises of representation, were union and plantation. Neither cultural materialism nor new historicism has shown itself to be sensitive to the conflictual British context of Shakespeare's texts. Ireland is a late entry to English Renaissance criticism, and its position within a simple oppositional model of Irish versus English, or British versus Irish, owes more to contemporary politics than to the vicissitudes of the early modern British state.

It is worth remembering that Jonson's famous poem addressed to Shakespeare and prefixed to the first Folio edition of 1623, having first proclaimed Shakespeare's exalted position among authors domestic and foreign, goes on specifically to situate the bard in a British context – the words 'English' or 'England' do not appear in the poem. While the line which is most often quoted declares that Shakespeare was 'not of an age, but for all time!' the preceding couplet contradicts that claim to transcendence and universality:

> Triumph, my Britain; thou hast one to show,
> To whom all scenes of Europe homage owe.[14]

The bard of Britain, in the wake of Anglo-Scottish Union and the subjection of Ireland, is set favourably against European literary figures both contemporary and classical. The subsequent reference to 'those flights upon the banks of Thames, That so did take Eliza and our James' reinforces the notion that Shakespeare is the poet of the British state, of two monarchs and four nations, whose power, artistic and administrative, centres on London. The 'rise of English' in the nineteenth century would reclaim Shakespeare as narrowly English. By the eighteenth century, with the Union of Parliaments in 1707 stripping Scotland of a further layer of political identity, and with the Ascendancy in Ireland at the height of its powers, the triumph of English literary culture rather than the triumph of Britain was the cultural claim. Samuel Johnson provides an instructive update on Ben Jonson's judgement. In 1765, Johnson could complain, with special reference to *King Lear*, perhaps Shakespeare's most British play, that Shakespeare 'commonly neglects and confounds the characters of ages, by mingling customs ancient and modern, English and foreign'.[15] Between Jonson and Johnson, Shakespeare has gone from being both British and for all time to forming the cornerstone of an emerging English canon, and any mingling of 'English and foreign' is viewed as a dramatic and generic failing. Given the difference between Jonson and Johnson, it is disappointing to see John Drakakis, in the Introduction to *Alternative*

Shakespeares, compound the two.[16] Chris Norris, in the same volume, accurately touches on Johnson's 'determination to hold Shakespeare up as the naturalized voice of a peculiarly *English* character and style'.[17] In the gap between Jonson and Johnson, the new word order of literature and language placed the term 'English' at the heart of *culture*, and reserved the epithet 'British' for *politics*.

Shakespeare is our contemporary exactly because the British Problem has the same currency, indeed, the same urgency, that it possessed when he grappled with it. Not all natives of English were, or are, unequivocally devoted to the political unification of the British Isles. The gradual displacement of English nationalism by British unionism was a painful process. The expansion of English sovereignty into other parts of the British Isles entailed a loss of sovereignty, not merely for Ireland, Scotland and Wales, but for England itself. This loss was also, paradoxically during the Renaissance, a loss of European identity, a loss for all the nations of the British Isles and a loss for Europe. Graham Holderness, in an arch aside on the continuing relevance of Shakespeare's treatment of national identities, expresses this tension succinctly:

> The interesting combination, on the part of Britain's Tory government, of pro-European commitment and chauvinistic resistance to European union, testifies to the problem facing British national ideology.[18]

That the British government had to resort to an electoral pact with Ulster Unionists in 1993 to get agreement on the Maastricht Treaty points up the way in which the Tory Party – still known in Scotland as the Conservative and Unionist Party – sees Britishness as a buttress against Europe and a means of sustaining its grip on 'the Nation'.[19] Yet 'one-nation conservatism' is not the sole province of the Tory Party.

In essence, the history of the emerging British state in the early modern period revolves around three overlapping themes: political unification; the supplantation of Celtic cultural forms by Anglo-Norman administration; and the anxieties aroused by the opposition of lowland and highland social structures. The Reformation put Union high on the agenda, as England began the retreat into Britain, a retreat from Europe that was also a westward and northward expansion of Englishness.

The current shift by English critics towards a British perspective sees in the process of union, conquest and plantation that constituted the state a problem, rather than the solution to a problem, which is how it came to be represented in a dominant English historiography.[20] Episodes enacted on the margins of English society can no longer be regarded as irrelevant, inconsequential or tangential to events unfolding at its centre, not least of all because the 'centre' of English culture, its pretensions to statehood, is located precisely in those margins.

As well as focusing attention on the political complexities of a multinational state, the British Problem also raises the question of British relations with Europe and the rest of the world. Ireland functioned in the period as a repository of expatriate Englishness, nascent Britishness and colonial otherness. It was represented at one and the same time as a backdoor for Spain, an outpost of barbarity, the last port of call for Renaissance humanism and a staging-post for America. It was the Achilles' heel of the multiple monarchy, since geographically it was situated outside the sceptred isle.

The encounter with other cultures is the key to cultural identity, and tangential texts and experiences can tell us something about mainstream literature and history. The colonial margins are crucial sites of struggle in the construction of metropolitan identity. Indeed, it is the non-English elements of the British Isles, represented as colonies or regions, that define and circumscribe Englishness. The largest country in any Union has a tendency to dominate, for example, Russia in the former Soviet Union. In the case of Britain, England has long functioned as a simplifying synecdoche for the complex whole that is the British state.

The fates of the three kingdoms of England, Scotland and Wales are intimately bound up together. In *Macbeth*, Duncan's sons find succour in the other two kingdoms:

Malcolm: I'll to England.
Donalbain: To Ireland I.

> (II.iii.3–4)

Macbeth, something of a Scottish nationalist, observes:

We hear our bloody cousins are bestowed
In England and in Ireland.

> (III.i.29–30)

In *King Lear* there is an attempt to make England's Celtic neighbours subject nations, but when you have only daughters, or when there is a woman on the throne as with Elizabeth, then there is a risk that the Celtic nations will infringe and impinge upon England. Goneril is wedded to Albany (Scotland) and Regan to Cornwall, while Cordelia goes off with France. But in one of the sources of Shakespeare's play, *The True Chronicle Historie of King Leir*, the third Celtic neighbour – besides Cambria (Wales) and Cornwall – is Ireland, not France. Cordelia is betrothed to 'the rich King of Hibernia'. Shakespeare's substitution of France for Ireland echoes that moment in *Henry V* when Ireland stands in for England. In the *True Chronicle*, the purpose of the proposed marriages of Lear's daughters is explained by a noble:

> To match them with some of your neighbour Kings,
> Bordring within the bounds of Albion,
> By whose united friendship, this our state
> May be protected 'gainst all forrayne hate.[21]

The neighbouring kingdoms are to act as buffer zones between England and Europe.

We 'other' Elizabethans

> This Shakespearian royalty, conceived in the reign of Elizabeth I, is not dead; it has lived since, within the story of Great Britain; and it is alive today, in the reign of Elizabeth II.[22]

What I want to attempt here is a kind of critical cartography, a provisional mapping-out of a problem I believe to be central to Shakespeare's texts, and to the culture that sustains, and is sustained by, those texts, upholding their exemplary status and their claims to universality. There are, traditionally, two ways of looking at Elizabethan society, as a beleaguered nation, insular and defensive, or as the embryo of an aggressively expansionist British Empire, as England writ large, England plus the 'National Regions' – to use contemporary BBC-speak. Both of these positions, Great British and Little English, elide the complexities of the British state. Few scholars engage with the British state as an entity made up of four nations and many nationalities. The 'British Problem', a new way of thinking about English history of the seventeenth century, can usefully be generalised as an approach to English culture in the early modern period, and Shakespeare in particular. The history of the formation of the British state, the national and colonial struggles that brought it into being, can backlight, not simply the histories, but the later tragedies, those plays written after the Tudor Myth had outlived its usefulness. Despite, or perhaps because, this problematic British history is also a volatile political present, it cannot be confined to an Elizabethan World Picture. We 'other' Elizabethans inhabit a new World Picture, or Order, that is both distant and derived from the first. The terms 'Elizabethan' and 'English' are obviously not coterminous. One rarely hears of 'Elizabethan Wales', although such a thing must have existed. 'Elizabethan Ireland' has been the subject of much historical attention, but the best book on the subject is called *The Elizabethans and the Irish*, as though Elizabethans were not Irish.[23] There was no Elizabethan Scotland. The first Elizabethan state excluded Scotland. Indeed, from a Scottish perspective there can be no Elizabeth II, since there was no Elizabeth I of Scotland. (Just as there were two James Is.) We 'Other' Elizabethans are reliving the reign of Elizabeth I. When England was Elizabethan, Scotland was Jacobean. Jacobean Scotland and Elizabethan England coincided historically. The time is out of joint. Britain is from its very inception anachronistic. Scotland had no place in the Tudor state. When England and Ireland and Wales were Tudor, Scotland was Stuart. Ulster and the Anglo-Scottish frontier were the two areas where Elizabethan England and Jacobean Scotland clashed, and these disputed territories were reinscribed into a British polity after 1603.

There is a tendency to view Renaissance England as a flat, homogeneous whole, whether in the idealised form of 'Merry England' or in the old historicist terms of the 'Elizabethan World Picture'. Jonathan Dollimore and Alan Sinfield have pointed out both the initial value of Tillyard's historicism over the universalising theories to which it was opposed, and its ultimate recuperation of that pervasive humanism.[24] The 'Jacobean World Picture' never caught on in quite the same way.

To focus upon the matter of Britain is not to lose sight of the continent, but to cut through the fog that obscures the English

Channel. It is one of the paradoxes of English Renaissance culture that a period characterised by Europeanisation can be viewed as a time in which England virtually turned its back on the continent in order to concentrate on matters 'domestic', in order, in fact, to domesticate the British Isles in the interests of English sovereignty. The Reformation isolated England from Catholic Europe. The Celtic fringe had to be tamed, brought under English jurisdiction, or it would offer access to Spain, by way of Ireland, or France, through Scotland. Shakespeare's histories deal with the problem of civil strife and foreign conflict, with English expansionism abroad and consolidation at home. But these terms, 'home' and 'abroad', are especially fraught in a British context, and it is difficult, and not necessarily desirable, to separate the question of English aggrandisement within the British Isles from the issue of war, and, by extension, competition for territory with its European neighbours. One thinks here immediately of John of Gaunt's speech, enlisted by Wilson Knight for his wartime revue:

> This royal throne of kings, this sceptred isle,
> This earth of majesty, this seat of Mars,
> This other Eden, demi-paradise,
> This fortress built by nature for herself
> Against infection and the hand of war,
> This happy breed of men, this little world
> This precious stone set in the silver sea,
> Which serves it in the office of a wall,
> Or as a moat defensive to a house
> Against the envy of less happier lands.
> This blessed plot, this earth, this realm, this England.
>
> (*Richard II* II.i.40–50)

This has been described – in my edition – as 'one of Shakespeare's most moving speeches', and it is moving, because it moves the map of England north and west to obliterate Scotland and Wales, which are no doubt included in the list of 'less happier lands' waiting to jump the moat. To Shakespeare's little Latin and less Greek, we must add, in the margin of this nascent National Curriculum, under Geography, 'Could do better'. But before we blame the bard for a map of misreading we ought to recall that the tendency to see England as an island, and as Britain, is part of a long historiographical tradition.[25] It is also the stuff of Shakespeare studies. A typical title would be *Shakespeare's Eden: The Commonwealth of England*.[26] The compilers of *Who's Who in Shakespeare's England* include an entry on James I, who 'reigned as James VI of Scotland from 1567, coming to the *English* throne in 1603'.[27]

There is a tension between the Little England speech delivered by John of Gaunt in *Richard II* and the colonialist rhetoric of the king, whose banishment of Bolingbroke prompts Gaunt to lament England's loss. The supreme irony of this passage is that the monarch's downfall was tied to his failed expedition to Ireland, an island in itself, but a lordship of the English Crown in Richard's day, and a subordinate kingdom in Shakespeare's time. Of course, there's never been an England in the sense suggested by John of Gaunt in this moving speech. When England was not a colony of Rome or France, it held colonies itself – Ireland from the twelfth century, Wales from the thirteenth – and was thus always something more or less than self-contained, never quite at home. England had entertained hopes of a continental empire in the fifteenth century, possessing Gascony, Normandy and Calais. Indeed, the infant Henry VI had been crowned King of France in 1422. As well as the other countries of the British Isles, England had to contend with Cornwall and the ubiquitous 'North' – anywhere north of Stratford. There was also the matter of the Western Isles, Orkney, the Shetland Isles, the Isle of Man, the Isle of Wight and the Channel Islands. The northern isles were controlled by Denmark until 1470. When Gaunt laments: 'That England that was wont to conquer others, Hath made a shameful conquest of itself', he is pointing up the vulnerability and instability of England as a geopolitical unity. England exists here only as conqueror or conquered, not as a nation in its own right. What others had England been wont to conquer in 1399? Or 1591, for that matter? Post-Reformation England had to buttress itself against Europe. Thomas Churchyard, in a text unambiguously entitled *The Miserie of Flaunders, Calamitie of Fraunce, Missfortune of Portugal, Unquietnes of Irelande, Trowbles of Scotlande: And the blessed State of ENGLANDE*, rehearsed the dual position of the Elizabethan state as an island cut off from Europe, an island that both includes and excludes Scotland, Ireland and Wales:

> This ILE is kirnell of the Nutte,
> and those that neare us dwell,
> (Our forraine neighbours rounde aboute,)
> I counte them but the shell:
> That holdeth in this kirnell sweete,
> as Nature hath asciende.
> And as some shells worme eaten are,
> yet kirnell sounde we finde.[28]

Islands beget islands. In *The Tempest*, ownership of the island, disputed by Prospero the planter and Caliban the native ('This island's mine'), is resolved by the claim of the Duke on behalf of the metropolis:

> *Sebastian*: I think he will carry this island home in his pocket, and give it to his son for an apple.
> *Antonio*: And sowing the kernels of it in the sea, bring forth more islands.
>
> (II.i.89–92)

The island-empire of England, the first 'British' Empire, what has been called 'the Atlantic archipelago', was fundamentally an anti-European phenomenon.[29]

In the Afterword to *Political Shakespeare*, perhaps the most influential collection of essays on Shakespeare to emerge in recent years, Raymond Williams recounts his experience of coming face-to-face with the volume and diversity of scholarship on the bard in Cambridge University Library.[30] There is a sense in which no study of Shakespeare can be considered too eccentric. His inclusiveness, though, is not as democratic as it might appear at first glance. Certain presuppositions underpin the majority of work on Shakespeare: that Shakespeare is English; that the language of the plays is English; that he is, by and large, sole author of the corpus that bears his name.

'Shakespeare's English' is a phrase which both names the language and literature he helped shape, and give international prestige to, and fixes, his nationality. Shakespeare is English. English is Shakespeare. This tautology lies at the heart of the dramatist and the discipline. To begin to question Shakespeare's Englishness, to see it as part of the problem rather than part of the solution to his cultural centrality, is to blot the landscape of 'this sceptred Isle'.

'Shakespeare's English' is part of that universalising humanist discourse that sees the language as belonging to the playwright, rather than the other way round. By reading it as 'Shakespeare is English', we lay stress upon the specificity of Shakespeare's national identity, but underplay the degree to which he lived and worked through the formation of a British political system. Shakespeare is English, and his canonisation went hand-in-hand with the naturalisation of the English language, a process that heralded, amongst other great things, the complex political struggle that saw the triumph of English as the dominant language of the British Isles. In 1500, half of the British Isles was Celtic-speaking. By 1650 only one tenth was Celtic-speaking. But Shakespeare is British, too. His works are part of the British Problem, but they are also part of the survival of a core English identity.

W. F. Bolton, in a recent study called *Shakespeare's English*, opposes the scene in *Henry V* in which Catherine's tutor, Alice, coaches her ward in English, and the exchange on the battlefield 'where all speak English, but none share a native tongue ... the "international" scene with Gower, Fluellen, Macmorris, Jamy and their cacophonic regional varieties of English, Welsh, Irish, Scots'.[31] Already we can see the familiar slippage between nation and region that characterises anglocentric British discourse. Within a page these 'cacophonic regional varieties of English, Welsh, Irish, Scots' have become 'regional varieties of English'.[32] Gower's language, far from being a regional variety of English, becomes the standard against which others are measured. The problem here is that there are Celtic languages – Welsh, Irish, Scots – which are not 'regional varieties of English'. The 'Franglais' spoken by the king, and by Pistol to M. Fer, is further evidence of the flexibility of English, its ability to cut the throat of other languages. As Terence Hawkes has observed, 'the language of British society has never been, and is not now, simply English'.[33]

It is one of the paradoxes of English Renaissance culture that a period characterised by Europeanisation can be viewed as a time in which England virtually turned its back on the continent in order to concentrate on matters 'domestic'. The Reformation isolated the English nation from Catholic Europe. England had declared itself an 'empire' in the Act in Restraint of Appeals in 1533, a word which in this context 'designated a sovereign territorial state which was completely independent of the pope and all foreign princes'.[34] In order to turn this 'empire' into an 'imperial monarchy', Henry VIII declared himself King of Ireland in 1541. The 'inland enemy', too, had to be eliminated. There had been an English Pale in Scotland in the fifteenth century, but the loss of Roxburgh in 1461 and Berwick in 1482 had put paid, temporarily, to English aspirations in the north. Scotland invaded England in 1513. In 1521, a Scottish humanist intellectual based in France wrote in Latin a proto-unionist *History of Greater Britain*, which argued that although there were two kingdoms on the island, all of its inhabitants were basically Britons. Published in Paris, the work was punningly known as *Britannicus Major*, after its author, who, by a curious quirk of history, bears the same name as the last prime minister.[35]

English investment in France effectively ended with the loss of Calais in 1558. The peace of Câteau Cambrésis in March 1559, and the departure of French troops from Scotland with the treaty of Edinburgh in July 1560, ensured that if England was going to be out of Europe, then Europe was going to be out of the British Isles. The end of the 'Auld Alliance' between Scotland and France, also known as 'the bridle of England', was forced home by London. The Battle of Kinsale in 1603 put paid to Spanish influence in Ireland, and with Anglo-Scottish Union the same year the first phase of England's shift from Europe to Britain was completed.

Henry V is a telling instance of a play ostensibly reconstructing a famous victory for England over France, which constructs the Elizabethan conquest of Ireland as both a lesser form of that victory, a variation on the imperial theme, and as a necessary prerequisite for the repetition of such a famous victory. Ireland, the ruin of Richard II, whose usurpation by Bolingbroke led ultimately to Henry's vanquishing of the French, returns as the 'second' of France. Yet Henry's Agincourt and Essex's Ireland were two quite different episodes. When Henry promises Catherine: 'England is thine, Ireland is thine, France is thine' (V.ii.230) we can spot the odd one out. What have Henry, formerly Prince of Wales, now King of England, and Catherine, the daughter of the king and queen of

France, to do with Ireland? Ireland is the battlefield in *Henry V*. While the interaction of the four nations that make up the nascent British State is figured, significantly, at the siege of Harfleur – a scene thought to have been especially written *after* James's accession as King of Britain – the nexus of British identity is not France, but Ireland. There is, as Gary Taylor points out, the 'revealing textual error' that substitutes Ireland for France: 'So happy be the issue, brother Ireland' (III.vii.51–5).

Shakespeare's histories suggest themselves as the most obvious repository of material on the formation of the British state. The questions of sovereignty and succession that are the stuff of both the 'Tudor Myth' and the 'Elizabethan World Picture' are raised explicitly in the two tetralogies. Indeed, the fact that these plays can be grouped together suggests a dramatic history of a process, or problematic, being worked out in the 1590s. In the first two tetralogies the 'civilising' of intra-British conflict, its representation as a threat to the 'nation', as equivalent to inter-English disputes, rather than as a challenge to the constitution of the state, is one of the most successful of Shakespeare's political ruses. Neither in the period in which the plays are set, nor in the period in which they were staged, is the unified Britishness invoked anything other than wishful thinking. The dramatic domestication of Ireland, Scotland and Wales prefigured their political domestication. The histories are prophesies.

1 Henry IV opens with the king extolling the virtues of a holy war as an alternative to civil war. Westmoreland interrupts to say that 'a post from Wales' has brought 'heavy news':

> Whose worst was that the noble Mortimer –
> Leading the men of Herefordshire to fight
> Against the irregular and wild Glendower –
> Was by the rude hands of that Welshman taken,
> A thousand people butchered,
> Upon whose dead corpses there was such misuse,
> Such beastly shameless transformation
> By those Welshwomen done, as may not be
> Without shame retold or spoken of.

(I.i.38–4)

The king is compelled to postpone the crusade:

> It seems then that the tidings of this broil
> Brake off our business for the Holy Land.

> (I.i.57–8)

Again, as with *Henry V*, the impression is given that intra-British conflict, like inter-English struggle, is an obstacle in the path of grander enterprises. But the 'tidings' that 'Brake off our business for the Holy Land' are yesterday's news. That business was, remember, intended as a diversion, to give the state a breathing space. This sceptred isle is an ill-sheathed knife, sitting uneasily in the scabbard. Hot on the heels of the post from Wales comes Sir Walter Blunt 'new lighted from his horse', with word from the North. Scots and English forces, under the Earl of Douglas and Harry Hotspur, have clashed, leaving:

> Ten thousand bold Scots ...
> Balked in their own blood.

> (*1 Henry IV* I.i.67–9)

For me, this is one of Shakespeare's most moving speeches, although editors rarely accord it the same emotional impact as Gaunt's lament for Little England. In *Macbeth*, we get a defence of English intervention in Scottish affairs when Malcolm declares: 'Gracious England hath lent us ... ten thousand men' (IV.iii.189–90). Presumably as a replacement for those lost in the earlier play. In *1 Henry IV* Westmoreland says of the slaughter of the Scots: 'It is a conquest for a prince to boast of' (I.i.77). Hotspur, son of the Earl of Northumberland, is the hero of the hour. The king expresses regret that his own son, Prince Henry of Wales, is not similarly heroic.

This short scene sets out, in sharp relief, the issues that will dominate this tetralogy, and indeed Shakespeare's histories as a whole. 'Civil' strife has to be suppressed by seeking an 'external' enemy. Unruly subjects, together with Welsh, Scots and Irish forces, pose a problem for the English polity. In *Henry V* it is worth recalling that when the Irish officer Macmorris first appears, he is in the company of the Scottish Captain Jamy. The heated exchange between Macmorris and Fluellen broaches the question of national identity:

> *Fluellen*: Captain Macmorris, I think, look you, under your correction, there is not many of your nation –
> *Macmorris*: Of my nation? What ish my nation? Ish a villain and a bastard and a knave and a rascal? What ish my nation? Who talks of my nation?

(III.iii.61–5)

Gower, the English captain, interjects with 'Gentlemen both, you will mistake each other' (III.iii.74). In Essex's *Lawes and orders of Warre* for the conduct of the service in Ireland, item number seven stated that there were to be 'No violent private quarrels in Campe or Garrison upon paine of death'.[36] Fluellen's breach of military etiquette, in selecting to debate military strategy in the field, undercuts his claim to 'know the disciplines of war' (III.iii.79).

Richard II's mistake was to do the British business without a sideline in foreign quarrels. He mortgaged the realm to fund his Irish expedition:

> From whence he, intercepted, did return
> To be deposed, and shortly murdered,

as Northumberland reminds us (*1 Henry IV* I.iii.149–50). Conversely, Henry V is seen to harness the Irish in the service of an overweening Englishness. Ironically, the latter play coincides with Elizabeth's costly campaign to quell Tyrone's Rebellion, and contains the only contemporary reference in all of Shakespeare's works, if one accepts a stultifyingly narrow conception of contemporary reference. As Gary Taylor says:

> Reflections of contemporary history have been suspected in many of Shakespeare's plays, but the allusion to the Irish expedition in 5.0.29-34 is the only explicit, extra-dramatic, incontestable reference to a contemporary event anywhere in the canon.[37]

This suggests an approach to drama, text and history that limits all three. The passage in question traverses such categories. There are at least three different kinds of history at work here. Henry's return to London is first compared with Caesar's to Rome, then, less enthusiastically, with Essex's anticipated arrival from Ireland:

> As, by a lower but loving likelihood,
> Were now the general of our gracious empress
> (As, in good time, he may) from Ireland coming,
> Bringing rebellion broached on his sword,
> How many would the peaceful city quit,
> To welcome him! Much more (and much more cause)
> Did they this Harry.

(V.Chorus.29–35)

This is British mythology at its most powerful. First, there is the appeal to classical precedent, in this case Imperial Rome, then the anti-European perspective, embodied in the defeat of the French, and finally the restless natives, Irish 'rebels' in this instance. The insistence that broaching Irish rebellion ranks lower in importance than the putative conquest of France ignores the reality of British state-formation. The juxtaposition of 'gracious empress' and 'peaceful city' suggests that colonial adventures and domestic order are intimately associated. Four different histories intermingle here. There is the history of a past investment in France, an investment that reached its zenith with Agincourt, and its nadir with the relinquishing of Calais in 1558, the year of Elizabeth's accession. There is the history of the Roman Empire, which England wishes to emulate. There is the 'contemporary' history of the Irish wars, whose successful conclusion, in a move of ideological deprecation, is described as 'a lower but loving likelihood' in comparison with Henry's triumph over the French. There is, too, the hopeful history of an Empire for the 'gracious empress', an Empire which consisted at Shakespeare's time of writing of France (wishful thinking), Ireland (not quite) and Virginia (in progress). Wales was not listed as part of the Crown's possessions, since the House of Tudor was of Welsh provenance. England also had a stake in Greenland at this juncture. Hardly the stuff that Rome was made of. But the British Myth – Tudor, Stuart, Hanoverian and Windsor – depends upon just this disavowal of so-called 'internal colonialism' – indigenous indigestion – its rhetorical relegation to a sideshow whose main event is Empire proper, a staging post to global influence. Ireland – together with Scotland and Wales –

has to be 'put down' in more ways than one, silently incorporated, demeaned, absorbed, rather than trumpeted as part of an imperialist project. Alluding to Empire abroad is the best way of concealing empire-building at home. In 1599, France was a competitor, not a colony. The siege of Harfleur had less significance than events in the Welsh marches, the Irish Pale and the Scottish frontier. Nostalgia for territories lost or forfeited goes hand-in-hand with the deliberate, strategic diminution of the Irish conquest. This is today's history, too. British sovereignty is threatened from within, by demands for Irish, Scottish and Welsh independence, and from without, by the prospect of European unification.

Richard's mistake was to concentrate the attention of his subjects on Ireland. Henry – and Shakespeare – averts the gaze, directs it to France. Richard articulated in too bold a fashion the project of the Tudor state-in-progress:

> Now for our Irish wars.
> We must supplant those rough rug-headed kerns
> Which live like venom where no venom else
> But only they have privilege to live.

> *(Richard II* II.i.155–8)

The other nations of the British Isles were presented as a thorn in the side of England's imperial ambitions, when in fact they were the root and branch of England's imperial ambitions. Two common sayings of the time were 'England's difficulty is Ireland's opportunity', and 'If that you will France win, Then with Scotland first begin', which an English lord recites at the opening of *Henry V*, elaborating thus:

> For once the eagle England being in prey,
> To her unguarded nest the weazel Scot
> Comes sneaking, and so sucks her princely eggs.

> (I.ii.169–71)

William Hazlitt pointed out the hypocrisy in this:

> 'The eagle England' has a right to be in prey, but 'the weazel Scot' has none 'to come sneaking to her nest', which she has left to

pounce upon others. Might was right, without equivocation, in that heroic and chivalrous age.[38]

In a variation on the theme, Diego Ortiz, in 1567, declared that: 'There is an English proverb in use among them which says – "He who will England win, In Ireland must begin"'.[39] All of these proverbs were reversible, but the basic point remained that between England and Europe lay the other nations of the 'British' Isles. Once again the British Myth constructs a history in which the threat from its neighbours, north and west, is a barrier to English aspirations. The subordination of the non-English nations of the emerging British state is posited as an essential prerequisite of Empire rather than an act of Empire in itself. The British Empire is first and foremost the British state, which represents the political subjection of the British Isles under English supremacy. 'England' and 'Empire' are the twin umbrellas that adumbrate the British Problem. England is substituted for the British state, and the Empire is exoticised, oriented elsewhere, made foreign, represented as being otherwise occupied than with, say, Ireland, or Scotland, or, Wales. The use of 'Empire' to mean extra-British activity overlooks the imperialism implicit in Britishness itself.

Contradictions abound, but they are constantly resolved by appealing to the British Myth, an origin-myth of 'national' unity that regionalises dissent. Brian Levack has analysed attempts made in the seventeenth century to convert the emerging British State into a British Nation.[40] The process is uneven. Wales had the Tudors, Scotland the Stuarts, but Ireland's entry to the state was not preceded by the gift of a royal house. The only Prince of Ireland was Tyrone, and Essex could not broach his rebellion.

Being British is above all a matter of flexibility and incorporation. In *Henry V*, the Welsh Captain Fluellen appeals to the king's Welsh origins:

> *Fluellen*: And I do believe your majesty takes no scorn to wear the
>   leek upon Saint Tavy's day.
> *King Henry*: I wear it for a memorable honour,
>   For I am Welsh, you know, good countryman.
> *Fluellen*: All the water in the Wye cannot wash your majesty's

Welsh plood out of your pody, I can tell you that; God pless it, and preserve it, as long as it pleases his grace, and his Majesty too!

(IV.vii.101–8)

When Williams enters in pursuit of the previously disguised king, Henry asks if the one he seeks is an 'Englishman'. Here, Henry has assumed another mask, that of Welshman. It pleases his majesty to 'preserve' his 'Welsh plood' no longer than is politically expedient. His earlier battle cry: 'God for Harry! England and Saint George!' made no mention of Wales or Saint David. When Henry goes among his men he hides his regal identity but reveals his ethnic origins:

Pistol: What is thy name?
King Henry: Harry *le roi*.
Pistol: Leroi? A Cornish name. Art thou of Cornish crew?
King Henry: No, I am a Welshman.

(IV.i.49–52)

Henry is something of a chameleon. What is *his* nation? The French envoy Montjoy had addressed him as 'Harry of England' (III.vi.118), and he had appeared to Williams 'but as a common man' (IV.viii.50). This is the same Hal who 'can drink with any tinker in his own language' (*Henry IV 1* II.iv.18). The would-be British monarch presents himself as classless and multinational.

With the passing of the Tudor regime, claims to Welshness lost their currency, and Wales was pressed into English service, not meriting a mention in Great Britain. In 'Zeale', a poem addressed to James I, Thomas Dekker and Ben Jonson wrote:

And then so rich an Empire whose fair breast
Contains four kingdoms by your entrance blest.[41]

The 'four kingdoms' are not the four nations of the British Isles represented in *Henry V*. One foot is kept on the continent as France takes the place of Wales.

We ought to recall that Essex did, in a sense, bring back rebellion broached on his sword – his own rebellion. The Essex Rebellion can be viewed as a displacement of Elizabeth's Irish War. Ireland could function as an alternative power-base. This was Richard's ploy in 1399 and Charles I's in the 1640s. But if that base failed, then the so-called 'mainland' or 'metropolis' would suffer.

History is not to be found exclusively in the histories, nor do we have to confine the question of contemporary reference to that allusion to Essex's Irish venture by the Chorus in *Henry V*. The politics of genre – and the question of history's relation to the present – is rather more complex than the accepted classification of the plays will allow. By categorising as tragedies those later histories which deal with an earlier period in the development of the British polity, we deprive them of their historical specificity. *Macbeth*, *King Lear* and *Cymbeline* address the fresh issues confronting the emerging British state in the light of Anglo-Scottish Union. The violence of the triple monarchy is displaced onto a mythical Scottish past, the Stuart succession is vindicated and, by extension, the Union. Ancient British history is rewritten in order to emphasise the dangers inherent in dividing the kingdom. Recent work on these plays goes some way towards establishing a British milieu. One thinks here, among others, of Paul Brown's excellent article on *The Tempest*, supplemented by an informed reading from Francis Barker and Peter Hulme; Donna Hamilton's incisive analysis of *Cymbeline*; Terence Hawkes' energetic piece on *King Lear*; and the historically grounded essays on *Macbeth* by David Norbrook and Alan Sinfield.[42]

By the Bishops' Order of June 1599 histories were proscribed: 'noe English historyes be printed excepte they bee allowed by some of her majesties privie counsel'.[43] After 1603, the Tudor Myth, instituted in order to justify the reign of Elizabeth, was no longer necessary. With the accession of James I, and a new royal house, it was replaced by a Stuart Myth of British 'national' unity, in which England's British problem, the problem of internal colonialism, had been momentarily resolved by the union with Scotland and the military defeat of Ireland. *King Lear* and *Macbeth* belong to a different *genre* from *Henry V*, not merely in the conventional sense – as tragedy rather than history – but as British rather than English texts.

These two powerful Jacobean dramas are, crucially, sites for the construction of a Britishness which is represented as both the fulfilment of a prophecy and the restoration of a fallen state. Lear's 'darker purpose', and the catastrophic consequences of his division of the kingdom, can be juxtaposed with Macbeth's vision of 'two-fold balls and treble sceptres'. English sovereignty was simultaneously undermined and enhanced by the Elizabethan reconquest of Ireland, Anglo-Scottish Union and the Ulster Plantation which followed on from these two events. Undermined, in so far as English cultural specificity was rendered diffuse by the 'island empire'. Post-reformation self-determination coincided with the birth of a modern Britishness. Enhanced, because England, as the dominant nation in the new political arrangement, with the biggest cut in the division of the kingdom, gained most from the concomitant loss of sovereignty implicit in the act of union.

The British Problem is above all a problem of representation, political and aesthetic. The tensions it produces can be seen in terms like 'internal colonialism', 'home internationals' (the name given to soccer matches between the four 'nations' of England, Scotland, Wales and Northern Ireland), and the BBC's oxymoronic 'National Regions'. English literature offers a way of preserving a national identity within a unionist framework. Between British Studies and English Studies lies the British Problem. The loss of national identity – arguably an originary loss – is compensated for by the institution of a national culture. It is a mark of the split between culture and politics that John of Gaunt's speech continues to dominate the canon of English literature, while Lear's 'darker purpose' haunts the British state. Shakespeare has been loaded unceremoniously into the English canon, but he remains the banished bard of Britain, no less alienated from the state that nursed him than was Bolingbroke by Richard II. We still await his triumphant return. The newly formed British Shakespeare Association (BSA), which held its inaugural conference in Stratford in February 2002, may provide the forum for such a repatriation.

The canon, being English, tends to gloss over other national identities, as well as eliding the differences between nationalists, unionists and republicans. Ben Jonson's position as an advocate of Union is well documented, although even there we find ambiguity and opportunism. Shakespeare's politics, his conception of 'this sceptred isle', despite Wilson Knight's conviction, are harder to pin down. Patriotism is not only 'not enough'. It is often 'too much'.

2
Postcolonial *Cymbeline*: Sovereignty and Succession from Roman to Renaissance Britain

Recent work in Shakespeare studies has begun to address the complexity of the multinational milieu in which Shakespeare wrote.[1] The chief aim of this chapter, in light of this fresh scholarship on the multiple historical contexts of Shakespeare's texts, is to articulate two current critical paradigms – postcolonial theory and the new British history of the seventeenth century that revolves around the question of the 'British Problem'.[2] Precisely because both approaches have their limitations – postcolonial theory tends to confuse England with Britain and to confine itself largely to the nineteenth and twentieth centuries, skipping the Renaissance, while historians of the British Problem concentrate almost exclusively on the decades of the middle part of the seventeenth century, skirting the sixteenth – they can be seen to impinge in important ways upon the late plays. I want to stake a claim for the space of 'Britain' in the time of Shakespeare as an exemplary postcolonial site. Drawing on the new British history, I shall maintain that this revisionist scholarship on the 1640s can be instructively read back into the early part of the seventeenth century, a time when England was moving from postcolonial nation to empire state. Drawing on postcolonial theory, specifically the notion of mimicry, I shall argue that the process of national liberation in early modern England involves a repetition of the colonial project, a common feature of postcolonial discourse. This act of repetition, relished and resisted in equal measure, is implicit in Shakespeare's Roman/British plays.

The formation of the British state, an experience characterised by successive crises of sovereignty, was both a prerequisite to Empire

31

and an act of Empire. As I argued in the previous chapter, the very legislation that freed England from Roman authority, the Act in Restraint of Appeals (1533), did so by declaring England to be an empire in its own right. The word 'empire' in this context 'designated a sovereign territorial state which was completely independent of the pope and all foreign princes'.[3] Claire McEachern has pointed up the irony of a 'nation' being founded as an 'empire', and noted the extent to which England was here defining itself in relation to Rome.[4] McEachern identifies the risk of repetition implicit in such a move:

> To call England an empire is to announce political sovereignty in the term by which it was known. Crucially, it is an announcement based as much in a competitive, mimetic resemblance to foreign authority as in a rejection of it.[5]

This 'competitive, mimetic resemblance' is at the heart of Shakespeare's late plays, especially those that deal directly with the formation of the British state. There is also a mimetic desire, a desire to emulate a Roman achievement about which there is deep ambivalence. A state forged in Wales and subsequently fitted with parts in Scotland before being exported to Ireland had an obvious blueprint. Britain was made in Rome. This was a problem for those English writers who feared that their country was in danger of being consumed by an enlarged state whose imperialist aspirations came to resemble all to closely those of its Roman counterpart, a rejuvenation rather than a rejection of Empire.

Concepts of anachronism and disjuncture are useful in thinking about Shakespeare's late plays, which resonate with belatedness and untimeliness.[6] Samuel Johnson castigated *Cymbeline* for its 'confusion of the names and manners of different times', but Shakespeare's justification of an innovative political union – by representing it as a process of reunion – demanded exactly such a level of con-fusion. According to Richard Hosley, in the introduction to his edition of the play, 'Johnson's aversion to the violent yoking together of Roman Britain and Renaissance Rome reveals a characteristic blindness to the essence of romance'.[7] Conversely, one could argue that the romance of empire is complicated by the act of betrayal, of two-timing. An anti-imperialist, anti-Roman Englishness yields to an imperial Britishness that emulates, even as it opposes, its former tyrant. The liberated colony is preoccupied with the mores and lessons of the erstwhile occupying power. England, Rome and Britain constitute a love triangle that can end only in tears, for at least one party.

In the first chapter of her book on Shakespeare's last plays, Frances Yates writes of 'The Elizabethan Revival in the Jacobean Age', and argues that 'there was built into the basically Protestant position of the Queen as representative of a pure reformed Church which had cast off the impurities of Rome, this aura of chivalric Arthurian purity, of a British imperialism, using British in the mythic and romantic sense which it had for the Elizabethans'.[8] This 'mythic and romantic sense' has always been inseparable from the modern economic sense, and it proved to be ideologically, as it was etymologically, inseparable from its Roman model. Romance is Roman. For Jacobeans in particular, struggling to come to terms with a new-found British identity, Arthurian romance could not conceal the outlines of a Roman tragedy. Philippa Berry, in a compelling essay on *Macbeth*, has shown how deeply embedded in early modern culture were notions of historical repetition: 'We can identify the existence of what can be termed "double time" in several of Shakespeare's histories, tragedies and Roman plays ... whereby the particular historical time of the play is implicitly paralleled or repeated by recent or near-contemporary political moments.'[9] Berry argues that the British monarchy in the Scottish play 'is mysteriously dependent upon its opposite yet originating shadow: the tyrannical and bloody image of a Scottish or Celtic king'.[10] I shall make a related case for *Cymbeline*, but as a dramatic endorsement of the Roman roots of Britishness, rather than a repudiation of its Celtic fringe.

Berry points out that in debates on Anglo-Scottish union the two kingdoms were often depicted as brothers.[11] In *Cymbeline* three versions of union coexist in the shape of a marriage threatened then resolved, long lost brothers reunited with their natural father, and a *pax Britannia* that mirrors the *pax Romana* of pre-Reformation days. The play's complexity stems in part from its multilayered treatment of the problem of British origins and the troubled issues of union and empire. The emphasis is on continuity within change, so that Britishness is seen as the resumption of an historical process rather than an absolute break with the past. Roger Warren speaks of 'the view of ancient Britain in the play – independent, yet related to the Roman empire'.[12] It is the fraught nature of the British postcolonial condition – 'independent, yet related' to its Roman counterpart – that Shakespeare is addressing with a subtlety suited to the subject. Always one to make a drama out of a crisis, Shakespeare takes the intractable historical material of union and state formation as his text. Giacomo is not the only Italian intriguer at large. The bard of Britain is himself performing sleights of hand, affirming a British monarchy that sees its reflection in Rome. What we are presented with in *Cymbeline* is a Union Jack in the box, a surprise package that delivers a sucker punch, a play that ostensibly celebrates the union of England and Scotland but which figures it, provocatively and controversially, cloudily enwrapped in a *rapprochement* between Britain and Rome. In a neat reversal, a newly expanded state is projected backward into Roman times, stealing James I's thunder, and giving all tribute to the reign of Caesar. With a foot in both camps, Roman Britain and Reformation England, *Cymbeline* marks the accession of James not as the advent of the Other, succeeding through some bizarre dynastic accident, but as the eternal return of the Same, coming to fruition ripely and rightly through ancient lineage.

Cymbeline is a nativity play, but it deals not with the birth of Christ, but with the birth of Britain, a birth that is not virgin but Virgilian. The contention of Emrys Jones that *Cymbeline* has to be read in its Jacobean context in order for its meaning and significance fully to be grasped has met with resistance, as have all topical readings of Shakespeare's plays.[13] Roger Warren maintains that this, arguably Shakespeare's most complex drama, needs no interpretative key 'since the play creates, arguably to a greater extent than many of Shakespeare's other plays, its own self-sufficient theatrical world, requiring no explanation beyond itself'.[14] This strikes me as a very British perspective, one that projects its own expansive insularity onto the text. Where Warren sees the location of the play within an immediate historical context as a mere embellishment on the part of the playwright I would want to argue for a central and profound preoccupation with origin myths and ideas of union as structuring the action of the play.

In an essay entitled 'Shakespeare, James I and the Matter of Britain', Christopher Wortham took three early Stuart plays by Shakespeare –

King Lear, Macbeth and *Antony and Cleopatra* – written roughly between 1604 and 1607, and argued strongly for their topicality.[15] One could make a case for seeing three later Stuart plays – *Cymbeline, The Tempest* and *Henry VIII*, written around 1609–13 – as meditations on the origins of Britishness, ancient and early modern, from Roman times to the Henrician Reformation and beyond to the Union of Crowns under James I and the Anglo-Scottish colonisation of Ireland that union engendered. These plays are postcolonial in so far as Shakespeare is working through England's post-Reformation history, the history of a nation wrested from an Empire that copied (in true deconstructive fashion) the thing to which it was ostensibly opposed, a history in which a new English nation grew into an Empire virtually overnight, then sealed its fate through an act of union that resulted in a net loss of English sovereignty in favour of a British Empire modelled on the Roman one that had only just been shaken off. At the end of *Cymbeline*, a play whose themes are reunion, reunification, repatriation, and reconciliation, this is presented positively, but its covert reintroduction of Catholicism by the back door would be interpreted much less generously and optimistically by those whose insular idea of Englishness did not extend to Britain. Even the 70 years of apparently unadulterated Englishness between 1533 and 1603 were complicated by the fact that England had 'Pales', 'Marches' and 'Borderlands' in its possession, territories that both supplemented and suppressed the development of Englishness.

The greatest ruse of anglocentrism is its eccentricity, its facility for displacing issues of identity onto England's neighbours and colonies, and thereby setting itself up as a standard or norm. Part of the Stuart Myth, of course, was to portray Britishness as a kind of homecoming. British identity is represented – like Protestantism, in fact – as a return to an original wholeness, to unity and integrity, to a pre-existent identity that was dormant during centuries of foreign tyranny, Roman and Norman (French). This Britishness is recycled, at the same time as it is collapsed into an Englishness that is literary and cultural, mythical and romantic. Modern critics tend to do what early modern writers specialised in – project into the past something that is new, strange and foreign and thus make it familiar, recognisable, in short, domesticated.

The history of late Shakespeare, of Jacobean or Stuart Shakespeare, is, like the history of England, nasty, British and short. Crucified between Rome and Britain, England was divested of its new-found sense of selfhood. *Cymbeline* seems obsessed with the very idea of Britain, its intangibility. Imogen, who 'chose an eagle' who is also a lion, asks:

> Hath Britain all the sun that shines? Day, night,
> Are they not but in Britain? I' th' world's volume
> Our Britain seems as of it, but not in't;
> In a great pool a swan's nest. Prithee think
> There's livers out of Britain.

(III.iv.137–41)

The mere incantation of the name of Britain, the watery grave of the dying Swan of Albion, serves to give it a force in language that is otherwise lacking. The delivery or deliverance of Britain is bound up with fantasy. Britain seems of the world but not in it precisely because it is an invention, and one with which Shakespeare's culture is only just coming to terms. Britain has been delivered, but 'There's livers out of Britain', parts of the body politic that are not quite incorporated, making it subject to liver failure, unless another organ or origin is available for a transplant. England, so recently delivered from Rome, finds itself caught up in another sprawling imperial corpus.

In *Cymbeline*, it is a question of autonomy and independence from Rome, but at the same time the imperial design was patented by Rome, and thus Britain pays tribute by default. Tribute and attribution are crucial to the drama. The villains of the piece are those, like the Queen – surely a reflection on Elizabeth? – who refuse to give credit where credit is due. For example, Cloten refuses to pay tribute to Rome, saying:

> Britain's a world
> By itself, and we will nothing pay
> For wearing our own noses.

(III.i.12–14)

Cloten is forswearing his own nose, or cutting it off to spite his face, because Britain may be a world by itself, but it is a world made in the graven image of the empire that conquered it of old, and from which it has freed itself only to be chained afresh. To deny this is to deny one's paternity and one's birthright. Paradoxically the real slaves are those who misread their own history. The solution to Britain's Roman legacy is not to shake it off, not to renounce Rome, but to succeed it, to step into its shoes, easier now that the imperial leather is on the other foot.

Cymbeline was written at a time when a new British imperial monarch with two sons, one the Duke of Albany, the other Prince of Wales, had effected a union between two warring kingdoms – Scotland and England – and made possible the conquest of a third, Ireland. Where Lear had divided the ancient kingdom of Britain with disastrous consequences, Cymbeline preserves its integrity while keeping the peace with Rome. It is hard not to hear a contemporary resonance in the closing speeches of Shakespeare's King of Britain:

> Although the victor, we submit to Caesar
> And to the Roman empire, promising
> To pay our unwonted tribute, from the which
> We were dissuaded by our wicked queen.
> Whom heavens justice, both on her and hers,
> Have laid most heavy hand.
>
> (V.iv.460–66)

The Soothsayer, Philharmonus, then hails a new Roman Britain, one that both pays tribute to Rome, and yet is paid tribute by Rome, as Rome's successor:

> The fingers of the powers above do tune
> The harmony of this peace. The vision,
> Which I made known to Lucius ere the stroke
> Of this yet scarce-cold battle, at this instant
> Is full accomplished; for the Roman eagle,
> From south to west on wing soaring aloft,
> Lessened herself and in the beams o' th' sun
> So vanished; which foreshadowed our princely eagle,
> Th'imperial Caesar, should again unite
> His favour with the radiant Cymbeline,
> Which shines here in the west.
>
> (V.iv.467–77)

When Cymbeline follows this with a declaration that 'A Roman and a British ensign wave / Friendly together' (V.v.480–1), he is ironically pointing up an imperial conjunction that would raise the troubled ghosts of religion and nationalism for years to come. A Brutus killed Caesar, only to become another Caesar. As we shall see in chapters 4 and 5, for Spenser, Ireland was another England, and another Scotland. For Bacon, Ireland was another Britain. For Shakespeare, England is another Rome.[16]

In *Cymbeline*, the soothsayer foretells that 'from a stately cedar shall be lopped branches which, being dead many years, shall after revive, be jointed to the old stock, and freshly grow; then shall Posthumus end his miseries, Britain be fortunate and flourish in peace and plenty'. (V.v.438–42) A 'stately cedar' might suggest a state that ceded, in the sense of ceding territory, in this case a state that ceded branches – limbs or members – that are now being grafted back onto the main body of the state. The Soothsayer elaborates:

> The lofty cedar, royal Cymbeline,
> Personates thee, and thy lopped branches point
> Thy two sons forth; who, by Belarius stol'n,
> For many years thought dead, are now revived,
> To the majestic cedar joined, whose issue
> Promises Britain peace and plenty.
>
>   (V.iv.454–59)

Multiplicity and plurality are the key to understanding Britishness. At the close of *Henry VIII* Cranmer's prophecy tells of how James will 'make new nations' (V.v.52). This proliferation of polities is a recurrent theme of the late plays, with union and plantation supplanting succession as the touchstone of sovereignty. The ceding of authority implicit in the transition from Tudor to Stuart government, and from English to British identity, was represented as a reunification and reinforcement of identity. As England receded, Britain was heralded as an outgrowth of an originary Englishness, as though the non-English nations of the flowering British state were branches of an English family tree.

The cedar is invoked once more at the end of *Henry VIII*, where Cranmer's prophesy foresees James I branching out:

> He shall flourish,
> And like a mountain cedar reach his branches
> To all the plains about him; our children's children
> Shall see this, and bless heaven.

(V.v.52–5)

Union and empire inevitably invoked images of amplification and expansion, and metaphors of natural growth abound in the literature of the period. In *The Tempest*, we recall, the Duke's followers say of his venture:

> *Sebastian*: I think he will carry this island home in his pocket, and give it to his son for an apple.
> *Antonio*: And sowing the kernels of it in the sea, bring forth more islands.

(II.i.89–92)

You reap what you sow. Linkage can entail shrinkage as well as growth. Colonies are both a necessary supplement – they shore up a deficiency in identity, or displace differences (for example, class) – but they are also dangerous supplements, as they can become sites of resistance to an imagined and imposed unity. A loss of sovereignty can follow when the latter end of a commonwealth forgets its beginning. *Cymbeline* offers an avenue out of English insularity and isolation, but all roads lead to Rome.

I want to conclude by looking very briefly at some prophetic writings of the seventeenth century that can be read in relation to Shakespearean prophecy in the late plays, specifically *Cymbeline* but also *Henry VIII*. We can learn from the future, as well as the past, and by focusing on the drama of British sovereignty as it unfolded in the turbulent years following Shakespeare's death we can see more clearly how difficult his task was, and how heretical his approach. As the jailer says in *Cymbeline*, 'what's past is, and to come the discharge' (V.iii.262). Prophecy, like theatre, is a kind of heresy, a form that allowed many women writers access to the male domain of history, and facilitated political interventions that might otherwise have been denied. Prophecy is a form in which the nation is figured, contested and invented. It points to the future, but is anchored in the past. What's past is prophecy. In the middle of the seventeenth century England found itself on the horns of a dilemma, torn between insularity and expansion, and haunted by empire and union. The constitutional crisis of the 1640s galvanised many writers, and it was a crisis that was often expressed in the form of allegory and prophecy:

> So againe looking backe to *Daniel* touching the *little Horne* declaring or sounding the brevitye of great *Brittaines* Monarchie, (Whose looke more stoute then his fellows) more over thus I considered the Hornes, and there came up another little Horne, before whom three of the first Hornes were pluckt up by the rootes, the truth of it as much to say, That he the first Heire of the red rose and the white. Whose ISUE three of them Crown'd Princes childlesse, deceasing without heires of their body, the Crown of England fell to Scotland, and great Brittaine so stiled, then wherefore blazoned by those great Beasts foure being from the name Bruite derived, whose Unicorns Horne become as short as his fellowes.[17]

This prophecy was made in 1644 by Lady Eleanor Davies (1590–1652), addressing – in fact, blessing – her daughter, Lucy, Countess of Huntingdon. Stitching together the story of Jacob and his sons (Genesis 29–45) and the beasts of Daniel's vision (Daniel 7), Davies offers a radical English Protestant critique of a Britishness that threatens to repeat the worst excesses of the Roman empire. For English Catholics, those whom the Reformation had effectively rendered strangers in their own country, a change of state and an outward expansion into empire, with its echoes of times past and opportunities for an intermingling of otherness, might have appeared inviting, suggesting an embracing of Europe after being disenfranchised. For Davies, the phrase 'Roman Britain' conjures up images of the present and a fateful future rather than the past. What's past is prologue. Endings are beginnings. These are old paradoxes.

In her defiance of Britishness and defence of Englishness Davies belongs to a tradition – one that would arguably include John

Milton – of besieged English Protestantism convinced that the expansion of the Tudor state in the wake of the Reformation had actually stifled rather than stiffened the resolve of the Reformation and that the advent of Stuart rule had effectively smothered a new-born Englishness. In her blessing of her daughter, so different from Cranmer's blessing of Elizabeth in Shakespeare's *Henry VIII*, Davies reminds her readers that the offspring of the father of the Reformation have failed to reproduce, resulting in the adoption of a child of empire, a British infant that apes Rome, fostering dissent.

Whereas the prophesies of Cranmer at the close of *Henry VIII* and the soothsayer at the close of *Cymbeline* hold out the promise of a fruitful future (both refer to a cedar that will have its branches restored) Davies sees something ceded, or surrendered, rather than seeded, or planted. When James accedes, England gives ground, or cedes. Davies, writing on the eve of what a modern anglocentric critical perspective calls the 'English Civil War' or the 'English Revolution' – she conversely alludes to 'Three devided kingdoms rent in peices' – discerns in the dynastic accident that brought James to the 'English' throne the seeds of destruction. As the former wife of Sir John Davies, Attorney-General of Ireland and author of a prominent treatise on that country's conquest under James I, Lady Eleanor was in a strong position to judge the progress of the British project.[18]

Davies' prophesy is, like many prophecies – including those that bring the curtain down on *Henry VIII* and *Cymbeline* – written after the fact. That is, the prophecies are histories, or reflections on events that have come to pass, epilogues rather than prologues. As well as playing with several senses of horn, Davies harps on the mythical meanings of Britishness. In her account, Bruite – Brute or Brutus – legendary founder of Britain, is changed from a brute to a beast, and one that recalls in too many respects the Beast of Rome, lately slain by England, now risen again in the guise of Britain. The risk of conversion, of becoming Roman, pervades *Cymbeline*. Posthumous cites Belarius, who urges his fellow Britons to 'Stand, / Or we are Romans' (V.iii.25–6).

Davies' lament for a lost Little England, an England that has made a shameful conquest of itself through buying into Britishness, purchasing power at the expense of integrity, is in keeping with a certain tradition of national narrative which figures the origin of the nation as a battle for recognition. Homi Bhabha remarks:

> In each case what is being dramatized is a separation – *between* races, cultures, histories, *within* histories – a separation between *before* and *after* that repeats obsessively the mythical moment of disjunction ... Colonial fantasy is the continual dramatization of emergence – of difference, freedom – as the beginning of a history which is repetitively denied.[19]

The crisis of the mid-seventeenth century that Davies records, and which she imputes to what historians now call the 'British Problem', is not new. As she herself maintains, its seeds were planted with the origins of the British enterprise, a Trojan horse that brought the beast of Rome back into England, the gift of empire that undermines the nation in the name of enhancing it.

The birth of Britain was an event that provoked Shakespeare into wordplay as devious as that deployed by Davies. The soothsayer's prophecy in *Cymbeline* plays upon the proper name of Posthumous Leonatus:

> Thou, Leonatus, art the lion's whelp;
> The fit and apt construction of thy name,
> Being *leo-natus*, doth import so much.

> (V.iv.444–6)

Britain is a posthumous being, bruited abroad, rumoured to be as roomy and rheumy as Rome, part-lion and part-eagle, a rough beast that lurches towards London. Born in the breach between England and Rome, it serves to fill that breach with the English dead, or with the death of Englishness, the Pyrrhic victory that *Cymbeline* anticipates, celebrates and commemorates. By figuring Britain as a second coming, an ancient kingdom restored to its former glory, Shakespeare was playing into the hands of the Roman precedent.

Multiple kingdoms call for multiple contexts. Even before James's accession English writers were working within a state that was not self-contained, a state that harboured more than one nation, which included Wales and Ireland. In *Henry VIII* Katherine alludes to her husband's 'dominions' (II.iv.16), and while the king himself speaks of 'kingdom' in the singular (II.iv.194), he refers to 'realms' in the plural (II.4.197). France figures here, Wales too perhaps, and also Ireland, a lordship of the English crown from the twelfth century and a kingdom from 1541, when Henry declared himself to be monarch of that realm. This raises the question of the integrity of Englishness. When was England itself alone, and when exactly was Britain conjured into being? Davies' prophecies, penned at the chilling dénouement of a particular phase of 'the British experiment', or the British Problem, ought to send us back to other crises of national identities, points of rupture and fragmentation, moments when the state is 'disjoint and out of frame'. One such time is, obviously, the early seventeenth century, when a newly united kingdom was coming to terms with a mixing of identities, with an openness to a previously threatening other, and with a multiplication of national contexts.

Like Yeats's 'Leda and the Swan', stratified allegory rather than straightforward history can best capture the postcolonial condition, and its legacy of violence. Mastered by the brute blood of Rome, did England put on its knowledge with its power? The poet, the prophet and the playwright can more eloquently express the complexities of nationalism and colonialism than either criticism or historiography. One could draw an analogy between Joyce's sense of Ireland struggling under a double yoke of British and Roman imperialism and Davies' perception of England suffering from an identical underlying complicity. Joyce wrote: 'I confess that I do not see what good it does to fulminate against the English tyranny while the Roman tyranny occupies the palace of the soul.'[20] Shakespeare understood, as did every English writer of his day, what it meant to be the servant of two masters.

How, finally, can one reconcile the voices of Shakespeare's optimistic imperialists with the dissenting tradition exemplified by a prophet of doom such as Eleanor Davies? One way of thinking about the differing attitudes to Englishness and Britishness that these writers exemplify is to accept the fact that disenfranchised communities respond in different ways to political change. Both Shakespeare and Davies, in the face of exclusion, could be seen to be voicing dissent, one championing a residual Catholicism that regarded British imperial interests as an opportunity for a more inclusive, more multicultural, more pluralistic, more European, more worldly state, more tolerant of religious difference than was

Reformation England, and the other advocating a radical Protestant counter-tradition that saw history repeating itself, in the shape of a Brute this time rather than a Beast.

Linda Colley's monumental study of the formation of British identity presents a providential Protestant view.[21] Murray Pittock has tried to counter this anglocentric Tudor mythology with a peripheral Stuart vision that is Catholic, Celtic and Gaelic.[22] The truth lies somewhere in between. There is more than one way to be British, more than one variety of Britishness, and more than one form of resistance. The constant vacillation between nation, state and empire is the stuff of drama, and is dealt with in telling ways by Shakespeare. The casual slippage between 'English' and 'British' in current critical discourse notwithstanding, the cultural cross-fertilisations and constitutional – and chronological – double-crosses of the seventeenth century continue to resonate. The discharge of history is not transparent, but remains clotted and ambiguous. Its colour and constituency is better known to the dramatist than to the critic or historian.

3
Shakespeare, Holinshed and Ireland: Resources and Con-texts

The texts of the Western canon play a dominant part in postcolonial literature, from the title of Achebe's novel, *Things Fall Apart*, drawn from Yeats' 'The Second Coming', to the influence of Shakespeare evident in Aimé Césaire's *Une Tempête* (1969), and Octave Mannoni's *Prospero and Caliban* (1950). Another pair of quotations from the same canonical texts might serve here as reminders of two issues central to postcolonialism, namely, the reversal or displacement of the core–periphery model of development, indeed the questioning of 'development' itself, and the issue of whether the colonial subject comprises both colonisers and colonised. 'The centre cannot hold' and 'This thing of darkness I acknowledge mine' aptly summarise much recent debate.[1] Ironically, Yeats was writing from a core hitherto regarded as peripheral. The idea that the Empire writes back signals the decentring or recentring of what was hitherto deemed liminal, while Prospero's owning of, and owning up to, Caliban, can be read alongside arguments around the colonial subject between Homi Bhabha and Abdul JanMohamed, for example, and the accusations of appropriation, and claims around what or who is properly postcolonial.[2]

The texts of a canonical author will always be heavily sedimented – in terms of history, culture, and language. When that author is arguably the greatest English dramatist and a national figure of world renown, then the potential for conflict is enormous and the stakes are high. In this chapter, rather than make any grand claims for corpus, canon or culture at large, I propose to enact a very provisional and localised intervention in the field. Taking two of Shakespeare's histories, I aim to focus on two passages from the Irish section of Holinshed's *Chronicles* that furnished a couple of key Irish references. Raphael Holinshed had gone to Ireland, possibly with the first Earl of Essex, Walter Devereux, in the early 1570s, and had there recruited Richard Stanyhurst as editor of the part of his projected history dealing with that country.[3] Stanyhurst is a complex and controversial figure, a descendant of the original twelfth-century English settlement in Ireland – the Old English – who, having first supported the Elizabethan reconquest – by the New English – finally fled to the continent as a recusant. The Irish *Chronicles*, partly as a consequence of Stanyhurst's divided loyalties, but also due to the unique status of Ireland as a nation in the process of recolonisation, with two English planter societies at loggerheads on its soil, remains a heterogeneous and hybrid collection of texts, some new works specially commissioned, others translations of earlier material. There is no doubt that the mere fact that it influenced a canonical author lends weight and *gravitas* to a text. Stephen Booth has argued that 'we care about *Holinshed's Chronicles* because Shakespeare read them'.[4] While Holinshed's *Chronicles* are widely recognised as a significant repository of source material for Shakespeare, they are seldom read in any detail, and certainly not with the attention accorded to the plays themselves. Despite our familiarity with them, the *Chronicles*, and especially the Irish writings, remain obscure. This is due both to the difficulties presented by the texts themselves and to the unusual nature of the Irish colonial situation, as well as to the tendency to note rather than annotate Shakespeare's sources, part and parcel of the resistance to history and topicality, if not to theory.

We know that Shakespeare leaned heavily on Holinshed for the history plays of the 1580s and 1590s. One would expect him to rely therefore on the Irish section of that work for his allusions to 'Irish' character. In tracing the historical pretexts of these dramatic nodal points, I want to speak of 'resources' rather than sources, in keeping with the most productive work on the interface between literature and history. In their incisive essay on *The Tempest*, Francis Barker and Peter Hulme use the word 'con-text' in order to highlight this problem: 'Con-texts with a hyphen, to signify a break from the inequality of the usual text/context relationship. Con-texts are themselves *texts* and must be *read with*: they do not simply make up a background.'[5] I wish to raise the kind of questions of identity, influence and interpretation that I believe are central to any discussion of Shakespeare and Ireland.

The Irish section of Holinshed's *Chronicles* provides two examples of an Old English legacy that becomes a New English inheritance. The texts I am going to concentrate on are John Hooker's translation of *The Conquest of Ireland* by Giraldus Cambrensis, a medieval Latin discourse given the oxygen of publicity by being published in English in a prominent Renaissance context, and Richard Stanyhurst's 'A Plaine and Perfect Description of Ireland', a peculiar collection of material – topographical, historical, and anecdotal – compiled by a Dubliner and prominent figure within the Old English colonial community in Ireland. Michael Cronin has written with authority and insight on the question of translation in an Irish context, and he has drawn attention to the peculiar juxtaposition in Holinshed of these two texts.[6] For my purposes, I would want to emphasise that these are respectively the views of members of an 'Anglo-Norman' and an 'Anglo-Irish' élite, both belonging broadly to an Old English community, that is, to the first wave of English colonisers that broke on the shore of Ireland.

I shall argue that both Gerald of Wales and Richard Stanyhurst are postcolonial figures in so far as they found themselves in that third space between native and coloniser. Too often, criticism of English views of Ireland confines itself to the early modern period, overlooking the first phase of English colonialism that preceded the arrival of Spenser and others, and restricts itself to denunciations of what is presented as an unremittingly pejorative discourse, 'nothing but the same old story'. Part of the problem with this approach is that it is insufficiently alert to the dangers implicit in rehearsing the negative opinions of the coloniser, affording them additional discursive purchase. Indeed, there is a thin line between exposure and reproduction. I hope to suggest that while it is important to record and tabulate instances of discrimination against the so-called margins, it is equally valuable to look for fissures within the putative metropolis.

English Renaissance representations of England's non-English neighbours were often interlinked, and this is acknowledged in pioneering studies of early modern images of the Celtic peoples.[7] Recent, more theoretically sophisticated discussions of colonial stereotypes in Shakespeare and his contemporaries have tended to concentrate on the Irish dimension of sixteenth- and seventeenth-century English colonial expansion.[8] At the same time, though, there has been a renewed interest in 'the matter of Britain', opening up the canon to a problematic 'British' context, throwing up issues of colonialism and nationalism, as well as raising the spectre of topicality, the haunt of the historicist, and the graveyard of Shakespeare criticism.[9] My own work attempts to map out the ways in which the formation of the British state entailed a policy of divide and rule, so that it is impossible to read Ireland in isolation from Scotland and Wales, or solely in relation to England, or to see it as a unified entity rather than as occupied by competing English colonial élites in the South, and as subject to a strong Scottish presence in the North. Roy Foster has spoken of 'varieties of Irishness', and, in the same way, it is essential to speak of varieties of Englishness, and of Scottishness.[10]

In *Henry V* the four nations that will make up the future united Kingdom are brought together on a French battlefield personified as four captains – Gower, Fluellen, Macmorris and Jamy (III.ii). In a decisive essay entitled 'Invisible Bullets', Stephen Greenblatt, taking colonialism as his starting-point for a reading of Shakespeare's histories, spoke of this famous four nation scene in these terms:

> By yoking together diverse peoples – represented in the play by the Welshman Fluellen, the Irishman Macmorris, and the Scotsman Jamy, who fight at Agincourt alongside the loyal Englishman – Hal symbolically tames the last wild areas of the British Isles, areas that in the sixteenth century represented, far more powerfully than any New World people, the doomed outposts of a vanishing tribalism.[11]

For Renaissance critics it is no longer possible, or at least no longer politically correct, to speak of a 'New World' without supplying the clothespins of scare quotes. To describe Scotland, Wales and Ireland as 'the last wild areas of the British Isles' or 'the doomed outposts of a vanishing tribalism' ought to be equally questionable, not least becaue of its allusion to a politically charged geographical entity called 'the British Isles'. Whose language is this? If it is the language of the sixteenth century, then it should be cited and sourced as such. Sadly, it is Greenblatt's language, and that of a whole critical tradition that simply assumes the incivility of the non-English nations of the emerging British state, and fires bullets that are all too visible.

The famous heated exchange between Macmorris and Fluellen broaches the question of national identity:

> *Fluellen*: Captain Macmorris, I think, look you, under your correction, there is not many of your nation –
> *Macmorris*: Of my nation! What ish my nation? Ish a villain, and a bastard, and a knave, and a rascal – What ish my nation? Who talks of my nation?[12]

The quizzical stance of Macmorris seems a suitable springboard for the interrogation of Shakespeare and Ireland. This is a crucial moment in a play that turns around the vexed issue of how to domesticate and unite the forces of a nascent British state against an enemy perceived to be more explicitly external and foreign. The standard interpretation is that Macmorris, as an Irishman, a native of a country colonised by England, is less comfortable with his identity than his fellow captains. But the episode can be viewed in a different light if we look at a likely source in Holinshed.

The medieval writer Giraldus Cambrensis – Gerald of Wales – is arguably the originator of modern English anti-Irish prejudice. His most recent biographer portrays him as a man stationed at the interchange of several conflicting cultures. Whatever his uncertain origins and divided allegiances, his two books on the twelfth-century invasion and colonisation of Ireland were hugely influential, and not just in his own time. Because of the anachronistic power of translation, they exercised a pervasive force in Shakespeare's day. The first of these, *The Topography of Ireland*, Giraldus originally delivered as a series of Latin lectures at the University of Oxford around 1187. Spurred on by the success of the *Topography*, and 'at the insistence of many men of rank', Giraldus set to work sometime around 1188–89 on *The Conquest of Ireland*. If in his first foray into Irish territory he had been chiefly preoccupied with 'the events and scenes of time past', then in his second Giraldus was primarily concerned with 'contemporary events'.[13] The *Conquest* appeared in an English translation by John Hooker in the second edition of Holinshed's *Chronicles* (1587).[14] Hooker's version of Giraldus, whom he called 'the best deserved and exact writer of the conquest and state of Ireland in his time', was dedicated to Sir Walter Ralegh, who had by then assumed the role of undertaker in the plantation of Munster, alongside Edmund Spenser.[15]

In the *Conquest*, Giraldus delineates divisions within the settler community, and between that community and the English Crown. In foregrounding the political differences between court and colony, he cites a speech by his uncle, Maurice Fitzgerald, a leading member of the newly established colonial élite, to illustrate the predicament of the vanguard of the adventuring class:

> Whie then doo we tarie? And wherefore doo we so linger? Is there anie hope of releefe from home? No no, the matter is otherwise, and we in woorse case. For as we be odious and hatefull to the Irishmen, even so we now are reputed: for Irishmen are become hatefull to our owne nation and countrie, and so we are odious both to the one and the other.[16]

The question of identity posed by Maurice is not based upon any coloniser–colonised duality, but centres on the cultural confusion experienced by an intermediate social grouping cast adrift between margin and metropolis. Cut free from their native moorings, Maurice and his fellow travellers are regarded as renegades by virtue of their displacement from the central authority from which they derived their impetus as adventurers. Denationalised, dispersed and disenfranchised, denied access to an increasingly exclusive English culture, the roots of the Anglo-Irish predicament are thus enmeshed with the originary moments of English colonialism. Theirs is an identity in limbo, the unfinished product of a hyphenated community torn between two cultures, English and Irish. Gerald's Maurice Fitzgerald bears a striking resemblance to Shakespeare's 'Irish' captain. In Macmorris we see a similar interrogation of easy assumptions of national identity.

Macmorris means literally 'son of Maurice'. In Spenser's *View*, we recall, Irenius had expressed his wish to see 'all the O's and Mac's, which the heads of septs have taken to their names, to bee utterly forbidden and extinguished' (p. 148). Sir James Ware, in a marginal note to Spenser's text, observed that:

> The custome of prefixing the vowell O to many of the chiefe *Irish* surnames, began soon after the yeere M. in the raigne of *Brien bororha*, (the sone of *Kennethy*) King of *Ireland*, As for *Mac* in surnames, it beareth no other signification, then *Fitz* doth among the *French*, and (from them) the *English*, and *ap* with the *Welsh*.

And although it were more anciently used then the other, yet it varied according to the fathers namc, and became not so soone fully settled in families. (p. 148)[17]

Names have always mattered within an Irish milieu, and how we spell 'Macmorris', as Andrew Murphy reminds us, determines our attitude to this 'Irish' character.[18] If we view Macmorris as an Old Englishman, that is, as an inhabitant of the English Pale in Ireland, and see Holinshed as the source of this character, this would suggest that the origins of his identity crisis, the apparently modern questioning of cultural identity, lie in the twelfth century.[19] Philip Edwards compares Macmorris with an 'Irish' captain in Essex's army, an angle that has been pursued by a number of critics.[20] In a revealing footnote to an essay on the Old English as 'conservative subversives', Ciarán Brady refers to a treatise written in 1598, on the eve of the Essex expedition, whose author insists that 'the extract of the English nation there [in Ireland] ought not to be excepted unto but rather employed against the Irish', lamenting that 'the descent of the English, to their great grief are here [in England] called and counted Irish though there are reputed and called English'.[21] This appears to be lifted verbatim from Holinshed, but of course such an acute case of mistaken identity is the Old English *modus vivendi* dating back to their very inception. Macmorris's nation may be in doubt not because he is Irish, but precisely because he is English. The matter is otherwise. As an Old Englishman, a descendant of the twelfth-century English settlement in Ireland, he could claim dual nationality. Shakespeare's 'stage Irishman' is quite probably a Palesman. Macmorris, or 'son of Morris', belongs to a clan which traces its ancestry back to the so-called 'Anglo-Norman' conquest. The Macmorris episode in *Henry V* offers one example of the way in which the Irish section of Holinshed's *Chronicles*, a peculiar mixture of medieval and early modern 'Old English' myths and anecdotes, came to be a source for a text celebrating a new kind of Englishness from which that community were to be excluded. There is some irony in the fact that an 'Anglo-Norman' aristocrat provided the blueprint for what conventional criticism considers to be the archetypal stage Irishman.

Before we leave Macmorris, it is worth noting that there was nothing unusual in the period about an Irishman fighting for England in France.[22] One of the first patriotic texts to be printed in praise of Tudor military power and English national supremacy was penned by an Irishman, or rather, an Old Englishman. Edward Walshe, in the aftermath of the English campaign in Boulogne, composed a tract entitled *The office and duety in fightyng for our countrey*. Walshe introduced his pamphlet as the text of a speech he delivered at the Siege of Boulogne (19 July–14 September 1544) before an assembly of Anglo-Irish forces – Irish kern and Old English troops – commanded by Richard, Lord Power of Curraghmore, together with a contingent from England.

Printed in London in 1545, and prefaced by a dedicatory letter to Sir Anthony Sentleger, Henry VIII's Irish viceroy, this text was apparently produced with an Irish market in mind as part of the Henrician drive towards unity in the lordship, now kingdom.[23] This same Walshe was the author of 'Conjectures', an Old English reform treatise addressed to the duke of Northumberland, with the distinction of being the first to employ classical precedents for sixteenth-century Tudor plantation schemes.[24] Walshe was listed in Holinshed, in Richard Stanyhurst's 'catalog of such learned Irishmen, as by diligent insearch could have bin found':

> Edward Walsh, he florished in the yeare 1550, and wrote in English 'The dutie of such as fight for their countrie, The reformation of Ireland by the word of God'.[25]

Walshe places great emphasis on language and ethnicity as markers and makers of nationhood:

> By her benefite, we fyrste learned to go on the grunde, and in amiable maner to frame oure babyshe tongues, to speak oure mother tounge or contrye language. By her benefite the stronge, the weke, the poore, the ryche, the noble, and thinferiour persons lyve together & are served together in their vocacion with ye necessaryes of theyr bodye…I wyl exhort that we, who the for knowledge of god hath destinied to be of the noble church and congregacion of Englande and Ireland: lack no courage to advaunce our selves defending the worthy fame which our fathers before us so long tyme have defended and preserved. And regardyng the great & noble magnanimitie of the very Ethnickis, let no defecte or slakenes be in us to perfourme so noble & worthy an enterprise.[26]

Here we have a jingoistic Palesman urging Anglo-Irish troops into battle against the French, whose efforts to repossess another pale, that around Calais, eventually proved successful. If ever the eccentricity of English ethnicity were evident, it is in this bizarre piece of early modern bellicosity. The phenomenon of Old English patriotism in this period was available to Shakespeare as an historical precedent for the four captains scene at the Siege of Harfleur in *Henry V*. If he was unable to advert to Walshe's unique discourse, Richard Stanyhurst covered the episode in Holinshed:

> king Henrie being fullie resolved to besiege Bullongne, gave commandement to Sir Anthonie Sentleger deputie to levie an armie of Irishmen, and with all expedition to send them to England. To these were appointed capteins the lord Powre, who after was dubd knight, Surlocke & Finglasse, with diverse others. They mustered in saint James his parke seven hundred. In the siege of Bullongne they stood the armie in verie good sted.[27]

Stanyhurst goes on to describe in great detail the severity used by the Irish against the French, who:

> with this strange kind of warfaring astonished, sent an ambassador to king Henrie, to learne whether he brought men with him or divels, that could neither be woone with rewards, nor pacified by pitie.[28]

This attribution of mercilessness to the native Irish perpetuated an image of Irish savagery at the very moment that English actions in Ireland were going 'beyond the pale' of conventional military practice. According to Steven Ellis:

> The rules of Irish warfare had traditionally differed from continental conventions, but by treating the natives as savages and persistently infringing all military conventions Elizabethan armies precipitated the savagery which characterized the conquest's eventual completion.[29]

By constantly imputing the contravention of military discipline to the Irish, the English, naturalised, and neutralised, their own violence as retaliatory, responsive, restorative.

In the thirty years between Walshe's patriotic manual and Stanyhurst's untimely contribution to Holinshed, Old English identity was compatible with the expansionist aims of Tudor government, and the increasing national self-consciousness of the native English. The Palesmen, as their crisis of identity deepened, presented themselves as Elizabeth's 'old ancient faithfull English subjects who never revolted sens the conquest', but by then the prefix 'old' had become confused with the condition of being 'obsolete'.[30] From 1579 to 1599, the alienation of the English Pale from the Crown was the single most important issue in Anglo-Irish politics. It was a time of national neurosis and cultural confusion. The impact of this changeover, the outcome of 400 years of colonial contact, is evident throughout Shakespeare's histories.

Having argued that the question put by Shakespeare's Macmorris points to the quandary of the Old English, I want now to explore another remote Holinshed resource that touches once more on issues of identity, influence, and origins. The next passage from Shakespeare that I want to examine is the speech uttered by Richard II on the eve of his Irish expedition:

> Now for our Irish wars.
> We must supplant those rough rug-headed kerns,
> Which live like venom where no venom else,
> But only they, have privilege to live.[31]

In the *Chronicles*, Richard Stanyhurst, an Old Englishman who could trace his family tree back to the roots of the original English invasion of Ireland, devotes a substantial part of his contribution, 'A Plaine and Perfect Description of Ireland', to the refutation of one 'maister Alan Cope', who in a dialogue between Critobulus and Ireneus had defamed the entire Irish nation by asserting that there were no snakes in Ireland because the people themselves were venomous enough. Stanyhurst's citation runs thus:

> And thereupon it is reported percase by some men, that there is nothing venemous or poisoned in Ireland, but the men and women. Which is taken to have beene spoken by most men for their brutish and savage manners.[32]

At this point one is already aware of a certain secondary quality to the evidence, in so far as Cope, in a dialogue, has one of the disputants quote what he introduces as a commonplace, 'And thereupon it is reported percase by some men'. It should be noted for future reference that Stanyhurst is almost wholly impervious to the question of the veracity or otherwise of the main theme of the passage from Cope's discourse to which he takes exception:

> Touching the principall question, whether S. Patrike did expell poisoned wormes out of Ireland, or whether it be the nature of the soile, as I said in the entrie of this discourse; so I saie againe, I weigh not two chips which waie the wind bloweth, bicause I see no inconvenience that may insue either of the affirmative or negative opinion.[33]

Stanyhurst is not even concerned specifically with the scurrilous report reproduced by Cope via Critobulus, the German half of the dialogue. It is not the quotation but the construction placed upon it which infuriates him:

> Here (good reader) thou must understand that M. Cope putteth the text downe and the glose. The text is, There is nothing in Ireland venomous but the inhabitants. The glose is, This is said to have been spoken for their brutish and savage conditions. Now well harpt by saint Lankfield. Here is a glose, I undertake you, sutable to the text.[34]

Stanyhurst then informs us that the trafficking in slander is a form of wit beneath such learned disquisitions, 'that these japes and gibes are onelie fit for ruffians, vices, swashbucklers & tospots'. In particular, Stanyhurst is outraged that a cleric should repeat such nonsense:

> And trulie they beeset a divine as well, as for an asse to twang quipassa on a harpe or gitterne, or for an ape to friske trenchmoore in a paire of buskins and a doublet.[35]

Stanyhurst further contends that by circulating such opinions in Latin – 'the language that is universallie spoken, throughout the greater part of the world' – Cope has added insult to injury, giving a popular prejudice a high cultural circulation.

A few facts are beginning to emerge from a controversy to which Stanyhurst has devoted approximately one-tenth of his discourse. Alan Cope, 'or some other that masketh under his visours', the author of a Latin dialogue, has permitted one of his speakers to repeat a common slander against the Irish, which is compounded by a superfluous gloss on the same. There the matter might have rested, had Stanyhurst not chosen such a prominent place to publish his elaborate refutation of Cope. Ironically, it was the publicity conferred upon a common slur that Stanyhurst had taken issue with in the first place.

John Derricke, in his *Image of Irelande* (1581), dedicated to Sir Philip Sidney, writes thus:

> O holie sainct, O holie man,
> O man of God I saie:
> O Patrick chiefe of all these karne
> if speake to thee I maie.
> What moved thee, the wriglyng Snake,
> and other wormes to kill?
> What caused thee on sillie beastes,
> to worke thy cruel will?
> What thyng incenst thee for to strike,
> them with thy heavie hande?
> When as thou leftest more spitefull beastes
> within this fertile lande.
> Thou smotest the serpentes venimous,
> and Furies didst subverte:
> And yet the footers of the boggs,
> couldst thou no whit converte?[36]

A marginal note observes: 'Irish karne more hurtfull then Serpentes'. Thus we have Stanyhurst, a representative of the Geraldines through the patronage of the Earl of Kildare, and a member of the Leicester-Sidney circle, condemning what he sees as a defamation of Irish character.[37] Four years later, in the midst of the Desmond war, the last stand of the Geraldines, another beneficiary of Sidney clientage – John Derricke – employs the self-same trope against the Irish.

Just as Giraldus furnished Shakespeare with an Anglo-Irish identity crisis which has come to be read as an Irish problem, so Stanyhurst provided him, through his laborious demonstration of Cope's iniquity, with a compelling image of Ireland that refers to there being nothing venomous or poisoned in that country but the natives, a phrase, we remember, 'onelie fit for ruffians, vices, swashbucklers & tospots' (the latter term appears in Feste's song at the end of *Twelfth Night*). Where does Shakespeare put it? Straight into the mouth of Richard II, where it will reside, and continue to tease, taunt and trouble critics long after Stanyhurst's discourse is nothing more than the exclusive resort of the historian of early modern Ireland.

Barnaby Rich, in *A New Description of Ireland*, misrepresents Stanyhurst's objections to Cope, implying that the latter's scepticism with regard to the 'foolish conceit houlden by the Irish, that Ireland was purged from venomous wormes, by the only praiers of S. Patrick' was the sole reason for his resentment, rather than the 'glose':

> Maister Stanihurst is so angry, that there should be any doubt or question made of that which hath beene so longe received and beleeved for an undoubted truth amongst the Natives of Ireland.[38]

Rich is guilty of glossing over the actual text of Stanyhurst's objections and reducing those objections to an obsession with a 'foolish conceit'.

In 1975, Nicholas Canny, one of the most important Irish historians in terms of recent debates on culture and colonialism in the period, in a discussion of the Old English élite, cites Stanyhurst's attack on Cope as an example of the growing sense of political and cultural identity within the Pale, expressed through their attitudes to the Irish as opposed to the more extreme programmes espoused by the New English:

> Stanyhurst was provoked into discussing the problem of converting the Irish to civility by a pamphlet, no longer extant, written in dialogue form by an Englishman named Alan Cope 'or some other that masketh under his visours'. We can gather from Stanyhurst's account that the general conclusion of the pamphlet

was that the Gaelic Irish were unreasonable men who could not be brought to civility by moderate means.[39]

Canny glosses the offending exchange between Ireneus and Critobulus, 'the two fictitious characters in the dialogue', as one in which both appear to have:

> attributed the perversity of the Irish to an error on the part of St. Patrick who in his effort to convert Ireland to Christianity had stopped short by banishing snakes from the country instead of the rancour from men's hearts.[40]

The plot thickens. In 1979 the playwright John Arden launched a blistering attack in the pages of the *New Statesman* on the anti-Irish attitudes, as he saw them to be, that were enshrined in the canonical texts of English literature.[41] John Bale and others came in for some rather violent polemical barracking. Spenser escaped with a minor knock which is worth quoting, because it engendered a serious response from an admirer in *Poetry Nation Review*:

> Spenser espoused genocide: and he is still read by schoolchildren in and around the A level for his melodious moral allegory. His posthumous influence upon such as Roy Mason deserves a monograph to itself.[42]

That monograph has yet to be written. The first literary target of Arden's kaleidoscopic tour through four centuries of unproblematically 'British' prejudice is Shakespeare, who as 'the very foundation of our national cultural export trade' has made most public the denigratory position on the Irish held by generations of English intellectuals. However, having singled out Shakespeare as the most famous defamer of the Irish, Arden employs an interesting metaphor in reassuring us that Shakespeare 'did not originate the poison'. Spenser is then briefly lashed, but only in order to get at 'Bilious Bale', the ideal whipping boy, and several citations from *The Vocacyon* ensue.[43]

The first response to Arden's article issued from the pen of Conor Cruise O'Brien, who wanted to know how Arden, as a dramatist, could hold Shakespeare responsible for the words he had his characters deliver.[44] Arden's rejoinder maintained that any author who reproduced such views and circulated or publicized them had to accept personal responsibility for the consequences.[45] Arden argued that Shakespeare's culpability stems from the fact that 'nowhere in the play is it challenged by any character or circumstance'. This is palpably untrue. In the very scene from which the offending quotation is taken, serious doubt is cast upon Richard's intention to fulfil his brag by both Northumberland and Ross, and surely the fate of the king is poetic justice? Moreover, the point that Richard mortgaged the realm of England to fund his Irish wars is reinforced in a later play, where Northumberland speaks of Richard's ill-fated journey to Ireland:

> From whence he, intercepted, did return
> To be depos'd, and shortly murdered.[46]

Conversely, Henry V is seen to harness the Irish in the service of an overweening Englishness. Ironically, the latter play coincides with Elizabeth's costly campaign to quell Tyrone's Rebellion, and contains what is generally agreed upon as the only reference to contemporary events in all of Shakespeare's works.[47] There is some irony in the fact that Shakespeare borrowed an allusion to Ireland as a land where only the people were venomous from Stanyhurst, that is, from a source where it was considered a remark worthy only of 'tospots'. Shakespeare's choice of an expression castigated by Stanyhurst, and designated suitable only for the lowest forms of life, leads one to suspect an acute criticism at the heart of Shakespeare's representation of English monarchical power. The exchange between Arden and O'Brien foregrounds some of the problems implicit in approaches to 'Shakespeare and Ireland' that are neither theoretically informed nor historically grounded. It exposes the degree of cultural investment in canonical authors in terms of oppositional discourses. The whole debate, if it deserves that term, is very much caught up in the language of 'guilt' and 'defence'.[48]

When Stanyhurst's biographer, Colm Lennon, arrived on the scene in 1981, his principal purpose was to reveal his subject as a lover of his country – this is the same Stanyhurst who wanted to eradicate the Irish language, and who stigmatised Irish soldiers as savages – and so the rebuke delivered to Cope features prominently in the discussion of Stanyhurst's native pride.[49] The ground of

Stanyhurst's main defence of Ireland's reputation is, as far as I can establish, his attribution of even greater savagery to the Germans than Critobulus accorded to the Irish. Hardly a major contribution to race relations. I'll have grounds more relative than this for countering colonial stereotypes. The final irony in this literary and historical cornucopia is that Alan Cope, as we might have guessed from the hints of Rich and Stanyhurst, is not the author of 'a pamphlet, no longer extant', but is something of a red herring. Stanyhurst had said that this author wore a mask, while Rich had him the composer of 'many matters', in which case one would expect something to survive. That something is not a pamphlet, as Canny assumed, but a copious religious dialogue published at Antwerp in 1566, written by Nicholas Harpsfield (1519–75), Archdeacon of Canterbury (1554–58), during the early years of his internment in the Fleet from 1558 to 1574. The dialogues were published with the aid of Alan Cope, a confidant of Harpsfield's, and later Canon of St Peter's in Rome. Harpsfield studied at New College, Oxford, where his elder brother, John, was appointed Regius Professor of Greek, which might partly explain Stanyhurst's allusion to that university: 'M. Cope never learned this kind of reasoning in the famous college of Magdalene in Oxford.' Stanyhurst studied at University College, Oxford, from 1563 to 1568. We can also now more easily understand that peculiar phrase of Stanyhurst's: 'Now well harpt by saint Lankfield'.[50] Thus by a somewhat circumlocuitous route we arrive back at Stanyhurst's original effort to ward off a common slur against the Irish. Such detours and digressions are the stuff of colonial and anti-colonial discourse (and Stanyhurst's Old English text can be read both ways).

In *Outside the Teaching Machine*, Gayatri Spivak writes: 'In postcoloniality, every metropolitan definition is dislodged. The general mode for the postcolonial is citation, reinscription, rerouting the historical.'[51] I have tried to illustrate two instances of rerouting that impinge upon Shakespeare and Ireland. What could be more serpentine than the route by which Harpsfield's vast and elaborate theological treatise became first Stanyhurst's German scapegoat and calumniator of the Irish, then Derricke's complaint to Saint Patrick, then Richard's racist rhetoric (as scripted by Shakespeare), then Rich's 'most arrogant and superstitious Papist', then Canny's lost pamphlet, then the basis for Arden's attack on just about everybody, then Lennon's example of Stanyhurst's defence of his native country? It is a catalogue of cultural confusion and a record of identity crises of which Lawrence Sterne would have been proud, and a rerouting which we may allow to stand here for the literary *fortuna* of many other undetected colonial cross-fertilisations. Together with the lament of Gerald of Wales on the predicament of his uncle, the story of Stanyhurst's snake serves both to inform and deform our understanding of the resources and con-texts that mark Shakespeare's representations of Ireland. These two extracts from Holinshed suggest that discerning ambivalence and hybridity may be the most fruitful way of tackling early modern views of Ireland, especially in the work of canonical authors, and particularly in a genre that invites such complexity, and points up the perils of reinforcing colonial stereotypes merely by repeating them. I hope that my own unpacking of a history of revisions, representations, and appropriations, liminal and tangential, has gone some way towards complicating the notion of a uniformly pejorative and unproblematically 'English' reading of two contested sites – 'Shakespeare' and 'Ireland'.[52]

4

Forms of Discrimination in Spenser's *A View of the State of Ireland* (1596; 1633): From Dialogue to Silence

In this chapter I propose to do two things. First, I shall suggest a specific Irish colonial context for Edmund Spenser's notorious prose dialogue, arguing that this particular form was a familiar feature of the literary landscape of early modern Ireland. I will then proceed to chart Spenser's confused cultural cartography in some detail, exploring a complex geography of difference in which the Irish are displaced, misplaced, and finally forced off the map altogether. Written around 1596, the first published edition of Spenser's *A View of the State of Ireland*, that of James Ware in 1633, advertised it as being written 'Dialogue-wise', yet few critics have been wise to the dialogue, or alert to the informed – and thus intentional – absence of the Irish from key passages of the text. In what follows, I remind readers of the dialogic status of Spenser's treatise, before going on to argue that the exchange is one which is closed to the Irish, making it much more monologic in tone and tenor than critics have hitherto assumed, but not in predictably pejorative ways. Indeed, the argument of this chapter is that a text that purports to treat of Ireland has other interests and preoccupations, a state of affairs which leads to its alleged subject matter being marginalised.

Dialogue-wise

Two recent contributions to Spenser studies by John Breen and Andrew Hadfield on the dialogue form in the *View* have added much to the ongoing debate on the poet's Irish experiences, and have begun to tackle Patricia Coughlan's complaint that 'the textual fact of its dialogue form has still not been sufficiently attended to.'[1] While Breen's insertion of Spenser's prose treatise into the established genre of the Renaissance dialogue is important and appropriate, here I want to develop Hadfield's tantalising suggestion that there is a highly specific Irish context for the dialogue form, and good historical reasons for English authors intent on treating Irish affairs to adopt this mode of writing.[2] Picking up on Hadfield's helpful suggestion, I shall argue that there is a more specific literary lineage to which the *View* can usefully be seen to belong, that of the early modern discourse on Ireland, a genre that draws frequently on dialogue as an ideal mode within which to express opinions that may not have been welcomed by the metropolitan authorities. I also wish to introduce an unpublished manuscript that raises the troubled matters of repression and representation central to the Irish dialogue, a text which has not been read alongside the *View* in any systematic way, and one which may in future yield a fruitful comparison.

First, though, some preliminary observations. John Breen has done a valuable service by reminding us all of the 'generic complexity' of Spenser's *View*. Breen is correct to argue that the *View* has to be read in the context of the Renaissance dialogue, but Hadfield is right to emphasise the form's dominant voice and forcefulness as well as its irony and playfulness. The dialogue form ought not to be used to exonerate Spenser from some of the more extreme views voiced in his prose treatise. There is arguably a 'monologism' at work within the 'dialogism.' Dialogue, for Mikhail Bakhtin, 'is not a means for revealing, for bringing to the surface the already ready-made character of a person; no, in dialogue a person not only shows himself outwardly, but he becomes for the first time that which he is, not only for others but for himself as well. To be means to communicate dialogically.'[3] The dialogue may be the most obvious literary form that suggests itself when 'dialogism' is discussed, but a monologue may in the end be far more dialogic than a dialogue. Dialogism is a textual principle, a mixing of voices within a single text. A dialogue may well consist, as some critics feel the *View* does, of two voices coming to the same conclusion.

'Aporia', a term Breen uses to refer to the rehearsing of contrary positions without assuming one, is not, in my reading, the mode followed in Spenser's dialogue. Whether or not one identifies

Irenius as Spenser it is difficult not to feel that there is a dominant line being pursued, and that Eudoxus is in step by the end of the text. The element of undecidability is minimal. Yet Bruce Avery has taken issue with the critical tradition that has argued for the one-sidedness of Spenser's dialogue. Those who claim that 'the *View*, though a dialogue, is essentially monovocal, seem to me to miss its most intriguing aspect: its polyvocality, its own contradictory mix of interpretations of, and speculations on, what might be the best view of Ireland.'[4] Avery's reasons for believing that the *View* is polyvocal soon collapse back into the old poet-planter dichotomy:

> These contradictions were part of Spenser's own experience. He was both a poet *and* a part of the political administration of the British [*sic*] colonial government; he was an Englishman, yet he spent most of his life in Ireland: hence the *View* seems to waver between Irenius's eyewitness accounts, which might square with Spenser's interpretation of his experience of the place, and accounts which would be acceptable to the home authority represented by Eudoxus.[5]

Or, as Breen puts it: 'The dialogue between Spenser's Irenius and Eudoxus is designed to complicate the authorial responsibility for what is spoken.'[6] Thus 'Spenser is the authority removed from the text.'[7] This fits in with the contention of Kenneth Gross that: 'There runs through the dialogue a deep strain of scepticism about the place and power of such structures of order as myth, custom and law.'[8] This is a different perspective from that of the tradition represented by Ciarán Brady which sees Eudoxus as a mere foil for the arguments of Irenius/Spenser:

> The dramatic pretence of the dialogue form was adopted by Spenser because it was imperative for him to show that when confronted with a true interpretation, a view, of the means by which Ireland came to its present condition, the sensitive, informed and critical English intelligence would concede the complete failure of its own central assumptions regarding the reform of Ireland, as in due course Eudoxus does.[9]

The dialogue suggests an interview of sorts, an exchange between an official and a member of the public. According to Helena Shire, it 'is a model for our modern form of communication, the interview on broadcast media between the specialist and the intelligent layman.'[10] Dialogue, though, does not necessarily imply a polite conversation or discussion. It can take the form of an interrogation. Coughlan observes that beneath 'a superficial diversity of roles' there lies certain fundamental positions, such as 'those of Master and Pupil, Objector and Answerer'.[11] She argues for 'the fictive mode of existence of the *View*, and against the treatment of it as an expository argument'. She also shows that Spenser and other English writers on Ireland were working from established literary models and within a circumscribed discursive space.[12] For Roland Smith, Spenser's choice of form is a means of juxtaposing or opposing Ireland's present state with its desired condition, so that the 'dialogue form emphasizes his strong inclination to draw contrasts between the reality of his Irish surroundings and the more ideal conditions which his proposed reforms would bring about'.[13] But Spenser is arguably less interested in 'the reality of his Irish surroundings' or any supposed colonial utopia, than he is absorbed by the uses to which myths can be put, and the ways in which Irish origin-myths impinge upon the reality of the surroundings he left behind in England.

Anne Fogarty, drawing on the work of Jacques Derrida, contends that Spenser's treatise is polyvocal, that 'the *View* is a form of bricolage, that is, a discourse which is patched together by borrowings from other linguistic systems and sub-systems.'[14] Fogarty says of Book VI of *The Faerie Queene* and the *View* that 'both of these works present equivocal and divided accounts of the political ideologies which they wish to sustain. In both cases, the "other space" projected by the text – the reordered Ireland of the *View* and the consolatory but doomed world of pastoral and faery in *The Faery Queene* – is realized with great difficulty.'[15] There is a tension in both cases between what is projected into the past and what is projected into the future, and between both lies the troubled question of a political present. If pastoral is the literary form that lends itself best to colonialism, then epic is the form that meets the needs of empire. Both rely on 'other spaces', the one as an end in itself, an alternative to metropolitan society, the other as a means to an end, unquestionably subject to the state. Much of the division and equivocation in colonial texts of the period arises from an awareness of the contradiction between local, small-scale ventures, many of them privately backed, and much larger state-sponsored enterprises. Plantations like that in which Spenser participated in Munster fell between two stools, being the product both of individual initiative and governmental subsidy.

Spenser's dialogue, according to Donald Bruce, is written in 'a form implying open-minded discussion.' Bruce maintains that:

> Irenius, the chief speaker, is neither Spenser's spokesman nor even a governmental recorder, since the *Viewe* was suppressed until 1633, when it could have little effect on official policy. Eudoxus, the second speaker, represents informed public opinion.[16]

The issue of suppression, or censorship, is a vexed one.[17] It could be argued that Ireland was both a site of unspeakable Otherness and a place where nothing but the same old story was endlessly related. It was at one and the same time an imaginative scene of pastoral retreat, and a domain characterised by political violence and martial law. It offered an archive of literary and cultural source material, as well as an opportunity, like that given to Spenser, to combine the roles of secretary and sheriff.

The individual writer found in Ireland a crux of identity as well as a crucible of ideology. The formation of a self – the fashioning of a gentleman – could occur here, but so too could dissolution and crisis. Spenser was very much a man made in Ireland, but also one ruined there. For some critics, including Donald Bruce, the form of the *View* enacts a self-effacement rather than a self-fashioning: 'Classical dialogue was a dramatic form, rendered objective by the self effacement of the author, who did no more than record disparate opinions, sometimes opposed to his own.'[18] Conversely, John Day sees the author slyly obtruding his countenance upon his cardboard creations: 'With only the barest fiction of conversation, no setting, and few digressions, the two thinly characterized speakers move methodically through an agenda.'[19] The hidden agenda is that of a Machiavellian figure who appears to stand back from his work the more to manipulate the reader.

According to Thomas Wright, Spenser, in composing the *View*, may have learned from Bryskett's *Discourse of Civill Life*, in which he had played a part, since this is a text which 'offers in a prose dialogue materials presented in Sidney's *Arcadia* and Spenser's *Faerie Queene*.'[20] John Day finds a more immediate influence in Richard Beacon's *Solon His Follie* (1594).[21] Beverley Sherry has pointed out Spenser's extensive use of dialogue in his poetic works: '*The Shepheardes Calender* is a series of dialogues in the tradition of the classical eclogue ... In *The Faerie Queene* there is a range of dialogue as well as indirect and reported speech.'[22] One could add the Spenser–Harvey correspondence and *Colin Clouts Come Home Againe* to this penchant for dialogue in Spenser.

Anne Fogarty has argued against the tendency to divide Spenser into planter and poet: 'Not infrequently Spenser's work is protected by a grim determination to keep the role of poet and of Elizabethan colonist permanently distinct.'[23] However, Fogarty herself may succumb to this temptation. The word 'gentle' does not mean soft or pacifistic, just as the word 'humanist' does not mean humanitarian. *The Faerie Queene* is a poem littered with corpses, arguably the most relentlessly violent verse in English literary history. The *View* is a model of civility in comparison. Yet critics of the calibre of Ciaràn Brady can still ask: 'How could the principal poet of the English Renaissance not merely tolerate or even defend, but actually celebrate the use of merciless and unrestrained violence against large numbers of his fellow men?'[24] The answer is, of course, with the greatest of ease (although in the second section of this chapter I will take issue with the notion of 'his fellow men').

David Baker argues that 'Irenius is not Spenser's spokesman in a simple sense, but one voice in a dialectic Spenser constructs between inadmissible scepticism of royal policy and articulations of the official "view", articulations Spenser usually puts in the mouth of Eudoxus.'[25] Ciaràn Brady recognises that the Renaissance dialogue was popular in Ireland, and that the form was perhaps inflected in a colonial context:

> The use of the dialogue form was by no means unusual in English Renaissance literature, and appears to have been somewhat in fashion in Ireland in the 1590s. But whereas typically the genre was employed as a useful pedagogical technique, as a means of conveying information and argument in a relaxed manner, Spenser made a clear effort to return to the formally dis-

putational character of the platonic original. Unlike the ciphers of the other Irish dialogues, Eudoxus is an intelligent, informed, if rather two-dimensional character.[26]

I am not so sure that Spenser differs so markedly from his English contemporaries in Ireland, but Brady is right to stress the disputational character of his treatise. The ciphers in the *View*, as we shall shortly discover, lie elsewhere.

Having rehearsed some of the positions taken up in recent Spenser criticism on the dialogue form of the *View*, I want to turn now to the place of the dialogue within a wider colonial milieu. The notion that there was, in the early modern period, a monolithic English 'discourse on Ireland' is fundamentally flawed. The 'discourse on Ireland' is a complex, fraught and heterogeneous genre. Within that diverse body of texts, the dialogue occupies a special position. The Renaissance dialogue in an Irish context raises questions of censorship and self-fashioning that impinge upon English Renaissance culture at large. It was Barnaby Rich, in the context of a dialogue written in 1615, who boasted: 'thos wordes that in Englande would be brought wythin the compasse of treason, they are accounted wyth us in Ireland for ordynary table taulke.'[27] 'Table-talk', from the cosy humanism of Bryskett's Dublin residence that provides the pretext for his *Discourse of Civill Life*, to the informed exchange between Irenius and Eudoxus, is the order of the day in early modern Ireland. Here was a unique space in which free-thinking intellectuals could say what they felt, not what they ought to say.

I want to conclude this section by introducing a contemporary dialogue that remains in manuscript, despite having been prepared for publication around the same time as Spenser's *View*. The 'Dialogue of Sylvanus and Peregrine' (1598), dedicated to the earl of Essex, is endorsed with the name of Sir Thomas Wilson (*c*.1560–1629), Keeper of the Records in Whitehall. The presence of an index, coupled with the dedication – a controversial one – suggests that it was intended for print. The *Dialogue* – at 74 folio pages or 40,000 words – is a substantial text. Its participants, Sylvanus and Peregrine – the names of Spenser's two sons, hence the historical association of the document with Spenser – meet at Westminster and expound upon the vicissitudes of Irish politics. They mirror the roles played by Eudoxus and Irenius respectively, with Sylvanus adopting the role of the probing questioner, and Peregrine assuming the air of one who is experienced in Irish affairs. Speaking of the *Dialogue* Rudolf Gottfried writes: 'the dialogue form – not common among Irish state papers – suggests that the *View* may have served as a model.'[28] I have already pointed out, however, that Spenser was by no means original in his choice of form.

The *Dialogue* is a composite treatise, a synthesis of divergent discourses divided into four books. The first book (ff. 284^r–312^v) deals with events from 'the latter ende of harvest 1597 untill March next ensuinge', and focuses upon King's county, or Offaly, part of the Leix-Offaly plantation. Peregrine claims to have little knowledge of Connaught (f. 331^r). Sir Edward Herbert, a courtier and Leix-Offaly planter, closely connected to the powerful 'Erle of Pembrook', is singled out for praise on account of a piece of counter-insurgency performed by him around harvest time. Sylvanus recalls Herbert as 'a suter at the Courte' who was well received by Elizabeth, and wonders that such a refined personage 'should lye in such a remoate place, and emongst such vyle neighbours' (ff. 284^v–285^v). Sir Warham St. Leger, reported present at Bryskett's house in the *Discourse of Civill Life*, and installed as Governor of Leix in 1597, is accused of aiding and abetting the rebels (f. 293^r). Peregrine entertains his interviewer with a 'Gallymauffery of knaves' (f. 304^r). The second book (ff. 313^r–331^r) 'entreateth of matters concerninge south Leimpster [Leinster]'. The third, covering Connaught and Ulster, is in two parts. In the first, Peregrine produces from the copious 'noates' to which he makes repeated reference, a discourse on Connaught in the form of a dialogue between an old soldier and Jacob, a trader in cattle (ff. 331^v–336^v).

This dialogue within a dialogue is followed by a report on events in Ulster entitled 'Ulster Occurences', which includes an eyewitness report of the defeat of English forces commanded by Sir Henry Bagenal (1556–98) at the Yellow Ford on 14 August 1598. It concludes with a list of the officers who perished in this encounter, and is dated 25 August 1598 (ff. 337^r–342^v). The discourse done, Sylvanus comments thus: 'How say you brother is it not tyme to top this lofty pyne?', to which Peregrine replies 'yee and chope the underwood too, or else all wilbe naught shortly' (f. 342^v).

The fourth book (ff. 343^r–354^r) concerns 'matters touching the Comon weale of the Contrie.' Peregrine unearths from his private collection of manuscripts a discourse supposedly related to him at his residence in Dublin by an elderly Palesman who dined there with three friends. This treatise appears to be culled from a variety of sources. It is a 'Gallymauffery' text. There is a tension around the perceived threat of Irishness, especially relating to language:

> ffirst by reasone of combinacon with the Irish as aforesayde in crept there Languadge to be allmost generall emongst us, that within a shorte tyme scorninge our oulde Englishe speeche which our Ancestours brought with them at the first conquest thinking it to base by reasone whereof we thought our selves mightely well appoynted to be armed with two Languadges so that beinge thus furnished we were able to goe into the Irish countries: and truck with them comodity for comoditie whereas they in former tymes were driven to bringe theires unto us and either bought ours againe with the mony they newly receaved for it or bartered ware for ware for ware, by an interpreter. Now this kynde of intercourse with the Irish breadde such acquayntaunce amitie and frendshipp betwene them and us, beinge so furnisht with theire Languadge that wee cared not contrary to our duties in ballancing our creditte, to make fosteredg, gossiping, and marriadge as aforesaid with them so that now the English Pale and many other places of the kingdome that were planted with English at the first Conqueste are growne to a confusion. (ff. 343^v–344^r)

In order to ward off the awesome spectre of a loss of selfhood through 'intercourse with the Irish', it was necessary to maintain the kind of 'internal dialogue' that proliferated among the literary representatives of the English colonial community.

   Interestingly, Eva Gold, in an essay which sees Spenser as a 'borderer', has suggested that the poet's own choice of dialogue is determined by just such a fear of a loss of identity:

> Spenser's anxieties – his own included – about the English tendency to 'degenerate' into the Irish may also account for the use of the dialogue form in the *View*. Why Spenser chose this form has occasioned some puzzlement, for it is not entirely clear why Spenser's material requires two voices. What may be important,

however, is not so much the relation between what Eudoxus and Irenius say, but rather the mere presence of Eudoxus. Eudoxus may be there to keep Irenius from losing his mooring to English identity.[29]

The question of self-fashioning is crucially linked to the need for dialogue, with the colonist having to converse in order to avoid conversion. Civil conversation is the key to cohesion within the colonial community. The process of identity formation is achieved through a deafening dialogue, not with, but over and against an Other whose exclusion from speech leaves a vacuum, a silence, a negative image, clearing a positively charged space in which the process of self-fashioning can occur.[30] The use of the dialogue form by English colonists in Ireland, Edmund Spenser included, reflects, on one level, a fundamental anxiety about identity, as well as an acute awareness of both the profit and the peril of being situated at a distance from the prying eye, and the cocked ear, of the state. It was by an act of self-censorship of sorts, a self-effacement that carved out a communal colonial sphere, that Spenser and his contemporaries imposed the binary opposition between coloniser and colonised that effectively ruled out debate, and kept the native Irish beyond the pale of 'civill conversation.' The planter-poets were in dialogue, but they were talking to themselves.

The texture of silence

Spenser's *View* is a far more sophisticated treatise than much of the criticism it has engendered would imply. Spenser's strategy in the *View* is not one of straightforward denigration of the Irish, but is rather one of displacement and subterfuge, no less racially motivated, in which the discussion of Irish identity is a side-show, and the main event is an interrogation of English, Scottish, British and European identity formation. It is precisely by means of a determined process of oversight, that is, by ignoring the Irish as such, that Spenser is able to effect the desired goal – the elimination of the native.

In an incisive essay on the representation of race in English Renaissance culture, Lynda Boose sees Spenser's *View* as a founding document of racism: 'If "race" originates as a category that hierarchically privileges a ruling status and makes the Other(s) inferior, then for the English the group that was first to be shunted into this discursive derogation and thereafter invoked as almost a paradigm of inferiority was not the black "race" – but the Irish "race".' Boose places the *View* within a discourse in which 'the derogation of the Irish as "a race apart" situates racial difference within cultural and religious categories rather than biologically empirical ones.'[31] My argument centres on the premise that the Irish are for Spenser less 'a race apart' than 'a race aside', and that they afford him a unique opportunity, through a series of subtle displacements, to explore questions of identity and difference that go beyond the immediate Irish context.

Despite the fact that Spenser's *View* is arguably one of the most difficult colonial discourses any reader may expect to encounter, standard criticism tends to portray it as an uncomplicated exercise in anti-Irish sentiment. The upshot of a peculiar conjunction of embarrassment and anger is that the text attracts commentary of the most simplistic sort. While inevitable as the necessary first stage in a critical process, the mere cataloguing of negative images obviously has its limitations, yet criticism of Spenser and Ireland continues to dwell on a perceived antipathy to all things Irish.

Spenser has been singled out for attention as being obsessed with 'race' in a way that his contemporaries were not. Brendan Bradshaw alleges that Richard Beacon and William Herbert, two of Spenser's fellow undertakers on the Munster Plantation, do not resort to the kind of ethnology employed by Spenser.[32] For Margaret MacCurtain, 'Spenser's delineation of the origins and history of the Irish could almost be termed an essay in anthropology.'[33] An earlier generation of Spenser scholars attached less weight to the time Spenser spends on issues of racial composition, colonial legacy, national identity, and cultural inheritance. Rudolf Gottfried's assertion 'that the antiquities are a completely separable element, a kind of historical decoration on the facade of the *View*; if they are also flimsy in character, they cause no weakening of its broad and solid structure' is no longer accepted wisdom.[34] Where Gottfried sees a façade, Ciarán Brady sees patience, purpose and planning in Spenser's ethnographic orientation. Yet having insisted on the centrality of Spenser's treatment of racial origins, Brady concludes that the sophisticated ethnology he constructs is merely a humanist pretext for homicidal policies: 'Thus the elaborate discussions of classical and modern authorities and the ingenious analysis of etymologies were intended to show that Spenser's credit as a scrupulous and sincere scholar remained good. The killing would be justified not simply on grounds of crude expediency but in terms of the highest humanist discourse as well.'[35] Tracey Hill likewise draws a direct link between the cultural denigration of the Irish and the need for colonial violence: 'In *A View*, the indigenous Irish are constructed as ethnically debased and intrinsically unruly; it therefore follows that a policy of extreme military repression is required to control them.'[36] In what follows I intend to take issue with the assumption that Spenser's discussion of origin-myths in the *View* is merely a humanist pretext for homicide.

My contention here will be that Spenser's chief strategy in the *View* is to efface rather than deface the Irish. From a theoretical perspective, I am concerned with what postcolonialism can learn from Renaissance texts like Spenser's and what readers of the *View* can gain from an awareness of postcolonial criticism. Spenser's text, published posthumously, remains timely. Sir James Ware's edition of 1633 was entitled *A View of the State of Ireland*. Ware dropped the 'present' from the title in an effort to forget the past. But the past, like the post, keeps coming back to haunt us. The *View* remains caught up in the present. Ware, in his preface, praises Spenser thus: 'His proofes (although most of them conjecturall) concerning the originall of the language, customes of the Nations, and the first peopling of the severall parts of the Iland, are full of good reading; and doe shew a sound judgment.'[37] Note that Ware pluralises national identity, in keeping with Spenser's preoccupation with multiple origins and identities.

The *View* is to a large extent an extended essay in multiculturalism. Its rehearsal of origins and identity, antiquity and early modernity, dialogism and development, make it an ideal starting-point for a meditation on the applicability of postcolonial theory to the period. The key terms of postcoloniality – ambivalence and hybridity – are seldom invoked in discussions of Spenser's Irish experiences. A theory most intimately and obviously associated with late modern, or even postmodern culture, postcolonial criticism can arguably both inform, and be informed by, early modern texts and contexts. In this regard, Spenser's treatise is an ideal test-case for the applicability of postcolonial theory to Renaissance texts.

Postcolonialism offers a valuable critical register for dealing with a text such as the *View*. Yet one recent response suggests that the simplified version of the poet's colonial ideology that obtains in Renaissance studies is being reproduced without significant alteration in a form of criticism which one would have expected to be more attentive to historical differences. Edward Said places Spenser unproblematically at the core of a particular Western colonial tradition: 'Since Spenser's 1596 tract on Ireland, a whole tradition of British and European thought has considered the Irish to be a separate and inferior race, usually unregenerately barbarian, often delinquent and primitive.'[38] In what follows, I aim to suggest that the perspective that sees Spenser's tract as part of nothing but the same old story of unadulterated anti-Irish racism from Giraldus Cambrensis to the present is fundamentally flawed, exactly because Spenser's overriding concern is not with the margins, but with the mainstream, that is, he is preoccupied with using the complexities of the Irish colonial milieu as a means of refiguring metropolitan identities.

One reason why it does not make sense to read the *View* in terms of a recognisable Anglo-Irish conflict that retrospectively superimposes a modern standpoint onto the sixteenth and seventeenth centuries is that Spenser's attitude to Englishness is as important as his opinion of the Irish. This fact has not generally been acknowledged by previous scholars, and as a result the traditional simplistic division between English and Irish cultures has been allowed to inhibit a properly historical reading of Spenser's work.

My starting-point is the treatment of national formation, for it is here, with Spenser's inventive ethnography, that the key to the author's attitude to his immediate political context is to be found. Spenser's genealogy of Ireland is compelling. He does not fix the Irish in an ethnographic present and a seamless past. Both speakers in the dialogue, Irenius the informed innovator and Eudoxus the searching sceptic, work together to undermine established prejudices. In fact, Irenius begins by insisting on the mixed and multiple origins of the country:

> Before we enter into the treatie of their customes, it is first needfull to consider from whence they first sprung; for from the sundry manners of the nations, from whence that people which now is called Irish, were derived, some of the customes which

now remain amongst them, have been first fetcht, and sithence there continued amongst them; for not of one nation was it peopled, as it is, but of sundry people of different conditions and manners. But the chiefest which have first possessed and inhabited it, I suppose to bee Scythians. (p. 44)

Note that Spenser cannot resist the pun, 'sithence' – 'since then' – foreshadowing 'Scythians.' Eudoxus interrupts at this point to ask: 'How commeth it then to passe, that the Irishe doe derive themselves from Gathelus the Spaniard?' Irenius explains:

They doe indeed, but (I conceive) without any good ground. For if there were any such notable transmission of a colony hether out of Spaine, or any such famous conquest of this kingdome by Gathelus a Spaniard, as they would faine believe, it is not unlikely, but that the very Chronicles of Spaine, (had Spaine then beene in so high regard, as they now have it) would not have omitted so memorable a thing, as the subduing of so noble a Realme to the Spaniard, no more then they doe now neglect to memorize their conquest of the Indians, especially in those times, in which the same was supposed, being nearer unto the flourishing age of learning and Writers under the Romanes. (p. 44)

Irenius, having dispensed with the Irish claim to Spanish provenance, comments: 'But the Irish doe heerein no otherwise, then our vaine English-men doe in the Tale of Brutus, whom they devise to have first conquered and inhabited this land, it being as impossible to proove, that there was ever any such Brutus of Albion or England, as it is, that there was any such Gathelus of Spaine' (p. 44). Several critics have commented on this provocative passage, undermining a prominent British origin-myth, which appears to be at odds with Spenser's attitude in *The Faerie Queene*, although Andrew Hadfield has argued eloquently for a consistent scepticism in both instances.[39] Judith Anderson says of the apparently anomalous undermining of the Brutus myth: 'Nowhere in Spenser's writings is the split between two different versions of truth more obvious than in his treatment of the Brutus legend, first in poetry and then in history. Nowhere else does he so thoroughly debunk popular myths of origin – indeed, popular antiquities – as in the *View*.'[40] Perhaps the most balanced perspective is offered by John Breen, who astutely observes: 'In the *View* Irenius appears to cast doubt upon the authenticity of the story concerning Britain's mythic origins ... However, it would be rash to suggest that, based on Irenius' comment, Spenser did not believe in the Brutus myth's romantic and nationalistic import.'[41] Again it is a matter of effect rather than essence. The Brutus Myth may be ridiculed in the *View*, but only in order to insinuate the Myth of Arthur, trading one origin-myth for another in a covert operation to assert a more pertinent prior British claim that will countermine the idea of England's Irish colony being a gift of the pope to Henry II.

Spenser's Irish genealogy is interlaced with conflicting perspectives on British origin myths. Kim Hall speaks of an 'ethos of language and national/ethnic competition ... concerned in many ways with the legal, cultural, and economic ramifications of the union of cultures under imperialism.'[42] Hall points out that in Spenser's text: 'Cultural and political differences between the English, the Scottish, and the Irish are distilled to problematic linguistic differences, the overcoming and assimilation of which is the first step in an imperialist project.'[43] Though written before the accession of James I, the *View* is a text of Union as well as of Empire, participating in the succession crisis of the 1590s and contributing to the debate around the three-way struggle between Ireland, Scotland, and England in the 1630s and beyond.

According to Tom Healy, 'Spenser proposes that Irish savagery excels anything that could be associated with England's most apparent enemy, Spain', but Spenser's refutation of the claim to Spanish descent is, as we have seen, qualified and strategic.[44] Moreover, Healy overlooks, as do many readers, a vital Scottish component.[45] Having despatched the myth of Brutus, Irenius next applies himself to the ethnic make-up of Ireland, arguing that the Scythians are Scots, and going so far as to declare that 'Scotland and Ireland are all one and the same.' When Eudoxus expresses astonishment at the existence of two Scotlands, Irenius assures his confused companion that he is not seeing double. There are not two countries called Scotland but two kinds of Scots, with one variety situated in the north of Ireland (p. 45). During this genealogical journey, Irenius concedes that he is drawing on bardic sources. Eudoxus warns him not to take the Irish chronicles too seriously, but Irenius responds by declaring that all chronicles are doubtful, before going on to claim that the Irish had letters before the English:

> neither is there any certaine hold to be taken of any antiquity which is received by tradition, since all men be lyars, and many lye when they wil; yet for the antiquities of the written Chronicles of Ireland, give me leave to say something, not to justifie them, but to shew that some of them might say truth. For where you say the Irish have alwayes bin without letters, you are therein much deceived; for it is certaine, that Ireland hath had the use of letters very anciently, and long before England. (p. 47)

Citing this passage, Ciaràn Brady notes that Spenser 'did not suggest that the Scythians or the Gaelic Irish were generally and totally infe-rior to more advanced civilizations; and in a number of cases, most interestingly in regard to the acquisition of literacy, he conceded that the Celts were far more advanced than the Anglo-Saxons.'[46] Having insisted on the validity, however qualified, of the Irish sources, Irenius then argues that the Gaules first inhabited Spain, then settled in Ireland. This comes as a great surprise to Eudoxus, since it flies in the face of the sources as he knows them:

> Surely you have shewed a great probability of that which I had thought impossible to have bin proved; but that which you now say, that Ireland should have bin peopled with the Gaules, seemeth much more strange, for all the Chronicles doe say, that the west and south was possessed and inhabited of Spaniards: and Cornelius Tacitus doth also strongly affirme the same, all which you must overthrow and falsifie, or else renounce your opinion. (p. 48)

But far from renouncing his opinion, Irenius presses his case, and continues with his iconoclastic ethnography. All are not Spaniards, he says, who come out of Spain:

> Neither so, nor so; for the Irish Chronicles (as I shewed you) being made by unlearned men, and writing things according to the appearance of the truth which they conceived, doe erre in the circumstances, not in the matter. For all that came out of

Spaine (they being no diligent searchers into the differences of
the nations) supposed to be Spaniards, and so called them; but
the ground-work thereof is neverthelesse true and certain,
however they through ignorance disguise the same, or through
vanity, whilst they would not seem to be ignorant, doe thereupon build and enlarge many forged Histories of their owne
antiquity, which they deliver to fooles, and make them believe
for true. (pp. 48–9)

Eudoxus wonders why it is 'that the Irish doe so greatly covet to
fetch themselves from the Spaniards, since the old Gaules are a
more auncient and much more honourable nation?' Irenius, in
keeping with Spenser's opportunistic approach to origin-myths, as
idiomatic strategies rather than stable identities, responds thus:

Even of a very desire of new fanglenes and vanity, for they derive
themselves from the Spaniards, as seeing them to bee a very honourable people, and neere bordering unto them: but all that is
most vaine; for from the Spaniards that now are, or that people
that now inhabite Spaine, they no wayes can prove themselves to
descend; neither should it be greatly glorious unto them, for the
Spaniard that now is, is come from as rude and savage nations as
they, there being, as there may be gathered by course of ages, and
view of their owne history, (though they therein labour much to
enoble themselves) scarce any drop of Spanish blood left in
them; for all Spaine was first conquered by the Romans, and
filled with colonies from them, which were still increased, and
the native Spaniard still cut off. (pp. 49–50)

When Irenius denies Spanish origins for tactical reasons – in order
to ward off Spanish claims – he does so by pointing to the mixed
origins of the Spanish. He proceeds to list the nations that overran
Spain, including the Carthaginians, Goths, Huns and Vandals, 'And
lastly all the nations of Scythia, which like a mountaine flood, did
over-flow all Spaine, and quite drowned and washt away whatsoever
reliques there was left of the land-bred people, yea, and of all the
Romans too.' Irenius details the conquests and colonisations of
Spain, and effectively does for Spain, in his radical ethnology, what
he is doing for Ireland – tears up the roots of its ancestry, leaving

'no pure drop of Spanish blood, no more then of Roman or Scythian':

> So that of all nations under heaven (I suppose) the Spaniard is the most mingled, and most uncertaine; wherefore most follishly doe the Irish thinke to enoble themselves by wresting their auncientry from the Spaniard, who is unable to derive himself from any in certaine. (p. 50)

Eudoxus cautions Irenius against speaking so sharply 'in dispraise of the Spaniard, whom some others boast to be the onely brave nation under the skie.' Irenius denies the charge:

> So surely he is a very brave man, neither is that any thing which I speake to his derogation; for in that I said he is a mingled people, it is no dispraise, for I think there is no nation now in Christendome, nor much further, but is mingled, and compounded with others: for it was a singular providence of God, and a most admirable purpose of his wisedome, to draw those Northerne Heathen Nations downe into those Christian parts, where they might receive Christianity, and to mingle nations so remote miraculously, to make as it were one blood and kindred of all people, and each to have knowledge of him. (pp. 50–1)

Thus the apparent 'denigration' of the Spanish leads into an acknowledgement of the mixed origins of all nations.

Irenius notes in passing the tendency of the Irish 'to call any stranger inhabitant there amongst them, Gald, that is descended from the Gaules', and having described Ireland as 'Scotia Major', and Scotland as 'Scotia Minor', he claims that 'Ireland is by Diodorus Siculus, and by Strabo, called Britannia' (p. 52). Eudoxus, recovering from the series of jolts his knowledge of history has suffered, summarises the story so far:

> Now thus farre then, I understand your opinion, that the Scythians planted in the North part of Ireland: the Spaniards (for so we call them, what ever they were that came from Spaine) in the West; the Gaules in the South: so that there now remaineth the East parts towards England, which I would be glad to understand from whence you doe think them to be peopled.

Iren. Mary I thinke of the Brittaines themselves, of which though there be little footing now remaining, by reason that the Saxons afterwards, and lastly the English, driving out the inhabitants thereof, did possesse and people it themselves. (p. 52)

On this last point, Roland Smith noted that: 'Spenser's theory that southeastern Ireland was "peopled from the Brittons" has been abandoned only recently by modern scholars.'[47] Smith maintains that 'Spenser's theory that "Irelande receved muche people afterwarde from the Saxons" has more to recommend it than has his theory of British migration.'[48]

Irenius concludes that the English displaced the British in Ireland, and that the Irish are more closely linked to the Scots than the Spanish. Reeling from these culture shocks, Eudoxus praises Irenius for 'This ripping of auncestors' (p. 53). No sooner has he sat back than Irenius has him out of his chair again. The English, it emerges, are the real villains of the piece. The Old English, the descendants of the original medieval colony, come in for more severe criticism than the Gaelic Irish. Irenius unsettles Eudoxus again by declaring that the chief abuses of the Irish are grown from the English, and indeed that the Old English are more reprehensible than the native Irish. Eudoxus is astonished to learn that of the remnants of the English pale not all remain English:

What is this that you say, of so many as remaine English of them? Why? are not they that were once English, English still?
Iren. No, for some of them are degenerated and growne almost mere Irish, yea, and more malitious to the English then the Irish themselves.
Eudox. What heare I? And is it possible that an Englishman, brought up in such sweet civility as England affords, should find such likeing in that barbarous rudenes, that he should forget his owne nature, and forgoe his owne nation! how may this bee, or what (I pray you) may be the cause thereof? (p. 54)

Irenius postpones his answer, and confesses to digressing from his original purpose – to set out the customs of Ireland – but the digression proves necessary, as a way of reinforcing the point that the present state of Ireland can only be understood with reference to its past, thus the detour that reconstitutes its various inhabitants. While the meditation on the Scottish/Scythian origins of the Irish yields to an examination of Old English corruption, Irishness remains through-out a mobile marker of wildness rather than an essential property. Irenius regrets that some of the Old English 'are almost now growne like the Irish', and 'have quite shaken off their English names, and put on Irish that they might bee altogether Irish'. Eudoxus is vexed at the notion 'that any should so farre growe out of frame that they should in so short space, quite forget their countrey and their owne names!', a cultural amnesia that he considers to be 'a most dangerous lethargie' (p. 68). But it transpires that the Old English have not so much forgotten their origins as remembered them all too faithfully. Their new-found and nominal Irishness is in fact good – or rather bad – old-fashioned Englishness. Thus it unfolds that the garments of the Irish, including the mantle, of which so much has been written in Spenser criticism, are English all along. Irenius, incurable iconoclast that he is, gives another turn of the screw when he boldly states, in response to the query from Eudoxus as to whether the mantle and other items of clothing are 'Irish weedes':

> No: all these which I have rehearsed to you, be not Irish gar-ments, but English; for the quilted leather jack is old English: for it was the proper weed of the horseman, as you may read in Chaucer, when he describeth Sir Thopas apparell and armour, as hee went to fight gainst the gyant, in his robe of shecklaton, which is that kind of guilded leather with which they use to imbroyder their Irish jackets. And there likewise by all that description, you may see the very fashion and manner of the Irish horseman most truely set forth, in his long hose, his ryding shooes of costly cordwaine, his hacqueton, and his haberjeon, with all the rest thereunto belonging. (p. 73)

Eudoxus finds it hard to believe that aspects of costume universally held to be Irish are actually English, but Irenius insists: 'No sure; they be native English, and brought in by the Englishmen first into Ireland.' Now we can begin to see the subtlety of Spenser's strategy. Not only are the Irish not Irish, and the Spanish not Spanish, but the English are not English.[49] Moreover, the Irish are really Scots, but they are Scots in English clothing. Irenius even claims the infamous Irish 'Galloglasses' as English: 'the which name doth discover them also to be auncient English: for *Gall-ogla* signifies an English servitour or yeoman' (p. 74). There is no point in doing as others have done and pointing out that this is a mistake on Spenser's part, and one of many. That would be to read as an historian the text of a poet. Like all such myth-takes, it is less an error than an angle.[50]

Later, Irenius compares the Old English with the Irish, 'which, being very wilde at the first, are now become more civill; when as these from civillity, are growne to be wilde and meere Irish' (p. 143). The English become Irish through conduct unbecoming. Meantime the Irish wax more civil, and thus less Irish. The Irish may even be growing English, but if so it's a new Englishness that stands for civility, not the old barbarous variety. Here, 'Irish' is not simply another word for 'barbarous', but a term of opposition, in this case opposition to another wave of colonisers. It is as if Spenser wishes to unravel Irish identity to the point of erasure. For the Old English, the loss of cultural memory – 'that he should forget his owne nature' – is catastrophic, but for the Irish to lose themselves is salutary.

Spenser presses home the idea of a time lag, arguing that the feudal nature of the Old English, their unwillingness to embrace modern English values, is the real problem. Irenius expounds a theory of culture that shows the first English colonial establishment to have been left behind by history. The Old English rebellions of the post-Reformation years – Kildare (1534), Butler (1569), Desmond (1579–83) – are put down to a regressive baronial state. In the *View*, Spenser is in many ways attacking his elders and betters. If one consequence of colonisation was the displacement of class, then another was the intensification of class struggle within the theatre of colonialism. Paradoxically, Spenser's perspective is on one level socially progressive, laying the blame for the present state of Ireland at the door of the first colonists, a 'caste' who are cast off, throwbacks to an earlier English culture:

Now this you are to understand, that all the rebellions which you see from time to time happen in Ireland, are not begun by the common people, but by the lords and captaines of countries, upon pride or wilfull obstinacy against the government, which whensoever they will enter into, they drawe with them all their people and followers, which thinke themselves bound to goe with them, because they have booked them and undertaken for them. And this is the reason that in England you have such few bad occasions, by reason that the noble men, how ever they should happen to be evill disposed, have no commaund at all over the communalty, though dwelling under them, because that every man standeth upon himselfe, and buildeth his fortunes upon his owne faith and firme assurance: ... [which] will worke also in Ireland. For by this the people are broken into small parts like little streames, that they cannot easily come together into one head, which is the principall regard that is to be had in Ireland, to keepe them from growing unto such a head, and adhering unto great men. (p. 140)

Spenser is not simply advocating social engineering here. He is saying something fundamental about class and individuality. Atomisation of the Irish is one way to ward off rebellion, and to break up those groupings that would otherwise be ripe for recruitment by overmighty subjects.

Irenius is at pains to establish that the English ruling class in Ireland are more blameworthy than the general population: 'for sure in mine opinion they are more sharpely to be chastised and reformed then the rude Irish, which, being very wilde at the first, are now become more civill; when as these, from civillity, are growne to be wilde and meere Irish' (p. 143). This fugitive Irishness into which the Old English are in danger of falling repeatedly assumes the form of an underdeveloped Englishness. It is a question of the arrested development of a colonial community, caught in limbo, and refusing to make way for a new generation of reforming native English.

In an authoritative intervention into Spenser studies, Deborah Shuger interrogates Spenser's use of classical republican sources in the *View*, which emerges in her reading as primarily an anti-aristocratic tract.[51] Shuger sees the central conflict in Spenser's work as one between a warrior aristocracy and a rural gentry, with Spenser on the side of the latter. Her key point is that the 'gorgic vision' of peace and civility through cultivation – in all its senses – 'ranges itself against a still-powerful attraction, even among scholarly humanists, to heroic barbarism.'[52] Spenser the aspiring gentleman is seduced by the glamour surrounding the overmighty subjects who block his progress. This opposition of English identities, Old and New, creates productive tensions, in prose and poetry alike. In mapping out his distance from the court, and in representing in aesthetic terms a feudal culture to which he was outwardly opposed, Spenser sourced reserves of social energy that radiate in his work. This context informs his forms, from his colonial pastoral to his epic of empire.

As for the Irish themselves, those who are not written out of the story, they are gullible rather than guilty. They follow the Old English, but, again ironically, unlike the latter, they are not beyond the pale. Naming is crucial as a means of taming. Thus Irenius observes:

> that whereas all men used to be called by the name of their septs [or clans], according to the severall nations, and had no surnames at all, that from thenceforth each one should take upon himselfe a severall surname, either of his trade and facultie, or of some quality of his body or minde, or of the place where he dwelt, so as every one should be distinguished from the other, or from the most part, wherby they shall not onely not depend upon the head of their sept, as now they do, but also in time learne quite to forget his Irish nation. And herewithall would I also wish all the O's and Mac's, which the heads of septs have taken to their names, to bee utterly forbidden and extinguished. For that the same being an ordinance (as some say) first made by O'Brien for the strengthning of the Irish, the abrogating thereof will asmuch infeeble them. (pp. 147–8)

This is a further example of a rhetorical strategy that seeks to abolish Irish identity at a stroke. If demonising is one colonialist approach to the Other, then dematerialising is another. Invisible natives are manifestly easier to handle than negative stereotypes.

Closing the earlier genealogical phase of his discourse, Irenius remarked: 'And thus you have my opinion, how all that Realme of Ireland was first peopled, and by what nations.' The Old English put out the British and are themselves now 'degenerate.' The Scots, or Scythians, are the other culprits. The Irish customs that Irenius abhors, and which critics often read as evidence of anti-Irish sentiment, are either Scythian, which for Spenser's purposes means

Scottish, or Old – and outmoded – English, leftovers from the feast of an earlier incursion, and fit now only for famine and the sword.

In the *View*, Spenser attacks the Spanish and the Scottish (Scythians), and dismisses the myth of Brutus, while retaining the claim that Arthur conquered Ireland (p. 52). Moreover, he reserves his strongest criticisms of native Irish society, not for the Gaelic Irish – whose aboriginality he throws into question – but for the 'Old English', the descendants of the initial phase of English settlement:

> for the chiefest abuses which are now in that realme, are growne from the English, and some of them are now much more lawlesse and licentious then the very wilde Irish: so that as much care as was by them had to reforme the Irish, so and much more, must now bee used to reforme them; so much time doth alter the manners of men. (p. 67)

In another shift of emphasis, Irenius repeats his claim that the Old English have become Irish – 'and are now growne as Irish, as O-hanlans breech, as the proverbe there is' – only to then cancel this out by attributing the most harmful Irish customs to the (Old) English themselves:

> You cannot but hold them sure to be very uncivill; for were they at the best that they were of old, when they were brought in, they should in so long an alteration of time seeme very uncouth and strange. For it is to be thought, that the use of all England was in the raigne of Henry the Second, when Ireland was planted with English, very rude and barbarous, so as if the same should be now used in England by any, it would seeme worthy of sharpe correction, and of new lawes for reformation, for it is but even the other day since England grew civill. (p. 70)

Implicit in this last point is the prospective alienation of the New English themselves, the future alienation of Swift, Yeats and Beckett, 'the last Anglo-Irishman.' As Patricia Coughlan remarks: 'As Scythians are to Greeks and wild men are to the civil, so the Irish are to the English: but so too, in a sense, are the colonists and officials in the field to the distant metropolitan policy-makers.'[53] Irenius goes further,

and maintains that it matters little when addressing the 'evill customes' of the Old English whether these originate among the Irish or
the English. What matters is that it is the 'degenerate' English who are
the problem. The twin pitfalls facing English colonists are fosterage
and intermarriage (p. 71). Patricia Fumerton contends that for Spenser
'fears of interracial alliance are very explicitly linked to fears of assimilation of the ruler by the ruled.'[54] But in a case like early moden
Ireland, where two colonial communities were competing for control,
things were arguably a little more complicated. For Spenser, an interracial alliance between the New English and the Gaelic Irish, with
the former clearly in charge, was preferable to an Irish-Scottish axis, or
the mixing of Old English and Gaelic Irish, particularly if the Spanish
were involved. In other words, there is more to race in the *View*
than alliance or assimilation, more at stake than the relationship
between ruler and ruled.

It is not simply a question of what has befallen the Old English
since their arrival in Ireland, but of how things have moved on in
England during their lengthy absence in the land that time
forgot. Indeed, it emerges that it is not so much that the Old
English have gone native as that they have retained earlier
English manners that are obsolete in the metropolis. It is the
medieval English culture of the first wave of planters that is now
erroneously regarded as Irish. This is one of the most curious
cases of mistaken identity in history. Spenser wants his readers to
do a double take in order to grasp the complex division of Ireland
along blurred ethnic lines. Thus many habits regarded as Irish are
in fact English, and if they seem uncivil this is because the original English colonists were far less cultured than their sixteenth-
century counterparts. Irenius excludes the English in Ireland from
England's newly established civility, thus justifying the fresh
influx of (New) English colonists. Spenser's antiquarian digressions on Irish origins are actually cleverly masked allusions to
contemporary affairs. Far from being an inveterate opponent of
all things Irish, Spenser is at odds with a particular form of
Englishness which sits uncomfortably with his own vision
of English national identity, and consequently his meditation on
English and Irish origins is more subtle than critics have allowed.
Moreover, the representation of the Irish as barbarous, through
the trope of Scythian origins, is complicated by the fact that

Spenser sees the Spanish and the Scots as the conduits of Scythian barbarity.

Few critics have grasped the extent to which Spenser's principal targets in his prose dialogue are the Scots and the Old English. Commentators quick to point out the anxiety about Spanish and Scythian influence fail to see that the twin threats of primitivism and invasion cohere in the spectre of the Ulster Scots, while in the southern provinces the Old English themselves constitute an internal enemy that is backward precisely because it represents an ancient and untenable form of 'English' identity. The Irish are not too barbarous to be Scottish, and the Spanish themselves are, according to Irenius, mixed like all races. In the case of the Spanish there has been a cultural traffic with North Africa that blurs the boundaries of what is European and what is 'outside' or 'other.' But lest we take this as a slur on the Spanish, as Eudoxus was wont to do, we ought to recall that for Irenius 'there is no nation now in Christendome, nor much further, but is mingled, and compounded with others' (p. 51). Spenser's scepticism regarding purity of origins is clearly an attempt to side-step the claims of the Old English to be more English than the New English, for not only is there no such originary Englishness, but in its earliest manifestation Englishness is so rudimentary as to be compatible with rude Irishness.

Spenserians have hitherto maintained that the elaborate ethnology that Spenser constructs in the *View* is either a facade or a front for colonial violence against the Irish. I would argue that the poet's strategy is very deliberate and intended to be highly persuasive in terms of reasserting the (New) English claim to Ireland in the face of Spanish and Scottish counter-claims, and arguing for the overthrow of the original English colony, now hopelessly corrupt. Spenser's insistence upon Scythian origins was structured by an underlying fear of Spanish and Scottish intervention in Ireland. Clare Carroll makes the link between the forms of otherness utilised by Spenser when she states that: 'In *A View* … by social level, religion, and what for Spenser is a non-European ethnic identity (alternately Scythian, African, or Moorish) the Irish are constituted as one inferior category.'[55] But Spenser wants at one and the same time to distinguish between the ruling Old English elite and their more subservient and malleable Irish subordinates, and to merge the 'non-European' with the 'European', since he uses Scythian to imply both Spanish and Scottish.

Spenser's varied and versatile use of past antiquities to inform and offset the ethnographic present has not always been appreciated. Critics have not looked to the *View* for ambivalence and hybridity, but for an anti-Irish polemic that they can comfortably and self-righteously denounce. The case I am trying to make is one that illustrates the ways in which Spenser actually deflects the gaze from the Irish to a Scythianism he imputes to Spanish and Scottish immigrants, and a barbarity he attributes to earlier English settlers. It is therefore a question, literally, of ignorance rather than knowledge, of *not knowing* the Irish, that is, of displacing them. The disappearing act, or sleight of hand, that Spenser effects, the way in which he effectively erases the local inhabitants from the canvas he is painting, is much more interesting, to me at least, than the conventional view that sees him as an unashamed calumniator of the Irish. Of course, it could be argued – after Macherey – that the text says what it does not say, and that the exclusion of the Irish is still a racist move, but the fact remains that Spenser's strategy is one of displacement and deferral rather than an unexamined essentialising animosity.[56]

A grounded and immediate attitude to cultural and national difference informs the *View*'s antiquarian ethnography. In its rehearsal of identity and difference, this important document draws an altogether more complex figure than is suggested by received opinion. The focus on Irishness and anti-Irish racism has concealed other ethnicities, and glossed over the tensions in Spenser's text, specifically the slippage between Old English and Irish, and Scythian and Scottish. By obsessing about Ireland critics have let England – and others – escape examination.[57] The discourse on racial origins is intimately bound up with the excavation of British and European origin-myths. Spenser's subtle and stealthy ethnography serves to stymie both Irishness and Old Englishness, and to insinuate New Englishness into the breach. His antiquities reveal anxieties about contemporary matters, including the matter of Britain, and this has not always been appreciated, except as a thin veil for his infamous anti-Irish views, so infamous as to require little elucidation. Spenser constructs knowledge of the Irish only as an absent Other, disoriented by barbarous foreign implants variously construed as Spanish, Scottish, and even English. Colonial identity is not a unified ideology whose goal is to alienate an integral native culture. In a problematic 'British' context, the meshing of Anglo-Irish and Scottish differences implies a delicate matrix of contested positions erected over an abyss. Any discussion of the *View* has to take its delving into – and spinning of – mythological origins seriously, since there is a question of policy at issue.

Michael Neill has argued eloquently that the 1541 act of kingly title, rendering Ireland a kingdom rather than a lordship, made assimilation a much more pressing demand for English colonists:

> For these propagandists Irish difference was something that simply *ought not to exist*; it was an unnatural aberration that the English were morally bound to extirpate. The most extreme form of this contradiction can be found in the writings of Spenser, who is at once among the more sympathetic and well-informed English observers of Irish culture and among the most extreme advocates of its destruction 'by the sword.'[58]

Spenser was indeed 'among the more sympathetic and well-informed English observers of Irish culture', and in this respect Neill comes closer to the truth of the matter than many other critics. But 'Irish culture', as we have seen, was far less singular than Neill's subsequent comments would imply, nor did Spenser merely advocate its destruction, as I hope I have shown.

My own feeling is that Spenser's deft interweaving of different elements of cultural and national identity in Ireland points to an awareness of the vicissitudes of what historians have come to refer to as the 'British Problem', that is, the painstaking process by which the British state was formed.[59] Ireland was, and arguably remains, a seed-bed of British identity as well as a fraught locus of colonial otherness, and standard criticism of the *View* that concentrates exclusively on its putative anti-Irish sentiments does not begin to do justice to the various twists and turns of this disturbing and challenging text. Spenser's English-oriented ethnogenesis, his concern with the Scythian connection as a way of asserting New English supremacy, reveals a preoccupation with the present, and with discrediting Spanish and Scottish claims to Ireland rather than debasing the Irish 'themselves.' There are elements of in-betweenness and anachronism in Spenser's troubling tract that ask our attention. In his 'ripping of auncestors', Spenser showed himself to be attuned to the ethnographic present. The critical tradition that sees the Irish as all too visible in the *View*, victimised and vilified, may find it difficult to accept that they are part of a mesmerising vanishing act. As a proponent of *recolonisation* at the expense of English and Scottish incumbents Spenser's creative energies were devoted, not to berating the native Irish, or even accounting for them, but to taking them out of the equation.[60]

5

'Another Britain'? Bacon's *Certain Considerations Touching the Plantation in Ireland* (1606; 1657)

> no man can, by care taking, as the Scripture saith, add a cubit to his stature, in this little model of a man's body: but in the great frame of kingdoms and commonwealths, it is in the power of princes or estates, to add amplitude and greatness to their kingdoms. (Bacon, 'Of Plantations')

The body of a text is like the frame of a kingdom. There is always the potential for growth. In the case of a marginal text which addresses the culture at large, this power of expansion is especially pronounced. Having examined in some detail the twists and turns of Spenser's *View*, I want now to look at a minor treatise by Francis Bacon which captures in an even more condensed form the tensions and texture of the Irish problem in a British context, or, perhaps more accurately, the British Problem in an Irish context.[1] Where Spenser is one of the foremost poets of the period, Bacon is a writer known chiefly for non-fiction, one of the most important essayists and political theorists of the English Renaissance, a figure who straddles disciplines and genres, and who participated in the making of policy. Bacon's belief in progress and the possibility of change, and the frequent analogies he draws in his writings between the acquisition of knowledge and the politics of empire, conquest and discovery, make his pronouncements on Ireland sharply relevant. His *Certain Considerations Touching the Plantation in Ireland* (1609), a short essay of some 4,500 words, has received scant notice either from students of Bacon or historians of early modern Ireland, and yet it is arguably one of the most articulate statements of the politics of plantation in the period.[2] Bacon's Irish treatise appeared on the eve of the Commission of 1609 which was crucial in laying the groundwork for the Ulster Plantation, and anticipated the publication of the *Conditions to be observed by the Brittish Undertakers of the Escheated Lands in Ulster* (1610).

Minor works by major authors can be used to say something about the corpus of the author, as Spenser's *View* is used to inform readings of Book V of *The Faerie Queene*, as Milton's *Observations* might be used to backlight his other prose works, especially those of that fateful year of 1649 – *The Tenure of Kings and Magistrates* and *Eikonoklastes* (which includes material on Ireland) – and as Bacon's Irish treatise has been used, as a way into his *New Atlantis*, in a recent article by Denise Albanese.[3] Bacon himself argued that occasional pieces could be used as opportunities to discuss wider issues.[4] Other relevant Bacon texts would include the parliamentary debate on naturalisation of the Scots, and on the Union in general; comments on Essex and Ireland; and the essays 'Of Empire' and 'Of Plantations'. Bacon's *Considerations* is a text which can usefully be read in the context of Bacon's discourses on union, plantation and empire. Most students of the Renaissance have encountered Bacon's *Essays*, and are familiar with his major works but, as with any canonical author, there are inevitably texts which slip through the net.

The *Considerations* is a remarkable display of Bacon's rhetorical brilliance. It is a finely wrought, densely woven and closely argued text, written in Bacon's axiomatic, aphoristic and legalistic style. It is a model of the essay form that Bacon largely piloted, juggling contraries and reconciling apparent contradictions. The text was first published in 1657 as part of the *Resuscitatio, or bringing into publick light several pieces of the works, civil, historical, philosophical & theological, hitherto sleeping; of the right honourable Francis Bacon ... Together with his lordship's life*, edited by his chaplain, William Rawley. Just as Spenser's *View*, written in 1596 but not published until 1633, participated in a later history than that which it described, so Bacon's considerations of the Ulster Plantation under James I became a text of the Cromwellian plantation of the 1650s.[5] I would like to submit it to another resuscitation, to incorporate it into a discussion of state and identity formation. In its preference for a style of reason rather than romance, Bacon's tract fits in with the work of Sir John Davies and anticipates the writings of Sir William Petty later in the century.[6]

I am not going to attempt here to situate Bacon's treatise in the context of its publication, but in the context of its composition. What I hope to suggest is that this text is a significant contribution to the delineation of the 'British Problem', part of Bacon's commitment to council and advice 'arising out of a universal insight and experience of the affairs of the world'.[7] In the *Novum Organum*, Bacon, in one of his familiar similes, remarked that 'Time is like a river which has brought down to us things light and puffed up, while those which are weighty and solid have sunk'.[8] The *Considerations*, I submit, is an item washed ashore that is worth salvaging.

*

The accession of James I as King of Britain marks a crucial juncture in relations between the three kingdoms of England, Scotland and Ireland. It also marked a turning-point in the career of Bacon. Knighted in 1603, he became King's Counsel in 1604, Solicitor-General in 1607, Attorney-General in 1613, a Privy Councillor in 1616, Lord Keeper in 1617 and Lord Chancellor in 1618. He entered the House of Lords as Baron Verulam in 1618, and was created Viscount St Albans in 1621. This was a remarkable rise to power, however deserved were the promotions. This period also marks a shift in the discourse on Ireland, which has to accommodate a Scottish perspective. In the language of colonialism, adventure and sensationalism give way to law and economics.

In 'On the Union' (1604), Ben Jonson employed the metaphor of marriage:

> When was there contract better driven by Fate?
> Or celebrated with more truth of state?
> The world the temple was, the priest a king,
> The spoused pair two realms, the sea the ring.[9]

Plantation suggests birth, and union marriage, but the offspring of this particular union, the Plantation of Ulster, has ensured that the marriage is an unhappy one. Ireland is born out of wedlock – outside of the sea's ring. In fact, Ireland is a child by a previous marriage, Henry II having been granted lordship by a papal bull of 1172. The Anglo-Scottish settlement annulled that previous bond, and created another union of sorts, the union of the north and south of Ireland, hitherto divided between Scots and English settlers in a kind of tug-of-war, and the union of the north and south of Scotland. A number of north–south divides were bridged by the Union of 1603 and the process of conquest and plantation that followed on from it.

On the face of it, the Union did not radically alter the colonial make-up of Ireland. The Scots continued to dominate in the north while the English settled primarily in the south. But the kind of Scots who planted themselves in Ulster did change. Highlanders and Islanders had hitherto been the most active settlers there. After 1603 an increasing number of Lowlanders began to arrive, even before the official planta-tion was underway. The Borders had been a key area of contention throughout the reign of James VI. In 1587 an Act was passed 'for the quieting and keping in obedience of the disorderit subjectis inhabitan-tis of the borders hielandis and Ilis'.[10] On the eve of the Ulster Plantation an instruction was issued that Islanders and Highlanders be excluded.[11] The threat of Irish and Scottish Gaelic Catholics coming together was too great for the government to countenance. Michael Hill has argued in a recent essay against drawing too clear a distinction between Highlanders and Lowlanders, pointing out that some Borderers were Celtic by culture: 'Only by distinguishing between the anglicized Lowlands and the Celtic Borders-Southwest can we under-stand the significance of a plantation of non-Highland Scots in Ulster from 1609 to 1625.'[12] As we saw in the previous chapter on Spenser, an Irish-Scottish alliance was something to be feared and fought against.

Addressing the Dublin Parliament in 1570 Sir Henry Sidney con-trasted the position of the English Pale in relation to the rest of Ireland, with that of England and Scotland. He was especially eager to justify the role of the English army in Ireland, objections to which were summed up in the question asked by the Old English, the predominantly Catholic descendants of the original twelfth-century English colony:

Whie should we not live withowte an armie as wel of Englande? Whie cannot our nobilitie, owre men of might in every border, our tenantes and servantes, withstande the Irishe nexte them, as well as the Northen Lordes and inhabitantes of Riddesdale and Titdesdale and those abowte the Scottish banke resiste the Scottes, facinge and pilfering as faste as our enemies?[13]

Sidney's response is telling:

> Touchinge Scotlande it is well knowen they weare never the men whome England neded to feare. They are but a corner cutt oute, and easelie tamed when they waxe owtragious. Your foes lie in the bosome of your cuntries, more in number, ritcher of grownd, desperate theves, ever at an inche, unpossible to be severed from yowe, withowte anye fence beside your owne valiantnes and the help of our souldiers. England is quiet within itself, thoroughlie peopled, on that side of Scotland which most requires it, guarded with an armie; otherwise the lordes and gentlemen and lustie yoemen that dwell on a rowe are readie to mayster their private vagaries; from all forrein invasions walled with the wide ocean. Weare theare suche a sea betwene you and the Irish, or weare they shutt up into an odd ende of the land, or had they no suche oportunities of bogges and woodes as they have, or weare they lordes of the lesser parte of Irelande, or weare they scattered into small handfulles, not hable to annoie whole townshippes and baronies as they doe, the comparison weare sumwhat alike. But alack, it fareth not so with you. You are besett rownde, your townes are feble, the lande emptie, the commons bare; everie country by itself cannot save itselfe.[14]

In Sonnet 30 of Philip Sidney's *Astrophil and Stella* the question is asked: 'How Ulster likes of that same golden bit / Wherewith my father once made it half tame.' Half tame, the other half awaiting Scotland, 'a corner cutt oute, and easelie tamed'. According to one historian of the Ulster Plantation, Elizabeth had abandoned an English enterprise in Ulster in 1575: 'Instead of advancing the English interest in the north and putting an end to the Scoto-Irish problem, it had only served to irritate the Irish and confirm them in their hostility to England.'[15] This enterprise, known as the Ulster Project, could be realised only through the joint endeavours of England and Scotland, sinking their mutual claims to the North of Ireland in an 'interracial alliance'.

After 1603 and the Union of the Crowns the newly-formed Stuart state could synchronise its efforts. The objections of some English writers to the Scottish presence in Ulster was stifled. Spenser was one of those who had opposed the idea of introducing Scots to Ireland as a means of controlling the Irish, on the grounds that the Irish and Scots were more likely to make common cause against the English than tame one another. He used the analogy of jumping out of the frying pan and into the fire. Bacon, writing in the wake of the Union of Crowns, was ready to set the Scottish meat in the Anglo-Irish sandwich sizzling again. This new political accommodation between two old enemies was made at the expense of a neighbour nation. The competing claims of Scotland and England to Ireland, centred on its unruly northern province, were resolved, and the foundation stone of the Protestant Ascendancy was laid.[16] The Scots had made considerable inroads into the eastern counties of Ulster in the sixteenth century. English settlement in the south-west had been less successful. The Munster Plantation had been overthrown in 1598.[17]

Contemporary commentators were quick to recognise the advantages of union. Sir Thomas Craig, author of a pro-union treatise, insisted 'that so long as the union lasts there will be no further trouble in Ireland'.[18] This was, of course, optimistic. Within a generation the War of the Three Kingdoms would have Ireland as its most fiery theatre. According to David Stevenson: 'Scottish penetration of Ireland, although intended to reinforce English interests there, had, by the time the covenanting crisis broke, begun to undermine them.'[19] Stevenson is referring of course to post-Union Scottish penetration, since the Scots had long claimed the right to be in Ireland in their own interests.

At the turn of the seventeenth century there was a genuine widespread belief that the Irish problems of England and Scotland were being solved. Michael Perceval-Maxwell points out that 'after Elizabeth's death, the migration of Scots to Ulster became a policy to be encouraged instead of a process to be deplored'.[20] Spenser's worst nightmare had come true – the Scots had a firm foothold in the north of Ireland – but by now it was an English colonial dream. The Flight of the Earls in 1607 left a political vacuum in Irish society. This vacuum was to be filled by an experimental British culture, planted in the wake of a union that was limited in scope, and largely unforeseen. The Ulster Plantation of 1609–10 was a combined Anglo-Scottish project, the word 'Brittish' being used, but with the coda that it included only 'Inland Scottish'.[21] Thus the Ulster Plantation – notwithstanding the Celtic identity of the post-Union planters from the Borders-Southwest – was a blow for Gaelic Ulster in more ways than one. Hiram Morgan has pointed out that with the departure of the Gaelic aristocracy and the Plantation of Ulster 'a new Pale was in the making'.[22] The focus of colonial activity was shifting from an English Pale around Dublin to a British Pale around Belfast. A fatal combination of the alliance the Ulster lords made with Spain and the union of England and Scotland rung the death knell of Gaelic Ulster.[23]

What is fascinating about Bacon's text is his conjuncture of union and plantation as complementary processes, and his recognition of the complication of interests in Ireland. There is nothing pastoral about Bacon's image of plantation. The link between colonisation and empire needs to be more thoroughly interrogated. The language of colonisation, the representation of that political enterprise, is crucial. The invention of Britain was a painful process entailing both unification, represented in a British origin-myth as reunification, and colonisation. Unlike Spenser, but like Sir John Davies, Bacon represented the plantation of Ireland as a matter of law rather than conquest. Bacon wrote on Calvin's case, the case of the Post-Nati (Scots born after 1603), and on the question of Irish sovereignty: 'And hereof many ancient precedents and records may be shewed that the reason why Ireland is subject to the law of England is not ipso jure upon conquest, but grew by a charter of King John, and that extended but to so much as was then in the king's possession, for there are divers particular grants to sundry subjects of Ireland and their heirs, that they might use and observe the laws of England.'[24]

In 'A Letter to the King upon presenting my Discourse Touching the Plantation of Ireland' Bacon presents his New Year's gift of a 'little book' whose 'style is a style of business, rather than curious or elaborate'. Bacon was moved to offer the king his opinion on the Ulster Plantation because of his grace 'in accepting of the like poor field-fruits touching the Union'. Bacon's discourse on the proposed plantation of Ulster grows directly out of his arguments around the Union. Bacon was a great advocate of 'the knowledge of causes', and the conditions of possibility of an event. The Plantation of Ulster was a consequence of the Union of Crowns, and Bacon was at pains to show how the two great enterprises of the early seventeenth century were founding moments in the new history of Britain. Perhaps only a political pessimist like Spenser could have predicted that it would all end in tears, or in flames, for it was a rising in Ulster that precipitated the three-kingdom conflagration of the 1640s.

Bacon's incisive tract reveals the colonial project that underpins the newly united kingdoms. Few histories of Anglo-Scottish Union focus on the Ulster Plantation. Few histories of the Ulster Plantation dwell on the Union. Bacon's *Considerations* brings the two together:

> And certainly I reckon this action as a second brother to the Union. For I assure myself that England, Scotland, and Ireland well united is such a trefoil as no prince except yourself (who are the worthiest) weareth in his crown.[25]

It is this 'trefoil' that intrigues me, the trefoil of Anglo-Scottish union and Irish plantation, the three-ply nature of the British Problem in an Irish context, a three-way struggle for sovereignty. The OED defines a 'trefoil' as 'a leguminous plant of genus *Trifolium* with leaves of three leaflets ... (thing) arranged in three lobes'. Leguminous plants have seeds in pods, and England and Scotland have now become as alike as two peas in a pod, the pod being Ireland, where the natives ate trefoils, or shamrocks, during the Munster famine, the tragedy that paved the way for Spenser's New English colony. The progress from Union to plantation is a kind of dialectic – English thesis, Scottish antithesis, British synthesis. The question of the 'trefoil' and the 'treble sceptre' should be part of the English Tripos. It should certainly be part of any serious study of the Renaissance. When a camera is mounted on a tripod, you do not see the tripod. Even a wide-angled lens can be anglocentric.

After 400 years we are still harping on Ireland and eliding the Scottish contribution. Scotland is the third term that gets lost in 'Anglo-Irish', the hyphen, or ligature that binds three nations under one heading, the third lobe of a trefoil, recalling a contemporary vision: 'And some I see / That two-fold balls and treble sceptres carry' (*Macbeth* IV.i.119–20). For Bacon, like Banquo, the future comes in twos and threes. Can Scotland be inserted into a seamless English narrative, or an uninterrupted discourse on Ireland? Only by an act of violence. Revisionist Irish history has not reinscribed Scotland. It remains within an 'Anglo-Irish' problematic. Cultural Materialism, Irish Revisionism and the New Historicism all seem content to leave this binary opposition intact. Yet the exclusion of Scotland from discussions of Ireland matters. It is the matter of Britain, the matter of the British Problem, the problem of identity and difference in a multi-nation state. How did Scotland and Ireland come to play Ariel and Caliban to England's Prospero?

Bacon justifies his intervention in the matter of the Ulster Plantation by adverting to the king's earlier acceptance of his views on the union. In doing so, Bacon recalls that his predecessor, Lord Chief Justice Popham (Sir John Popham, who died on 7 June 1607), 'laboured greatly in the last project, touching the plantation of Munster: which nevertheless, as it seemeth, hath given more light by the errors thereof, what to avoid, than by the direction of the same, what to follow'. Bacon became Solicitor-General on the 25th of June, 1607, serving in the post Popham had held when Munster was planted. Bacon wrote to Sir John Davies on 26 December 1606, urging him to be a 'labourer' rather than a 'plant'.[26]

*

In the *Considerations* Bacon tells the king that 'God hath reserved to your Majesty's times two works, which amongst the acts of kings have the supreme preeminence; the union, and the plantation of kingdoms' (116). Bacon employs a telling metaphor for the act of founding 'estates or kingdoms': 'for as in arts and sciences, to be the first inventor is more than to illustrate or amplify; and as in the works of God, the creation is greater than the preservation; and as in the works of nature the birth and nativity is more than the continuance: so in kingdoms, the first foundation or plantation is of more noble dignity and merit than all that followeth' (116). There are two kinds of foundation, 'the first, that maketh one of more; and the second, that maketh one of none'. These correspond to 'the creation of the world' and 'the edification of the church'. James I is responsible for 'both these kinds of foundations or regenerations': 'The one, in the union of the island of Britain; the other, in the plantation of the great and noble parts of the island of Ireland. Which enterprises happily accomplished, then that which was uttered by one of the best orators, in one of the worst verses, *O fortunatum natam me consule Romam!*' may be far more truly and properly applied to your majesty's acts; *natam te rege Britanniam; natam Hiberniam.'* Pursuing the metaphor of creation, of different kinds of creation – artistic, scientific, divine, etc. – Bacon declares: 'For indeed unions and plantations are the very nativities or birth-days of kingdoms.' But there is a dark side to these birthdays: 'For most part of unions and plantations of kingdoms have been founded in the effusion of blood. But your majesty shall build *in solo puro, et in area pura,* that shall need no sacrifices expiatory for blood; and therefore, no doubt, under an higher and more assured blessing' (117). In 'Of Honour and reputation' Bacon asserted: 'If a man performe that which hath not beene attempted before ... he shall purchase more Honour, then by effecting a matter of greater difficulty or vertue, wherein he is but a follower.'[27]

Bacon divides the main body of his text into two sections, aims and means. The first deals with 'the excellency of the work' (of plantation), and the second with 'the means to compass and effect it' (117). The first is divided into 'four noble and worthy consequences that will follow thereupon', these being 'in point of honour, policy, safety, and utility'. These are cultural, demographic, military and economic, having to do with reputation, population, national security and profit.

The first of the 'four noble and worthy consequences' is 'honour':

> whereof I have spoken enough already were it not that the harp of Ireland puts me in mind of that glorious emblem or allegory, wherein the wisdom of antiquity did figure and shadow out works of this nature. For the poets feigned that Orpheus, by the virtue and sweetnes of his harp, did call and assemble the beasts and birds, of their nature savage and wild, to stand about him as in a theatre; forgetting their affections of fiercenes, of lust, and of prey; and listening to the tunes and harmonies of the harp; and soon after likewise called the stones and woods to remove, and stand in order about him: which fable was anciently interpreted of the reducing and planting of kingdoms; when people of barbarous manners are brought to give over and discontinue their customs of revenge and blood, and of dissolute life, and of theft, and rapine; and to give ear to the wisdom of lawes and governments; whereupon immediately followed the calling of stones for building and habitation; and for trees for the seats of houses, orchards and inclosures, and the like. This work, therefore, of all other most memorable and honourable, your majesty hath now in hand; especially, if your majesty join the harp of David, in casting out the evil spirit of superstition, with the harp of Orpheus, in casting out desolation and barbarism. (117–18)

Bacon's use of the Orpheus myth as a practical illustration of the civilising process of colonial power is typical of his approach to classical mythology, an approach he advocated eloquently in the *Wisdom of the Ancients*, written the same year as the *Considerations*, where philosophy stands for Orpheus, and where, significantly, it can be shipwrecked and resurface as part of an expatriate culture 'in some other remote nation'.[28] Judith Anderson has argued that: 'Throughout Bacon's writings, the dominant tenor of his observations about the poetic imagination is negative and distrustful.'[29] In addressing the related projects of union and plantation, Bacon can be seen to be wrestling with a reconciliation of the poetic and the politic. As Clark Hulse points out: 'Bacon ultimately insists that fables were used "to teach and lay open, not to hide and conceal knowledge".'[30] Negativity and distrust could be set aside where there was a clear need for myth and magic to be enlisted in the aid of *realpolitik*. In this regard, Bacon appears here in the guise of Prospero, the bookish humanist compelled by circumstance to resort to spells.

Bacon's second 'worthy consequence' is a matter of policy, less a consequence than 'the avoiding of an inconvenience, which commonly attendeth upon happy times, and is an ill effect of a good cause', namely surplus population, 'an effect of peace in fruitful kingdoms'. The 'surcharge or overflow of people ... doth turn external peace into internal troubles and seditions'. In Bacon's speech on naturalisation of 1604 he had challenged those who maintained that it would provoke internal dissent: 'I demand what is the worst effect that can follow of surcharge of people? Look into all stories, and you shall find it none other than some honourable war for the enlargement of their borders, which find themselves pent, upon foreign parts.'[31] Bacon offers as examples Spain and France, recently unified as nation-states. He alludes to the historical unity of England, and suggests that 'we now scarce know whether the Heptarchy were a story or a fable'.[32] The 'Heptarchy' alludes to the supposed seven kingdoms of Angles and Saxons in the seventh and eighth centuries. Bacon is not one of those who sees the unification of Britain as a return to a former state. He does not wholly subscribe to the origin-myths of Brutus and Arthur: 'It doth not appear by the records and monuments of any true history, nor scarcely by the fiction and pleasure of any fabulous narration or tradition of any antiquity, that ever this island of Great Britain was united under one king before this day.'[33] Yet elsewhere he alluded to the king's 'heroical desire to reduce these two kingdoms of England and Scotland into the unity of their ancient mother kingdom of Britain'.[34] But this is not necessarily a contradiction. Britain could be unified in different ways. According to Bacon, there are four parts to a perfect union: 'Union in Name, Union in Language, Union in Laws, and Union in Employments'. Bacon asserts that Britain has 'one language, though of several dialects'.[35] There are two conditions that will bring about 'a Perfect mixture', 'Time', and the scientific principle 'that the greater draw the less':

> So we see when two lights do meet, the greater doth darken and drown the less. And when a smaller river runs into a greater, it leeseth both the name and the stream.[36]

Bacon, in his *History of King Henry VII*, records that some of Henry's counsellors cautioned 'that if God should take the King's two sons without issue, that then the kingdom of England would fall to the King of Scotland, which might prejudice the monarchy of England. Whereunto the King replied; That if that should be, Scotland would be but an accession to England, and not England to Scotland; for the greater would draw the less: and it was a safer union for England than that of France'.[37]

In another treatise, 'Certain Articles or Considerations Touching the Union of the Kingdoms of Scotland and England', Britain, according to Bacon, is now united:

> In sovereignty. In the relative thereof, which is subjection. In religion. In continent. In language. And now lastly, by the peace by your Majesty concluded with Spain, in leagues and confederacies: for now both nations have the same friends and the same enemies.[38]

That phrase, 'in continent', is crucial, because the British project is, on one level, an alternative to the continent, an attempt to establish 'another Europe'. It is also incontinent in so far as its purpose is to insulate England's colon against foreign incursion. The fact that we can still speak of British *and* European history is one measure of the success of that project. Eva Haraszti has pointed out that while: 'The term European history means in Britain, Continental history ... For

Continental historians European history includes the history of Great Britain as well.'[39] In Bacon, as in Spenser and Shakespeare, one can see the rudiments of that process of separation by which political union within a reinvented Britain enables a distinct (multi-) national identity to be forged over and against Europe. England could not have effected such a strategic isolation on its own. A '(two) island empire' was the only (temporary) solution.

'Scotland', Bacon acknowledges, 'is now an ancient and noble realm, substantive of itself':

> But when this island shall be made Britain, then Scotland is no more to be considered as Scotland, but as a part of Britain; no more than England is to be considered as England, but as a part likewise of Britain; and consequently neither of these are to be considered as things entire to themselves, but in the proportion that they bear to the whole. And therefore let us imagine ... that Britain had never been divided, but had ever been one kingdom: then that part of soil or territory which is comprehended under the name of Scotland is in quantity (as I have heard it esteemed, how truly I know not) not past a third part of Britain; and that part of soil or territory which is comprehended under the name of England is two parts of Britain; leaving to speak of any difference of wealth or population, and speaking only of quantity. So then if, for example, Scotland should bring to parliament as much nobility as England, then a third part should countervail two parts; *nam si inequalibus equalia addas, omnia erunt inequalia.* And this, I speak, not as a man born in England, but as a man born in Britain.[40]

Only in his imagination, of course, was Bacon 'a man born in Britain'. There was no 'Britain' when Bacon was born, though he was certainly, in career terms, a man *made in Britain*. And the notion that 'Scotland is no more to be considered as Scotland ... no more than England is to be considered as England', but both are to be overnight British successes, is a piece of wishful thinking on Bacon's part.

In the *Considerations* the 'internal' threat to peace through over-population can be warded off through colonial enterprise:

> Now what an excellent diversion of this inconvenience is ministred, by God's providence, to your Majesty, in this plantation of

Ireland? wherein so many families may receive sustentations and fortunes, and the discharge of them also out of England and Scotland may prevent many seeds of future perturbations. So that it is as if a man were troubled for the avoidance of water from the place where he hath built his house, and afterwards should advise with himself to cast those waters, and to turn them into fair pools or streams, for pleasure, provision, or use. So shall your Majesty in this work have a *double commodity*, in the avoidance of people here, and in making use of them there. (118)

Avoiding people here (in Britain), and making use of them there (in Ulster). This *double commodity* follows like a second Brother. In the speech on naturalisation, Bacon named the benefits as 'surety' and 'greatness':

Touching surety ... it was well said by Titus Quintius the Roman touching the state of Peloponnesus, that the tortoise is safe within her shell ... But if there be any parts that lie open, they endanger all the rest. We know well, that although the state at this time be in a happy peace, yet for the time past, the more ancient enemy to this kingdom hath been the French, and the more late the Spaniard; and both these had as it were their several postern gates, whereby they mought have approach and entrance to annoy us. France had Scotland, and Spain had Ireland; for these were the two accesses which did comfort and encourage both these enemies to assail and trouble us. We see that of Scotland is cut off by the union of both these kingdoms, if that it shall be now made constant and permanent. That of Ireland is likewise cut off by the convenient situation of part of Scotland towards the north of Ireland, where the sore was: which we see, being suddenly closed, hath continued closed by means of this salve; so as now there are no parts of this state exposed to danger to be a temptation to the ambition of foreigners, but their approaches and avenues are taken away: for I do little doubt but those foreigners which had so little success when they had these advantages, will have much less comfort now that they be taken from them ... For greatness ... I think a man may speak it soberly and without bravery, that this kingdom of England, having

Scotland united, Ireland reduced, the sea provinces of the Low countries contracted, and shipping maintained, is one of the greatest monarchies, in forces truly esteemed, that hath been in the world.[41]

Bacon goes on to suggest that the British state is the fulfilment of the imperial 'dream of a Monarchy in the West'.[42] Ironically, his Irish treatise first saw light under a Protectorate.

One of the English objections to the Union was that the country would be swamped with Scots, in the same way that 'sheep or cattle, that if they find a gap or passage open will leave the more barren pasture, and get into the more rich and plentiful'.[43] Bacon, speaking in defence of the Union, countered this particular fear in three ways. First, he suggested that Scottish migration would be limited by the fact that 'we see it to be the nature of all men that they will sooner discover poverty abroad, than at home'. So much for Scottish fortune-hunters. Second, he claimed 'that this realm of England is not yet peopled to the full', and could thus afford to accommodate any such prospective Scots invasion.[44] Finally, Bacon put his finger on a key feature of the Union, its third term, as it were – the mutually profitable carve-up of Ireland:

there was never any kingdom in the ages of the world had, I think, so fair and happy means to issue and discharge the multitude of their people, if it were too great, as this kingdom hath, in regard of that desolate and wasted kingdom of Ireland; which being a country blessed with almost all the dowries of nature, as rivers, havens, woods, quarries, good soil, and temperate climate, and now at last under his Majesty blessed also with obedience) doth, as it were, continually call unto us for our colonies and plantations.[45]

In their comedy *Eastward Ho!* (1604) Chapman, Jonson and Marston included a proposal for shipping 100,000 Scots to the New World, where 'we should find ten times more comfort of them ... than we do here'.[46] In the event, the (relative) surplus population of Scotland was planted in Ulster under Anglo-Scottish/British jurisdiction. There was a perception in English minds of Scots massing on the Borders. Ireland earthed the political energy generated by the Union, displaced its anxieties and excesses.

*

Bacon's incisive tract reveals the colonial project that underpins the newly united kingdoms. Bacon's fusion of union and plantation ties in with the ideas in his 'Example of a Summary Treatise touching the Extension of Empire', a version of the essay 'Of the True Greatness of Kingdoms', a subject he dealt with in depth in the unfinished work *Of the True Greatness of Britain*, composed in 1608 on the eve of the Ulster settlement. Lisa Jardine links Bacon's attitude to naturalisation of the Scots with the harnessing of military expertise in the interests of an expansionist British state.[47] Bacon believed in the politics of 'linkage', in strategy and policy, in making connections between different political processes. Ian Box has argued that it was Bacon's 'concern for national glory through military might' that prompted him to profess 'support for the unification of Scotland and England'.[48] Implicit in this policy was a drive towards complete union. The union of plantation, the joint enterprise of Ulster, came before the union of parliaments. It should be noted, however, that, apart from Ireland, Scotland and England pursued separate colonial strategies until after the parliamentary union of 1707. History has it that this second Union was prompted by the disastrous Darien enterprise, Scotland's go-it-alone effort at colonisation, but there were pressures closer to home that made political union desirable, and those pressures included the unfinished business of Ireland. Bacon was an architect of the Westward Enterprise, a New Atlanticism that drew on European examples, classical and contemporary, but constituted, on another level, as I have suggested, a turning away from Europe. Robert Faulkner has analysed Bacon's imperialism in detail, in particular his theory of overpopulation as a cause of colonies.[49] In 1624 Sir William Alexander remarked: '*Scotland* by reason of her populousnesse being constrained to disburden her selfe (like the painfull Bees) did every yeere send forth swarmes.'[50] Alexander was promoting settlement in Nova Scotia, so he had an investment in representing Scotland as overflowing. But so did the English with their ideas of Scots massing on the Borders.[51]

The third consequence of Bacon's *Considerations* pertains to the security of the British state. The plantation of Ireland would make the new polity safe 'in discomforting all hostile attempts of foreigners, which the weakness of that kingdom hath heretofore invited' (118). Bacon uses three examples to illustrate his point:

> the tortoise is safe within her shell: but if she put forth any part of her body, then it endangereth not only the part that is so put forth, but all the rest. And so we see in armour, if any part be left naked, it puts in hazard the whole person. And in the natural body of man, if there be any weak or affected part, it is enough to draw rheums or malign humours unto it, to the interruption of the health of the whole body. (119)

Bacon had used the metaphor of the tortoise before, in the speech on naturalisation already cited, and in a letter of advice to the Earl of Essex, his patron, following his appointment as Lord Lieutenant of Ireland in March 1599, where he observed 'how far forth the peril of that State is interlaced with the peril of England, and therefore how great the honour is, to keep and defend the approaches or avenues of this kingdom, I hear many discourse; and indeed there is a great difference, whether the tortoise gather herself within her shell hurt or unhurt'.[52]

Bacon's fourth and final consequence is 'the great profit and strength which is like to redound to your crown, by the working upon this unpolished part thereof'. Here, Bacon invokes Ireland as both within and outwith the new united kingdom, 'another Britain' to supplement the first:

> For this island being another Britain, as Britain was said to be another world, is endowed with so many dowries of nature, considering the fruitfulness of the soil, the ports, the rivers, the fishings, the quarries, the woods and other materials; and specially the race and generation of men, valiant, hard, and active, as it is not easy, no not upon the continent, to find such confluence of commodities, if the hand of man did join with the hand of nature. (119)

This passage does not quite square with the earlier claim that James had enacted two kinds of foundation, 'the first, that maketh one of more; and the second, that maketh one of none ... The one, in the union of the island of Britain; the other, in the plantation of the great and noble parts of the island of Ireland.' Here, 'another Britain' implies making two of one in the act of making one of none. There is a difference between making one of another and making another one. But this is a classic instance of imitation and originality being brought together.[53] Bacon's political theory found it difficult to countenance a Britain that appeared virtually *ex nihilo*. He therefore needed 'another Britain', one that was constructed in an active enterprise. The first had arisen, as David Stevenson remarks, 'through the dynastic accident of James VI of Scotland ascending the English throne as James I in 1603'.[54] The second would be a decisive act of social and political engineering, part of the *vita activa*, a programme in which Bacon himself would play an active part. It is ironic that Bacon should be conjuring up another Britain at the very moment at which he was writing *The Beginning of the History of Great Britain*, which first surfaced, like the *Considerations*, in the *Resuscitatio* of 1657. Bacon's forging of another Britain in the immediate aftermath of the founding of the first reinforces the claim that 'the art of discovery grows with discovery'. The invention of Britain can be reproduced, patented, multiplied. The use of the term 'mainland Britain' to imply that Ireland is an offshore island is proof of the relevance of Bacon's evocation of another Britain. Geography is political. The 'British Isles' is disputed terminology as well as disputed territory. The north of Ireland is intimately bound up with the beginnings of modern Britishness. In her essay on the *New Atlantis*, Denise Albanese opens with Bacon's Irish discourse and the reference to 'another Britain', which she astutely ties to a subsequent reference to Caesar, the implication being that Britain is now in the position of imperial Rome.[55] But in keeping with the reversion to 'England' in literary studies she concludes her argument with an allusion to 'early Stuart *England*'.[56]

Bacon represented the Ulster Plantation as 'a second brother to the Union'. This recalls that strange substitution in the first folio edition of *Henry V* (V.ii.12): 'So happy be the issue, brother Ireland', where it has been conjectured that the contemporary preoccupation with the Irish wars led to Ireland supplanting France. A 'textual error' of greater magnitude has permitted England to stand for Britain, and 'another Britain'. There was always the risk that these two brothers might not agree. Was there room for 'another Britain' so soon after the forging of the first? It is worth recalling that when the Irish officer Macmorris first appears in *Henry V* he is in the company of the Scottish Captain Jamy. This had been Spenser's fear – that Ireland and Scotland would unite against England.

Sir William Herbert, one of the principal undertakers in the Munster Plantation, had spoken at the beginning of the 1590s of 'foreign aggression and evils which proceed from elsewhere, namely the ravages, furies and arms of the Scots', and hoped that in the future 'the province of Ulster will be most like the province of the North of England'.[57] Another author writing at the end of that fateful decade had hoped that 'her Majesty shall make Ireland profitable unto her as England or mearly a West England'.[58] After the union, it was no longer a question of a West England, or a North England, but of another Britain. Ulster became, not a province like the North of England, but a province in which Highland and Island Scottish settlers were to be displaced by Lowlanders and Borderers, a province which would become a crucible of British identity. Sir John Davies, in his *Discovery* (1612), praised the execution of the Ulster Plantation: 'his Majesty did not utterly exclude the Natives out of this plantatiõ, with a purpose to roote them out, as the Irish wer excluded out of the first *English* Colonies; but made a mixt plantation of *Brittish and Irish*, that they might grow up togither in one Nation'.[59] But what would that 'one Nation' be? It is worth dwelling for a moment on the full title of Davies's text: *A Discoverie of the True Causes why Ireland was never entirely Subdued, nor brought under Obedience of the Crowne of England, untill the Beginning of his Majesties happie Raigne.* Although Davies does not say it, the reason James was able to unite the 'whole Island from Sea to Sea' was that it was now under obedience of the Crown of Britain.[60] It was the Union that sunk Anglo-Scottish differences over Ulster, 'the most rude and unreformed part of Ireland, and the *Seat* and *Nest* of the last great Rebellion'.[61] In a letter to Salisbury dated from Coleraine 28 August 1609, Davies spoke of the welcome the commissioners had received from the Londoners there: 'We all use our best Rhetorick to persuade them to go on wth their plantation; w[ch] will assure this whole Iland to the Crowne of England forever'.[62] The Crown of England? This is the best rhetoric indeed, rhetoric that can speak of 'Brittish' settlers and yet insist on English sovereignty.

In an influential essay entitled 'The Creation of Britain', Jenny Wormald notes that the Lord Chancellor, Ellesmere, Bacon's predecessor in that office, endorsed the latter's letter of April 1605 calling for the writing of a British history: 'Sir Francis Bacon touching the story of *England*'. Wormald comments: 'It is a lovely example of deeply ingrained Englishness wrestling with the British vision demanded by a new king of England; and it is presumably one of the earliest examples of that habit which infuriates inhabitants of the other parts of the British Isles to this day: the habit of using "England" as synonymous with "Britain"'.[63] Arguably as infuriating as the habit of counting Ireland as part of the 'British Isles', but then, Bacon, in alluding to Ireland as 'another Britain', anticipated that particular habit. The Union of Great Britain and Ireland of 1800 would give way, in time, to a continuing claim to the Six Counties of Ulster, as an exemplary conflictual site of British identity. Bacon's brief treatise is a timely reminder of the way in which the plantation of Ulster is intimately bound up with the historical foundations of Britishness.

6
Fording the Nation: Abridging History in *Perkin Warbeck* (1633)

In chapter 5, I cited Francis Bacon's *History of King Henry VII* as a text preoccupied with questions of union and succession. Bacon, we recall, alludes to Henry's advisers warning 'that if God should take the King's two sons without issue, that then the kingdom of England would fall to the King of Scotland, which might prejudice the monarchy of England. Whereunto the King replied; That if that should be, Scotland would be but an accession to England, and not England to Scotland; for the greater would draw the less: and it was a safer union for England than that of France'. In this chapter, I want to suggest that the new British historiography, combined with the recent turn towards the matter of Britain in Shakespeare studies, can be employed to good effect in a reading of John Ford's *Perkin Warbeck* (1633), the story of the pretender who threatened to usurp – with a little help from friends in France, Scotland, Ireland and Cornwall – the throne of Henry VII, King of England and Wales.[1] The English history play is a dramatic form most often viewed within a single national milieu rather than in the context of an emerging multination state. It is associated with the maintenance of the Tudor Myth and the projection of the Elizabethan World Picture, and with a particularly triumphant version of English nationalism.

In the three chapters on Shakespeare, I tried to show the extent to which the work of England's national bard is bound up with the disputed borders of Britishness. Here, I want to take as my starting point Ford's late historical drama, and to use this somewhat anachronistic literary text in order to argue for the centrality of issues around Britishness to the drama of the Renaissance. I have argued that Shakespeare's history plays, the most notable instances of the genre, and indeed other plays within the Shakespeare canon, can be seen to have been concerned with a rehearsal of the themes of a united British kingdom. Shakespeare's subtle and searching interrogation of the conflicting allegiances is made explicit in Ford's reprise of the chronicle play.

It is impossible to read *Perkin Warbeck* without referring back to Shakespeare's histories, and, more generally, to the Tudor Myth that those plays helped constitute, but the relationship between Ford's work and Shakespeare's remains contested. Some critics see Ford's revival of the history play as a compliment to Shakespeare, while others regard it as part of a critique. It is certainly not possible to read Ford's history play outside of the genre that it revives. Yet Ford does more than hark back to a genre that is no longer in vogue. Histories had been proscribed by the Privy Council in 1599. After 1613 less than a dozen history plays are recorded. There were several reasons for the history play dying out, including censorship, Union, and changing audience tastes, reflected in the move to a more inward-looking drama. When the Tudor Myth ran out of steam, so too did the English history play.

As we have seen, there are various ways in which the four nations that together will form the basis of a future British state interact in Shakespeare's histories. For instance, Richard II's ruin followed on from his disastrous campaign in Ireland, and in *Henry V* the nations are represented at Harfleur by four captains. What preoccupies me is the extent to which, in Ford's play, perhaps predictably, the power-base of the pretender is in the Celtic Fringes, as it were. Perkin draws his strength first from France, then Ireland, Scotland, and finally Cornwall. Ford had expressed an interest in the new British state at an early stage in his career. In *Fames Memoriall* (1606), he had commended Lord Mountjoy, the Irish Viceroy who had succeeded Essex in Ireland, thus:

> As oft as *James* the monarch of our peace,
> Shall be in after chronicles recited,
> In that to heavn's applause and subjects ease
> *England* and *Scotland* he in one united,
> A sight with which true *Britains* were delighted:

So oft shalt thou eternall favour gaine,
Who recollected'st *Ireland* to them twaine.[2]

The claim that Mountjoy recollected Ireland in the wake of Anglo-
Scottish Union glosses over the fact that England and Scotland were
at loggerheads over Ireland, and that the Union of Crowns offered
an opportunity not merely for recollection but for an active forgetting of the recent past. What Ford's play unmasks is the extent to
which English monarchical history is an almost unrelenting tale of
regicide, usurpation and competing claims to the throne. Henry IV
usurped Richard II in 1399. Richard III's brother Edward IV usurped
Henry VI in 1461; Richard took the throne from Edward's son,
Edward V, in 1483. 1485 witnessed the invasion and accession of
Henry VII, who defeated Richard III at Bosworth. It is here that
Perkin Warbeck makes his brief appearance on the stage of British
history. In fact, there were other pretenders abroad at this time, one
of whom, Lambert Simnel, was crowned Edward VI in Dublin in
1487. Ireland was the springboard for claimants to the English
Crown, and from 1460 was the power base of the Yorkist cause.

   If, as I have been arguing throughout this book, every text has
several contexts, then *Perkin Warbeck* is no exception. Ford's
drama is an untimely example of a Stuart history play that con-
fronts questions of identity in the three kingdoms at the inception of the Tudor Myth. It is the last English history play, and
constitutes a retrospective meditation on a volatile political form.
The play is a triple play. It participates in three historical junc-
tures – set in the 1490s, it recalls the history plays of the 1590s,
and both anticipates and participates in the political upheavals of
the 1630s. It ostensibly charts the progress of Perkin Warbeck,
from the moment he disembarked at Cork in 1491 posing as
Richard IV, to his execution at Tyburn on 23 November 1499.
First performed in the year of the first printing of Edmund
Spenser's *A View of the State of Ireland* (1633), Ford's play was published hard on the heels of the appointment of that text's dedica-
tee, Thomas, Viscount Wentworth, and later Earl of Strafford, as
Lord Deputy of Ireland. Strafford was a key factor in triggering the
War of the Three Kingdoms, as was Spenser's provocative prose
dialogue, and I shall maintain that Ford's play contributes to this
troubled moment. The play was reprinted in 1714, and revived in

1745, on both occasions to coincide with a fresh threat from a pretender to the British throne.[3]

Ford's full title reads: '*The Chronicle Historie of Perkin Warbeck. A Strange Truth*'.[4] The 'Strange Truth' of *Perkin Warbeck* is that it is a compelling instance of a revisionist literary text, a play that both revives and revises the Tudor Myth, parodying the genre of the history play, mocking established models of monarchical authority, and displacing the centre of power from London to a host of locations on the so-called 'margins' of metropolitan English culture – Cornwall, Ireland, Scotland. The play was dedicated to William Cavendish, first Earl of Newcastle, who would act as a royalist leader in the coming War of the Three Kingdoms. Interestingly, in view of the action of the play, Cavendish was allegedly involved in plots laid in 1643 and 1644 to lead Charles I's English supporters in an invasion that would be backed up by Scottish and Irish troops.[5] Ford, addressing Cavendish, acknowledges his act of resuscitation in reviving a dying art form:

> Out of the darkness of a former age (enlightened by a late both learned and honourable pen) I have endeavoured to personate a great attempt, and in it a greater danger. In other labours you may read actions of antiquity discoursed; in this abridgement, find the actors themselves discoursing: in some kind, practised as well what to speak, as speaking why to do.

Ford's abridgement of the British Problem in *Perkin Warbeck* truncates and telescopes the questions of sovereignty and statehood implicit in a multiple monarchy. Chronologically, his tale comes between two reigns marked by Shakespeare in his histories, namely those of Richard III and Henry VIII. The action of the play, set on 'The Continent of Great Britain', can be read as a dramatic representation of the gap between form and content in a nascent British state, as the splitting and repetition of royal authority is seen to unhinge the whole political structure. In keeping with a central motif in his other plays, Ford asserts: 'Eminent titles may indeed inform who their owners are, not often what'. The contest over ownership of 'The Continent of Great Britain' is exactly to do with its defining principle and locus of power.

Ford's purpose in writing *Perkin Warbeck* is patriotic. He means to present a native narrative, 'a history couch'd in a play', and no ordinary history, but:

> A history of noble mention, known,
> Famous, and true; most noble cause our own;
> Not forg'd from Italy, from France, from Spain,
> But chronicled at home; as rich in strain
> Of brave attempts as ever fertile rage
> In action could beget to grace the stage.
> We cannot limit scenes, for the whole land
> Itself appear'd too narrow to withstand
> Competitors for kingdoms. Nor is here
> Unnecessary mirth forc'd, to endear
> A multitude. On these two rests the fate
> Of worthy expectation: Truth and State.

The problem is that if, in one reading, 'Truth and State' are 'Competitors for kingdoms', then Perkin Warbeck may be seen to represent the former and Henry VII the latter. Moreover, the term 'State', juxtaposed, or more precisely here opposed to 'Truth', arguably unseats monarchical government. What we are presented with is a contest between force and forgery, in which force wins out in the end, but with forgery recognised as the stuff of drama, dreams and national identity.

The opening scene contains a spectre that is strangely familiar to Renaissance audiences, the ghost of conflicts past that vexes the nascent British state:

> Still to be haunted, still to be pursued,
> Still to be frighted with false apparitions
> Of pageant majesty and new coin'd greatness,
> As if we were a mockery king in state,
> Only ordain'd to lavish sweat and blood
> In scorn and laughter to the ghosts of York,
> Is all below our merits; yet, my lords,
> My friends and counsellors, yet we sit fast
> In our own royal birthright. The rent face
> And bleeding wounds of England's slaughter'd people

> Have been by us, as by the best physician,
> At last both thoroughly cur'd and set in safety.
> And yet for all this glorious work of peace
> Oneself is scarce secure.

(I.i.1–14)

Haunted by the ghosts of York, Henry, apparently the rightful ruler, is himself reduced to a spectral existence, because the currency of 'new coin'd greatness' ruins established economies of power. This experience of being possessed by poltergeists is the perennial condition of the British state. The most significant modern historical account of the reign of Henry VII alludes to Perkin Warbeck as 'a Yorkist ghost that could not be easily laid'.[6] In Ford's play, Durham extends the king's metaphor, noting that:

> The rage of malice
> Conjures fresh spirits with the spells of York.
> For ninety years ten English kings and princes,
> Threescore great dukes and earls, a thousand lords
> and valiant knights, two hundred fifty thousand
> Of English subjects have in civil wars
> Been sacrific'd to an uncivil thirst
> Of discord and ambition.

(I.i.14–21)

These words are eerily prophetic when one considers that Ford was writing on the eve of another civil war, one that would claim yet another king, this time to be supplanted by a protector rather than a pretender.

The metaphor of haunting is a recurrent figure in representations of threats to monarchical authority in the drama of the period. One thinks here of Banquo and Hamlet's father. Consider the use of the same trope in Marlowe's *Edward II*, where the king asks:

> Shall I still be haunted thus?

and Lancaster responds:

> Look for rebellion, look to be deposed.
> Thy garrisons are beaten out of France

> And lame and poor lie groaning at the gates;
> The wild O'Neil, with swarms of Irish kerns,
> Lives uncontrolled within the English pale;
> Unto the walls of York the Scots made road,
> And unresisted drave away rich spoils.[7]

This would have resonated in the 1590s, and indeed in the 1630s, and beyond. It finds an echo in another history play, Shakespeare's *Henry IV Part One*, which opens with a speech by the king that anticipates that of Ford's Henry VII, and which has the same root, namely fear of 'internal' challenges to royal authority:

> So shaken as we are, so wan with care,
> Find we a time for frighted peace to pant,
> And breathe short-winded accents of new broils
> To be commenced in strands afar remote.
> No more the thirsty entrance of this soil
> Shall daub her lips with her own children's blood,
> No more shall trenching war channel her fields,
> Nor bruise her flowerets with the armèd hoofs
> Of hostile paces.[8]

The spectre of a war between kin, a civil war, beckons. Intra-British hostility haunts the pages of *Perkin Warbeck*, as it does those of Shakespeare's histories. The aggrandisement of England by prosthesis, through the incorporation and mutilation of Wales, Ireland and Scotland entails the twitching of phantom limbs, as these nations assert what little independence they still possess, and England finds itself in turn possessed by its possessions, having nightmares of history in its north and west wings. Union may be a reality, but unity is a pretence. In *Perkin Warbeck* the pretender himself is frequently alluded to as a phantom. Henry tells one of his advisors:

> We know all, Clifford, fully, since this meteor
> This airy apparition first discradled
> From Tournay into Portugal, and thence
> Advanc'd his fiery blaze for adoration
> To th'superstitious Irish; since, the beard
> Of this wild comet, conjur'd into France,

> Sparkled in antic flames in Charles his court;
> But shrunk again from thence, and hid in darkness,
> Stole into Flanders, flourishing the rags
> Of painted power on the shore of Kent,
> Whence he was beaten back with shame and scorn,
> Contempt, and slaughter of some naked outlaws.
> But tell me, what new course now shapes Duke Perkin?

(I.iii.35–47)

'For Ireland', is Clifford's reply, confirming the king's conviction that 'Some Irish heads work in this mine of treason', but he goes on to reveal that Warbeck's Irish associates have urged the pretender:

> To fly to Scotland to young James the Fourth,
> And sue for aid to him. This is the latest
> Of all their resolutions.

(I.iii.64–6)

Perkin shapes the new course of British history, which will see a shift in English investment from Wales to Scotland. Henry VII complains of feeling like 'a mockery king in state'. (I.i.4) He rails against Warbeck, and observes that:

> Foreign attempts against a state and kingdom
> Are seldom without some great friends at home.

(I.i.84–5)

'Home' and 'foreign' are, of course, vexed categories in a British context. The English Empire conjured into existence in 1533 was declared to be independent of foreign princes. But where does 'home' end and 'foreign' begin? It comes as no surprise, either to the historian of the early modern period, or to the student of the British Problem, to learn whence Perkin Warbeck found support for his claim:

> first Ireland,
> The common stage of novelty, presented

> This gewgaw to oppose us; there the Geraldines
> And Butlers once again stood in support
> Of this collossic statue.
>
>   (I.i.105–9)

The Geraldines and Butlers are opposing Irish factions who have the Yorks and Lancasters respectively as their English analogues, but here they are lumped together and Ireland as a whole is represented as a seed-bed for rebellion. Since the pretender is an 'airy apparition' of a king, Henry curses 'th'superstitious Irish' (I.iii.39).[9] Having launched himself from Ireland, the pretender next seeks protection at the court of James IV, before finding 'Ten thousand Cornish' willing to fight for him. War beckons, the perk in the pretender's purse. Historically, Perkin Warbeck (1474?–99) would be much closer in age to James IV (1473–1513) than to Henry VII (1457–1509), hence Durham's reference to 'young James the Fourth'. Henry will later say of James that 'The Scot is young and forward' (II.ii.152). As well as nation, there is a question of generation here. The incumbent in Ford's time, Charles I (1600–49), close in age to Ford's Henry, would well understand his predecessor's predicament. If the Tudor Myth depended on the vindication of that dynasty, then the Stuart Myth subjects it to interrogation, chiefly from the so-called 'margins' of the British state, a state in turmoil in Ford's time, and merely a distant prospect in the time of Henry VII. Mildred Struble sees *Perkin Warbeck* as being implicated in contemporary debates about divine right and the grounds of legitimate rule, so that Ford's strategy was 'to contrast the Tudor interpretation of majesty, under Henry VII, and the Stuart interpretation, just beginning, under James IV' in order to unravel the divided inheritance of Charles I.[10] Building on this claim, my own view is that *Perkin Warbeck* is less a deconstruction of the Tudor Myth than a reconstitution of it that uncovers its ideological roots and routes, and at the same time passes comment on the first thirty years of Stuart rule.

If *Richard II* is ever-present in Ford's revival of the history play, then other Shakespeare histories hover in the background. In the news from Cornwall there are shades of *Henry IV Part One*, where news of the activities of the Scots and Welsh broke off the king's business, which was to deflect attention away from British conflict through a crusade to the Holy Lands. Similarly, in *Henry V* Shakespeare has an exchange between the English king and Canterbury that rehearses the familiar spectre of a Scottish invasion. Henry warns:

> We must not only arm t'invade the French,
> But lay down our proportions to defend
> Against the Scot, who will make raid upon us
> With all advantages.

Canterbury tries to assuage the king's fears but misconstrues its main source. Thinking that the king is worried about cross-border raids, he says:

> They of those marches, gracious sovereign,
> Shall be a wall sufficient to defend
> Our inland from the pilfering borderers.

Henry, however, has a more substantial consideration in mind than mere 'pilfering borderers':

> We do not mean the coursing snatchers only,
> But fear the main intendment of the Scot,
> Who hath been still a giddy neighbour to us,
> For you shall read that my great grand-father
> Never unmasked his power unto France
> But that the Scot on his unfurnished kingdom
> Came poring like the tide into a breach
> With ample and brim fullness of his force
> Galling the gleanèd land with hot assays,
> Girding with grievous siege castles and towns,
> That England, being empty of defence,
> Hath shook and trembled at the bruit thereof.[11]

The 'bruit' of a Scottish invasion is the brutal fact of the British Problem. Ford, unlike Shakespeare in his early histories, is writing in the wake of Anglo-Scottish union, when the border between England and Scotland has become blurred, and the respective sovereignties of those two countries were at once fused and confused.[12] The margins have folded back to reveal another centre. Patricia Parker has argued that the scene in *Henry V* that brings together the Welsh, Scottish, English and Irish captains 'is less a demonstration of integrity than of the argument and disunity that prevent these diverse forces from answering Henry's unifying call'. Parker sees Shakespeare's play as being preoccupied with 'England's control over its border or borderers', and this too is the crux of *Perkin Warbeck*.[13]

James IV's own justification for helping Warbeck is revealing. The Scottish king points to the precedent of seeking foreign assistance to resolve domestic disputes:

> The right of kings, my lords, extends not only
> To the safe conservation of their own
> But also to the aid of such allies
> As change of time and state hath oftentimes
> Hurl'd down from careful crowns, to undergo
> An exercise of sufferance in both fortunes:
> So English Richard, surnam'd Coeur-de-lion,
> So Robert Bruce, our royal ancestor,
> Forc'd by the trial of the wrongs they felt,
> Both sought and found supplies from foreign kings,
> To repossess their own.

> (II.i.18–28)

In *Macbeth*, we recall, Duncan's sons, like Perkin Warbeck, and like Charles I, seek succour and redress in two neighbouring kingdoms:

> *Malcolm*: I'll to England.
> *Donalbain*: To Ireland I.[14]

Macbeth observes:

> We hear our bloody cousins are bestowed
> In England and in Ireland.

> (III.i.29–30)

In this case it is from England that an intervening army is despatched. In *Perkin Warbeck*, while James is extolling the virtue or, rather, the necessity of seeking foreign aid, Henry is complaining of domestic disorder:

> We are followed
> By enemies at home that will not cease
> To seek their own confusion.

> (II.ii.125–7)

Fresh intelligence arrives, informing Henry:

> That James of Scotland late hath entertain'd
> Perkin the counterfeit with more than common
> Grace and respect, nay, courts him with rare favours.
> The Scot is young and forward; we must look for
> A sudden storm to England from the North;
> Which to withstand, Durham shall post to Norham
> To fortify the castle and secure
> The frontiers against invasion there.

> (II.ii.149–56)

Ironically, when he comes to refer to Henry's Tudor origins, James IV undermines at a single stroke both his adversary's Englishness and his legitimacy:

> The Welsh Harry henceforth
> Shall therefore know, and tremble to acknowledge,
> That not the painted idol of his policy
> Shall fright the lawful owner from a kingdom.

> (II.iii.62–5)

Henry's identity is no more fixed or firm than that of Warbeck, but is incontinent and unstable. Having moved from the Irish to the Scots, Warbeck next elicits help from Cornwall. The Scottish threat to English dominion is followed by another hazard to the integrity of England, as Daubeney brings the news of a Cornish interest:

> Ten thousand Cornish,
> Grudging to pay your subsidies, have gathered
> A head, led by a blacksmith and a lawyer;
> They make for London.

> (II.iii.129–32)

'Welsh Harry', as James called him, celebrates the victory over the 'Cornish rebels' on 'Saint George's Fields'. (III.i.9) This victory, it has been noted, was achieved historically by virtue of a heavy reliance 'on the loyalty of the Welsh contingents'.[15] In *Henry V* the king, despite his claims to Welsh origins, had been addressed as 'Harry of England' (III.6.118), and had cried 'God for Harry! England and Saint George!' (III.i.34) We can see here a gap opening up between Tudor and Stuart interpretations of history. After the accession of James I, it was no longer necessary to appeal to Welsh origins or to an ancient British identity, since a new British political system, a constellation that included Scotland, was now a reality. While Shakespeare's Henry V made much of his Welsh origins, arguably in order to compliment the Tudor regime, Ford offers a case for preferring the English pretender – supported most notably by the Scots, but also aided by Irish and Cornish elements – over the English incumbent who owes his existence to the Welsh.[16] Ironically, Henry VII had never been Prince of Wales, an office he conferred on his son, Arthur, in 1489.[17] We can juxtapose Henry VII's Welshness and defensive Englishness to Perkin Warbeck's resort to sources of support ostensibly outside the Anglo-Welsh axis, in Ireland, Scotland and Cornwall. Interestingly, in Ford's day there was a significant influx of Irish immigrants into Wales:

> Between 1628 and 1631 there was another mass movement of people from Ireland to England, Scotland and continental Europe. On 27 August 1628 the English privy council noted that 'of late great numbers of poore Irish people have been landed in divers parts of Wales'. They ordered that 'no such Irish' be permitted to land and in the ensuing months heavy penalties were imposed on all shipowners who transported them.[18]

Is the risk to be avoided here simply that the Irish might gain a foothold in Wales, or is it that the Welsh and Irish might combine at some vanishing point in the future and together confront the authority of England? Remember that an alliance between the Irish and Scots was the pre-Union, pre-British nightmare from which England wished to awake.

Perkin Warbeck shares the concerns of Shakespeare's histories. Throughout Ford's play, national boundaries are broached by invasion and the forging of alliances. When he weds Katherine Gordon, daughter of the Earl of Huntly, Warbeck declares:

> An union this way
> Settles possession in a monarchy
> Establish'd rightly, as is my inheritance.

> (II.iii.78–80)

'An union this way', that is, through marriage, 'Settles possession in a monarchy'. A union any other way may be not quite so secure. For example, the dynastic accident that brought James I to the throne, or any other acts of incorporation or conquest. The wedding itself sees a marriage of cultures. Warbeck's Irish followers fear being upstaged at the celebrations that follow the ceremony:

> 'tis fit the Scots
> Should not engross all glory to themselves
> At this grand and eminent solemnity.

> (II.iii.139–41)

The father of the bride, Huntly, mocks the mixture of Scottish and Irish entertainment:

> Is not this fine, I trow, to see the gambols,
> To hear the jigs, observe the frisks, b'enchanted
> With the rare discord of bells, pipes and tabors,
> Hotch-potch of Scotch and Irish twingle-twangles,
> Like so many quiristers of Bedlam
> Trolling a catch!

> (III.ii.2–7)

In a scene that seems both to recall and parody Ben Jonson's *Irish Masque at Court* (1613) the Irish and Scottish entertainers appear.[19] The stage direction reads:

Enter at one door four Scotch Antics accordingly habited; enter at another four wild Irish in trowses, long-haired, and accordingly habited. Music. The masquers dance.

Whereas Jonson's *Irish Masque* was ostensibly a compliment to the conversion powers of James I, as the rude Irish masquers revealed themselves to be sophisticated Anglo-Irishmen, in Ford's play the entertainment for James IV is more ambiguous, designed both to expose the lack of cultivation in evidence when popular Scottish and Irish traditions converge, and to suggest that Scotland and Ireland have more in common culturally than either has with England. If the Irish-Scottish combination amuses Huntly, it also serves to point up the difference between the English and Scottish courts. As Jonas Barish observed: 'Not only does love bulk large at the Scottish court – we hear nothing of it in England – but there is also ceremony and revelry, music, dancing, feasting, and masquing.'[20] In short, culture. Perkin offers an alternative Englishness to Henry's mixture of grim severity, military prowess and underhand political manoeuvring, and thus promises the possibility of another kind of Anglo-Scottish interface than that of an incorporating union. Warbeck, having thanked James for his 'unlimited' favour, speaks of the alliance that must ensue when the pretender takes his proper place on the English throne:

> Then James and Richard, being in effect
> One person, shall unite and rule one people,
> Divisible in title only.
>
> (III.ii.106–8)

While Warbeck seeks the assistance of the Celtic nations that encircle England, Henry has a 'charm' that will break the spell Warbeck has woven over James IV. He has a Continental card up his sleeve. Facing Scottish forces, Surrey remarks:

> The Scots are bold,
> Hardy in battle; but it seems the cause
> They undertake, considered, appears
> Unjointed in the frame on't.
>
> (IV.i.10–13)

Not only is the time out of joint, but the frame is too. The national context of the dispute over the English throne is criss-crossed by various kinds of foreignness. We learn of Henry's attempts to disengage James from Warbeck with promises of a British and European peace, in the shape of friendly relations with both Spain and England. Outflanked by Henry's politicking, Warbeck finds succour in the news that the Cornish are entreating him to land in Cornwall with a force and lead them against Henry. Astley, one of Warbeck's followers, sums up the situation thus:

> that if this Scotch garboils do not fadge
> to our minds, we will pell-mell run amongst the Cornish
> choughs presently and in a trice.
>
> (IV.ii.57–9)

Warbeck is hopelessly outmanoeuvred by Henry. While the pretender draws support from Scotland, Ireland and Cornwall, the incumbent outflanks his adversary through some devious intrigues with Spain. Warbeck's 'antic pageantry' is no match for Henry's plotting. Hialas, the Spanish agent, proposes a union between Henry and James, recalling Warbeck's earlier appeal for one between himself, as Richard IV, and the Scottish king:

> France, Spain and Germany combine a league
> Of amity with England; nothing wants
> For settling peace through Christendom but love
> Between the British monarchs, James and Henry.
>
> (IV.iii.1–4)

Hialas urges James to accept the offer of a way of avoiding a damaging Anglo-Scottish war:

> To this union
> The good of both the church and commonwealth
> Invite 'ee.
>
> (IV.iii.14–16)

By marrying Margaret, Henry's daughter, James will forge an alliance in blood that will bind Scotland and England together, aligned against the challenger forged in Ireland, that 'common stage of novelty'. The Scottish king cannot resist the prospect of such a pleasing outcome to his predicament. As the king of a nation whose

support for the claimant to the throne of a more powerful neighbour has placed his country in jeopardy, James is relieved to discover such an easy way of saving face:

> A league with Ferdinand! A marriage
> With English Margaret! A free release
> From restitution for the late affronts!
> Cessation from hostility! and all
> For Warbeck not delivered but dismiss'd!
> We could not wish it better.

> (IV.iii.56–61)

Warbeck's dry remark when he discovers James's acquiescence is
telling:

> The Tudor hath been cunning in his plots.

> (IV.iii.109)

With the Scottish door closed to Warbeck, Cornwall affords another
vantage point from which to assail Henry. Like the English Pales in
France and Ireland, and the Marches of Wales and Scottish
Borderlands, Cornwall offers an alternative power base. Within the
compass of a pale the English state is simultaneously at its most
forceful and its most vulnerable. In keeping with the pretender's
facility for picking losers to back him, the Cornish are duly routed,
though Warbeck is still at large, albeit ensnared 'Within the circuit
of our English pale' (IV.ii.3).

If Ford's treatment of the British Problem shifts the gaze to the
perceived margins of the state, then his play also has a crucial
European dimension. Indeed, then as now one cannot separate
developments in Continental Europe from issues affecting 'The
Continent of Great Britain'. Jane Ohlmeyer's suggestion that the
War of the Three Kingdoms in the 1640s was actually a War of Five,
given the involvement of France and Spain, can be pushed back into
the fifteenth-century, so that the British Problem is inseparable from
a wider European Problem.[21]

Perkin is more mercurial than martial, but he is majestic. Ford's
strength in the play, and its revolutionary import, is that the pretender emerges as a much more charismatic figure than the

enthroned Henry, and that the real centre of 'The Continent of Great Britain', certainly in terms of the play, is the court of King James. Ford's version of events is in places dependent on historical sources, and yet, at the same time, in its sympathetic portrayal of the self-styled second son of Edward IV, it flies in the face of established historiography, and flatly contradicts previous canonical accounts of the pretender – one thinks here immediately of Thomas Gainsford's *True and Wonderful History of Perkin Warbeck* (1618) and of Francis Bacon's *History of the Reign of Henry VII* (1622).

Philip Edwards points out the way in which the story of Perkin Warbeck would have had a contemporary resonance in the 1630s: 'A charismatic figure of lost royalty would have had a great emotional appeal at a period when many of Charles's subjects looked on the occupant of the throne as the dried husk of a king.'[22] By placing in doubt the status of the English crown at the inception of the Tudor Myth, Ford problematises and ultimately undermines, or countermines, one particular version of British origins, by reminding us that altercation and dissent lie at the heart of the Tudor regime. As Alexander Leggatt writes: 'A kingship that can be thus imitated, fought over, or simply earned is a kingship that has lost its unique, sanctified character and become a role or an office like any other.'[23] But Ford does not merely illustrate the contingency of kingship. He shows that there are other kingdoms whose claims to sovereignty impinge upon the English Crown.

The question of British identity at the heart of the play, and its implicit promotion of compromise, foundered with the advent of conflict in the three kingdoms in the 1640s. Promoting a narrow English national perspective on history is arguably not Ford's chief aim. In his play the fact that the court of James IV is given far more attention than that of Henry VII reflects, I would argue, an overriding preoccupation with British statehood rather than English monarchy. After reading Ford's play, a piece of Caroline drama set on the cusp of the Tudor regime, and clearly informed by late Elizabethan history plays, one returns to Shakespeare with a fresh insight into the shaping of 'The Continent of Great Britain'.

Alexander Leggatt is one of a number of commentators who have juxtaposed the character of Shakespeare's Richard II with Ford's Perkin Warbeck, but this is not the only possible comparison.[24] Mark Thornton Burnett has contrasted Warbeck with Marlowe's

Tamburlaine, claiming that where Tamburlaine exits wishing he had done more, Warbeck is defeated by the rightful king.[25] But do we read the conclusion of Ford's play as an instance of Faustian defiance, or as the resignation and submission of Richard II? Is Perkin Warbeck, the royal pretender, another Richard II, eloquent but impotent, or is he, like Marlowe's Tamburlaine, a self-made man with a gift for moving speeches? If *Perkin Warbeck* as a whole is most obviously and most often compared with Shakespeare's *Richard II*, a more interesting and potentially fruitful comparison may be yielded by setting it alongside *Henry V*. Indeed, while I would take issue with H. J. Oliver's assertion that '*Perkin Warbeck* in its own way is just as patriotic as *Henry V*', I find this view more palatable than Joan Sargeaunt's insistence that 'Ford is not really concerned at all with the fortune of England, with its traditions, its politics, and its countryside'.[26] Both, of course, are only half right. Ford is interested in a critique of English patriotism that takes as its basis an expanding 'British' context. Ford is arguably concerned above all with the fortunes of Britain. Questions of sovereignty in the sense of both personal rule and political dominion are rehearsed throughout the play.

Within this interlocking multiple monarchical matrix, one may detect the shadow of republicanism, a republicanism that thrives in the non-English nations that make up the British state. The historical irony is that it was only when those nations threatened to usurp English authority that an English republic came into being, under Cromwell, for the express purpose of asserting English supremacy within the three kingdoms. One may also discern here the rudiments of another concern of Ford's, the idea of advancement through merit. But the play furnishes us with more than a classic instance of Renaissance self-fashioning. It shows that the fashioning of a state from a number of nations and monarchies is a painful process, fraught with danger. The matter of sovereignty is complicated if an expansion of the state results in a questioning of monarchy. More than one crown in a state can amount to less than one crown. I would go so far as to suggest that what we have in Ford's play is a confrontation between two possible futures for Britain, a federal republic or a centralised monarchy. Moreover, the Continent of Great Britain is shown to be reliant upon the Continent of Europe, one composite monarchy among others. According to J. H. Elliott: 'If sixteenth-century Europe was a Europe of composite states, coexisting with a myriad of smaller territorial and jurisdictional units jealously guarding their independent status, its history needs to be assessed from this standpoint rather than from that of the society of unitary nation states that it would later become.'[27] Again, it's a question of going backstage, of getting behind the proscenium arch of the theatre of Britishness, viewing its halfway houses, its staging posts, its dress rehearsals and its endless encores. That Warbeck should be sustained by Cornwall, Ireland and Scotland is wonderfully appropriate given the way in which the Tudor Myth, centring on England and Wales, depended upon the suppression of Irish and Scottish elements in the nascent British state. What we get in the Stuart Myth, which reconfigures the relationship between the four nations, is the return of the repressed elements of the British state. Wales loses credibility and visibility, Scotland becomes crucial, and Anglo-Scottish partnership proves a necessary prerequisite for the complete conquest of Ireland.

In the figure of Perkin Warbeck, guardian of a 'Strange Truth', the English claimant who derives his strength from the 'borderlands' of 'Great Britain', one may hear the rumble of an impending conflict. It would be tempting to see Ford as the Stuart revisionist of Tudor nationalism, but if Ford's is arguably a critical nationalism sensitive to the interplay of the three kingdoms, then Shakespeare is far less jingoistic than his most conservative English readers would attest. Much of Shakespeare's work, and not only in the histories, was concerned with rehearsing tensions made explicit in Ford's reprise of the chronicle play. I prefer to see both playwrights as struggling with a problem that in recent years has been rather too exclusively the province of the professional historian.

As an English historical drama that foregrounds the non-English components of the British political state-in-formation, *Perkin Warbeck* provides an example of what Patricia Parker, with reference to Shakespeare, has termed 'the edification from the margins ... that can be gained by attending to what might appear the simply inconsequential'.[28] Ford's play is more than merely an ironic reflection on an outmoded theatrical genre. Rather, the play reveals a complex engagement with notions of Britishness that is also present within those earlier historical dramas that have too readily been seen by critics, radical and conservative alike, as professing a narrow English nationalism. That traditional standpoint is shown to be limited in light of Ford's belated elaboration on the form. If the literary critic desires a model for exploring the British Problem in English Renaissance literature then it may be that, in addition to the sterling work of the born-again British historians, the literary texts of the period, particularly those hitherto seen to be preoccupied with a specific national context, will supply productive analogues. A recent essay on reading Renaissance drama speaks of 'the difficult and challenging work of locating the text in its histories, and identifying histories in the text; and of plotting the significances of those traces for our own historical location'.[29] My own very provisional perusal of Ford's revisionist history play is, I would hope, with all its faults and failings, a modest step in that direction.

7
Milton's *Observations* (1649) and 'the Complication of Interests' in Early Modern Ireland

On 28 March 1649, Cromwell's parliament commissioned John Milton 'to make some observations upon the complication of interests which is now among the several designers against the peace of the Commonwealth ... to be printed with the papers out of Ireland which the House hath ordered to be printed.'[1] Milton's *Observations upon the Articles of Peace with the Irish Rebels* duly appeared on 16 May appended to a series of documents comprising the articles of James Butler, Earl of Ormond's peace with the Irish confederates (dated 17 January), his proclamation of Charles II as king; the ensuing exchange of letters (9 and 14 March) between Ormond and Colonel Michael Jones, Governor of Dublin; and an attack on the English parliament by the Scottish Presbytery at Belfast, dated 15 February. What Milton has to say about 'the complication of interests' between the Old English, the Irish 'rebels', and the Ulster Presbytery highlights the difficulties attending the representation of Ireland in the early modern period, and, more particularly for my purpose, points up the difficulties that arise within a multiple monarchy.

The argument of this chapter is simple. Milton's *Observations* is not an anti-Irish treatise in any simple sense, but is rather a complex text that affords its author an ideal opportunity to explore further the vicissitudes of the British Problem.[2] Caught up in a rhetoric of accusation and apology that serves to veil its wider context, criticism of this tract has obscured its real significance, specifically as a document that deals explicitly with a struggle over sovereignty within a troubled British milieu. Indeed, as we shall see, Milton's greatest concern in the *Observations* is not with Ireland at all, but with Scotland.

The *Observations* is clearly a hybrid document. The text as a whole occupies around 65 quarto pages, 44 pages being taken up by the reproduction of the documentation to which Milton was to reply. Milton's agenda is clear from the proportion of space he devotes to each portion of the document. The 33 pages of the Articles of peace elicit only four and a half pages of commentary, Ormond's two-and-a-half page letter to Colonel Jones gets as much, and the four and a half pages of the Representation of the Scottish Presbytery receives eleven pages of refutation. Milton justifies a single response to these various documents thus: 'there will be needfull as to the same slanderous aspersions but one and the same Vindication against them both.' (p. 300) Milton elaborates further:

> Nor can we sever them in our notice and resentment, though one part intitl'd a *Presbytery*, and would be thought a Protestant Assembly, since their own unexampl'd virulence hath wrapt them into the same guilt, made them accomplices and assistants to the abhorred *Irish* Rebels, and with them at present to advance the same interest: if wee consider both their calumnies, their hatred, and the pretended Reasons of their hatred to be the same; the time also, and the place concurring, as there lacks nothing but a few formall words, which may be easily dissembl'd, to make the perfetest conjunction; and between them to divide that Iland. (p. 300)

In other words, Milton's response to the Republic's request that he uncover the 'complication of interests' in Ireland is a deconstructive one. That is, he takes an apparent opposition and proceeds to dismantle it in order to reveal an underlying complicity, in this case the threatening conjunction, from an English standpoint, of Scottish and Irish interests. Milton's task is to show the extent to which both Dublin and Belfast appear to be conspiring against London. That is, the Old English of the South (the descendants of the twelfth-century English settlement in Ireland, chiefly Catholic), and the new Scottish settlers in the North, are at one in their resistance and opposition to Cromwell's regime. It is a tale of two Pales, the long-standing one around Dublin and the recently planted one around Belfast, and of their shared antagonism towards the metropolis. In its concern with questions of sovereignty and with the hegemony of the English parliament the *Observations* demands to be read alongside two other texts of that tumultuous year – *Eikonoklastes* and *The Tenure of Kings and Magistrates.*

Ireland has long occupied an ambiguous position in English culture, as a convenient colonial pretext for further expansion abroad, as a vexed site of imperial interest in itself, and, crucially for my purposes, as a testing-ground for theories of British identity. Like all texts addressing the fraught matter of three kingdom politics, Milton's *Observations* is multilayered. Influenced by Spenser, it looks back to the colonial crisis of the 1590s, and the Nine Years War that stretched English authority in Ireland to the limit; it draws on the atrocity literature of the 1640s that followed on from the Ulster Rising of 1641; it taps into what Paul Stevens terms 'Leviticus thinking', the radical Protestant exclusionism that represented the Irish as unclean; it is part of a longer tradition of civil discourse on Ireland; and, last but not least, it recognises Ireland as a highly localised conflictual milieu within which wider political struggles were to be fought out.[3] There is a long tradition of seeing Ireland as the place where Milton's radicalism was compromised, a tradition that draws on Marx's insight that 'the English republic under Cromwell met shipwreck in Ireland.'[4] This is the view of Christopher Hill, who explains Milton's complicity in a discourse of discrimination thus: 'Even relatively liberal thinkers *assumed* the total inferiority of the Irish and their culture.'[5] Hill's view, that Ireland was the graveyard of English radicalism, is shared by Paul Stevens, who notes that: 'In Ireland, Milton's revolutionary rhetoric becomes colonizing rhetoric.'[6] Both Hill and Stevens, in different ways, use religion to explain (away) Milton's apparent anti-Irish rhetoric.

What Milton has to say about the 'complication of interests' between the Old English, the Irish and the Ulster Presbytery is important in terms of the 'British Problem.' Milton's discourse on Ireland impinges directly upon the question of his imperial vision. Ireland represents the earliest and most fraught of England's colonial projects, and Milton's unraveling of England's Irish problem shows him to be both seduced by and estranged from the simplistic anti-Irish hysteria of his contemporaries. Ireland, for Milton, constitutes an obstacle in the path of reform in England and an impediment to the establishment of an anglocentric British state in preparation for a British Empire, yet Milton's anger is targeted not at the Irish *per se*, but at the twin threats of Catholicism and Presbyterianism, of Old English and Ulster Scots. In this, Milton comes close to the Spenser of *A View of the State of Ireland*.[7] We know that Milton was familiar with Spenser's *View* because two entries in Milton's commonplace book show that he had read the first published edition of 1633.[8] Milton and Spenser both belonged to a radical Protestant tradition that championed English sovereignty and supremacy within the burgeoning British polity, yet their work touching Ireland has tended to be quarantined and corralled, cut off from their preoccupation with the matter of Britain, lest it contaminate their theories of origins and identity. By dwelling on an unproblematic Hibernophobia, critics can gloss over their own implication within an anglocentric discourse. It is above all a question of using the margins as a site of displacement, and as a way of avoiding any engagement with mainstream Englishness.

One way of reading the *Observations* would be to place it within an English colonial ambiance, where the 'discourse on Ireland' is essentially a discourse of civility against a perceived barbarism. Here, Milton's text would belong to a genre of political writing about Ireland from an English perspective which stretches from Giraldus Cambrensis to the present day, and tells 'nothing but the same old story.'[9] Another approach would be to see the colonial conflict in terms of religion, the terms of Hill and others. Don Wolfe asserts that both Milton and Spenser 'regarded the Irish as barbarous, savage, uncouth, but, worst of all, papistical in religious belief.'[10] But as Norah Carlin has astutely pointed out, there was more than a fear of Catholicism at work in English texts on Ireland in the 1640s, and the old, pre-Reformation ethnography constantly came into play.[11] The relationship between the discourses of civility and religion is problematic, and criticism of each tends to revolve around the status of Englishness. A complication of interests calls for a complication of discourses. To a discourse of civility and one of religion, one must add a discourse of sovereignty, a fusion of Protestant humanism and English nationalism.

One reason why the old Anglo-Irish or English-Irish oppositional model simply will not do, especially when dealing with texts as subtle and nuanced as Milton's, is that the cultural composition of early modern Ireland was much more complicated than this structure allows. Two varieties of Englishness, old and new, were competing for control, with the native Irish, and the Scots in the north of the country, adding to what was essentially a four-way struggle. If Spenser's *View* rehearses in detail the complexities of the various allegiances, Milton's text can be seen to be similarly engaged with a multi-national struggle. Milton's targets in the *Observations* are Spenser's targets in the *View* – the native Irish, the Old English, and the Scots. Milton is as scathing of the Scots as was Spenser. He rails against the Belfast Presbyterians:

> who from a ground which is not thir own dare send such defiance to the sovran Magistracy of *England*, by whose autoritie and in whose right they inhabit there. By thir actions we might rather judge them to be a generation of Highland theevs and Redshanks, who beeing neighbourly admitted, not as the *Saxons* by merit of thir warfare, against our enemies, but by the courtesie of *England* to hold possessions in our Province, a Countrey better than thir own, have, with worse faith then those Heathen, prov'd ingratefull and treacherous guests to thir best friends and entertainers. (pp. 333–4.)

By characterising them as 'treacherous guests', Milton is reasserting Spenser's claim that the Scots were not to be trusted in Ulster.

Milton was, like Bacon and Spenser before him, attuned to the multilayered nature of the British Problem in an Irish context. Rereading early modern English views of Ireland, one becomes increasingly aware of a pronounced British dimension that has been airbrushed from the canvas in modern historiography. I have already illustrated the extent to which Spenser's *View* and Bacon's *Certain Considerations* can be read as problematically British rather than simplistically Irish texts. What is called for in analysing English political writings of the period is a broader perspective, both temporal and geographical. This means going back and reading Spenser's *View*, and the whole English tradition of representing Ireland, and it means refusing to accept the form of the British state as merely a prerequisite of empire, or seeing Ireland as simply a halfway house. So-called 'internal colonialism' is a phrase that conceals the extent to which the formation of the British state, an experience characterised by successive crises of sovereignty, was both a prerequisite to Empire *and* an act of Empire in itself. When David Armitage argues that Milton was a poet against empire one has to ask: Which empire? What concept of empire is being employed?[12] My own feeling is that both Spenser and Milton were colonial republicans.[13]

The Articles of Peace called, among other things, for the repeal of Poynings' Law which made the English parliament sovereign in Ireland. Ormond's letter to Jones accused Cromwell of trying 'to change the Monarchy of *England* into Anarchy.' According to Merritt Hughes: 'The dominant feeling in Milton's discussion of Ormond's terms with the Confederates is resentment at their threat to England's sovereignty.'[14] Hughes further asserts that: 'By English standards in Milton's time, Ormond's Articles of Peace were simply articles of treasonable surrender.'[15] But what exactly were English standards, given the multiple and divided nature of Englishness? As we shall see, at stake is the whole question of who speaks for England, and who truly represents the best interests of the nascent British state.

The 'Necessary Representation' of the Scottish Presbytery described the trial of the late king as 'against both the Interest and the Protestation of the Kingdome of *Scotland*', and demanded of the English parliament 'that they doe cordially endeavour the preservation of the Union amongst the well affected in the Kingdomes, not being swayed by any Nationall respect: remembring that part of the Covenant; *That wee shall not suffer our selves directly, nor indirectly, by whatsoever Combination, perswasion, or terrour, to be divided, or withdrawne from this blessed Union, and Conjunction'* (p. 299). The members of the Belfast Presbytery deny being 'broachers of Nationall and divisive motions', throwing that charge back at 'the Sectaries in England' (p. 296).

As with Spenser's *View*, selective quotation rather than comprehensive reading is the hallmark of criticism of Milton's treatise. The lines that are most often quoted from the *Observations* are those that describe the Irish as a people 'who rejecting the ingenuity of all other Nations to improve and waxe more civill by a civilizing Conquest, though all these many yeares better shown and taught, preferre their own absurd and savage Customes before the most convincing evidence of reason and demonstration: a testimony of their true Barbarisme and obdurate wilfulnesse to be expected no lesse in other matters of greatest moment' (p. 304). But if we return these lines to their original context we see that Milton is referring to a specific Article:

The two and twentieth Article more ridiculous then dangerous, coming especially from such a serious knot of Lords and Politicians, obtaines that those Acts prohibiting to plow with horses by the Tayle, and burne oates in the Straw, be repeald: anough if nothing else, to declare in them a disposition not onely sottish but indocible and averse from all Civility and amendment, and what hopes they give for the future, who rejecting the ingenuity of all other Nations to improve and waxe more civill by a civilizing Conquest, though all these many yeares better shown and taught, preferre their own absurd and savage Customes before the most convincing evidence of reason and demonstration: a testimony of their true Barbarisme and obdurate wilfulnesse to be expected no lesse in other matters of greatest moment. (pp. 303–4)

Now, there is no question that this is an instance of anti-Irish rhetoric, in so far as it is opposed to the attempt by the Old English to resist English laws and culture, but it is also highly specific, and directed against a ruling elite. Granted, Milton speaks of '*Irish* Barbarians' (p. 308), and of 'the villainous and savage scum of Ireland' (p. 323), but he is no less critical of their Scottish counterparts. And Milton could aim invective at his own English countrymen. In *Eikonoklastes* he declares: 'It were a Nation miserable indeed, not worth the name of a Nation, but a race of Idiots, whose happiness and welfare depended upon one man.'

Milton's central argument against the Articles of Peace is that they risk 'alienating and acquitting the whole Province of *Ireland* from all true fealty and obedience to the Common-wealth of *England*' (p. 305). It is a question of the relationship between a 'Province' and a 'Commonwealth.' Milton's reaction to the fourth Article, which urged the prosecution of all those 'as shall divide one Kingdome from another', is to throw this charge back at the accuser: 'And what greater dividing then by a pernicious and hostile Peace, to disalliege a whole Feudary Kingdome from the ancient Dominion of *England*?' (p. 307). As Merritt Hughes observes: 'For an antimonarchist, Milton was strangely sorry to see Ireland freed from the feudal obligations which Wentworth had so successfully asserted in order to increase Charles's rents from crown lands.'[16] Both Milton and Spenser wanted to see democracy at home and absolutism abroad, or at least to have legislative control ascendant at the core, while unlimited executive authority is simultaneously exercised and exorcised in the colonies.

David Underdown points out that it is as much of a problem to see Cromwell's conquest exclusively as an episode in Irish history as to see it solely as an episode in English history.[17] Underdown maintains that: 'The conquest of Ireland was as essential to the survival of the Republic as the conquest of Scotland, and for much the same reasons. The danger of an Irish-based Stuart invasion had been present in English minds ever since 1642.'[18] Yet having mentioned Scotland, Underdown proceeds to remind his readers that 'it is an Anglo-Irish relationship that we are dealing with, and ... we shall not get at the reality of it by confining ourselves either to England or to Ireland.'[19] Or to both, I would add. What about Scotland? One Irish historian has pointed out that in the Ulster Rising of 1641: 'The most striking incongruity appears in the treatment of the Scots.'[20] Aidan Clarke reveals that Turlough O'Neill, one of the Irish leaders, 'wrote to Sir Robert Knight late in November to apologize for the inadvertent killing of some Scotsmen, and to propose a conference so that "both the nations being formerly one should still so continue".'[21] Another Irish leader, Philip McHugh O'Reilly told his followers: 'You are not to meddle with any of the Scottish nation except they give you cause.'[22] Clarke finds significance in the fact that 'the settlers in Ulster had been drawn from two mother countries: the assumption that their natural sympathies and interest would converge with those of the administration, valid in plantation days, had no relevance to a new situation in which hostilities between Scotland and England presented the Scots with a conflict of loyalties which many of them had little difficulty in resolving.'[23] Clarke concludes: 'Thus, as developments outside Ireland altered relationships within it, the short-sightedness of the convenient Anglo-Scottish partnership in the plantation became evident: colonisation without anglicisation was not adequate to the purpose.'[24] It was certainly not adequate to Milton's purpose.

The underlying complicity between the Scots and the Irish – complicit in so far as they oppose English political supremacy – is, for Milton, the key component of the complication of interests. The English government was swift to recognise the pivotal role of Scotland in the renewed Anglo-Irish conflict. Charles I had been in Scotland when the Ulster Rising broke out on 23 October 1641. On 3 November 'a committee for Irish affairs was set up and ordered to consider "how this kingdom shall make use of the friendship and assistance of Scotland, in this business of Ireland".'[25] Milton places the Articles of Peace side by side with the Necessary Representation of the Belfast Presbytery in order 'to observe in some particulars the Sympathy, good Intelligence, and joynt pace which they goe in the North of *Ireland*, with their Copartning Rebels in the South, driving on the same Interest to loose us that Kingdome, that they may gaine it themselves, or at least share in the spoile: though the other be op'n enemies, these pretended Brethren' (p. 317). Again and again Milton returns to his theme, that the Presbyterians, professed opponents of Catholicism, 'have joyn'd interest with the *Irish Rebells*' (p. 325). Milton represents this complicity in religious terms:

> But as it is a peculiar mercy of God to his people, while they remain his, to preserve them from wicked confederations: so it is a mark and punishment of hypocrites to be drivn at length to mix thir cause, and the interest of thir *Covnant* with Gods enemies. (p. 325)

What the Belfast Presbytery share with the Old English is a critical attitude to the newly established Republic. Milton asks: 'What meane these men? is the Presbytery of *Belfast*, a small Town in *Ulster*, of so large extent that their voyces cannot serve to teach duties in the Congregation which they oversee, without spreading and divulging to all parts farr beyond the Diocesse of *Patrick*, or *Columba*, their writt'n Representation, under the suttle pretence of Feeding their owne Flock?' (pp. 317–18). It is a question of orbit and sphere of influence, of jurisdiction, England's over Ireland, and the Belfast Presbytery's over its own flock. Milton's commission is to spread and divulge English overlordship to all parts far beyond the diocese of Cromwell. The Necessary Representation is, to Milton's mind, an overreaching document, one that makes exorbitant claims, and his duty is to remind the Ulster Scots of their limited remit. Milton turns the screw further by comparing the presbyters to bishops:

> And surely when we put down Bishops, and put up Presbyters ... we did not think that one Classick Fraternity so obscure and remote, should involve us and all State affairs within the Censure and Jurisdiction of *Belfast*, upon pretence of overseeing their own charge. (p. 318)

The Belfast Presbytery indulge in as much 'impudence and false-hood as any Irish Rebell could have utter'd; and from a barbarous nook of *Ireland* brand us with the extirpation of laws and liberties; things which they as little understand as ought that belongs to good letters or humanity' (p. 327).

Milton is emphatic in his defence of English interests. Addressing the Presbytery, he justifies the execution of Charles to which they objected:

> But they tell us, *It was against the interest and protestation of the Kingdom of Scotland.* And did exceeding well to joyn those two together: heerby informing us what credit or regard need be givn in *England* to a *Scotch* Protestation, usherd in by a *Scotch* interest: certainly no more then we see is givn in *Scotland* to an *English* Declaration, declaring the interest of *England*. If then our interest move not them, why should theirs move us? If they say, wee are not all *England*; we reply, they are not all *Scotland*: nay, were the last year so inconsiderable a part of *Scotland* as were beholding to this which they now term the Sectarian Army, to defend and rescue them at the charges of *England* from a stronger party of their own Countrymen, in whose esteem they were no better then Sectarians themselves. (p. 330)

It is a question of representation, *necessary representation*, because representation is necessary. Milton's closing lines reiterate his belief that despite, or rather because of their own protestations, the Belfast Presbytery are engaging in 'a co-interest and partaking with the *Irish* Rebells', adversaries turned accomplices:

> Against whom, though by themselves pronounced to be the enemies of God, they goe not out to battell, as they ought, but rather by these thir doings assist and become associats. (p. 334)

Milton is accusing the Scots of playing into the hands of the Irish merely by opposing England on a single issue. England's enemy is its enemy's friend. Guilt by association.

If the 'British Problem', by virtue of its incorporation of a Celtic dimension into an anglocentric narrative, entails the possibility of a repetition of the original colonial project, that is, of expansion and appropriation, it is also a timely antidote to a lot of Anglo-American scholarship on the period that tended to gloss over or minimise the parts played by Scotland and Ireland in English history. Before the advent of the 'British Problem', the complexities of British history were seldom foregrounded. This can be easily illustrated by reference to a work published in 1972, the year before Pocock's plea. Lawrence Stone, in *The Causes of the English Revolution, 1529–1642*, offers a classic instance of the old anglocentric position. Stone devotes a brief passage to 'two chance events' that sparked off civil war in England. One was the death of the moderate leader-in-waiting, the Earl of Bedford, the other was the 'Irish Rebellion'. Both 'chance events' are dealt with summarily under the heading of 'The Triggers, 1640–42.' This is English historiography before the 'British Problem' was acknowledged:

> With hindsight one can see that the Irish situation had been becoming more and more explosive for a decade, but to contemporaries the rebellion, with its accompanying massacres and the loss of all English control outside the port towns, *came like a bolt from the blue*. Its timing could not have been more unfortunate, *since the plain need to crush it* made necessary the resurrection of central power in its most extreme and dangerous form, an army. Ever since the collapse of the government in 1640, there had been a vacuum of power, a situation which, *had it not been for the Irish Rebellion*, might have been allowed to continue for some time until the political crisis had been settled. But now there arose the necessity of raising an army, and therefore the question of who was to control it.[26]

The Ulster Rising was neither a 'chance event, nor 'a bolt from the blue.' Its origins went back much further than a decade, and 'the plain need to crush it' was not universally felt. Indeed, one could argue that the singular achievement of the short-lived English Republic was the subjection of Ireland.

Ireland is inevitably the most politically fraught component in the new British history, since the terminology itself is problematic. Indeed, one could argue that the British Problem represents, on one level, a way of turning round the Irish Question, in order to interrogate the other constituent parts of the British state. It is not surprising then that the most challenging work on this topic comes from those Irish historians who, while aware of the advantages of a wider perspective, are also wary of its overweening tendencies, provide committed but qualified accounts of the role of Ireland, and they do so generally without lapsing into the language of 'borderland', 'Celtic Fringe', or the anomalous 'British Mainland' that characterises the new Britocentrism as much as it did the old Anglocentrism, keeping intact the outmoded core–periphery model that the British Problem, at its most pressing and sceptical, promises to overturn.

For Milton, the Ulster Rising, far from coming out of the blue, provided an indication of the perennial threat of Catholicism. In *Eikonoklastes*, contemporaneous with the *Observations*, he wrote:

> For it cannot be imaginable that the Irish, guided by so many suttle and *Italian* heads of the Romish party, should so far have lost the use of reason, and indeed of common Sense, as not supported with other strength then thir own, to begin a Warr so desperate and irreconcilable against both England and Scotland at once.[27]

Milton, in the face of royalist claims to the contrary, accuses the king of provoking discord in the three kingdoms. Milton writes of Charles I's attitude to the Irish: 'He holds them less in fault then the *scots*, as from whom they might *allege* to have fetch'd *thir imitation*; making no difference between men that rose necessarily to defend themselves, which no Protestant Doctrin ever disallow'd, against them who threatn'd Warr, and those who began a voluntary and causeless Rebellion with the Massacher of so many thousands who never meant them harme.'[28]

Throughout *Eikonoklastes*, Milton repeatedly makes the connection between events in Ireland and royal policy with regard to Scotland, and he advocates religion and civility as the proper cohesive force to maintain the British state, while insisting on the pre-eminence of the English parliament. The Bishops 'seek to rouze us up to … a cursed, a

Fraternall *Warre*. ENGLAND and SCOTLAND dearest Brothers both in *Nature*, and in CHRIST must be set to wade in one anothers blood; and IRELAND our free Denizon upon the back of us both.'[29] In nature and in Christ, but the three kingdoms were to form a triangle with England at the apex. It is Milton's pro-English feelings, as much as any anti-Irish sentiment, that underpins his belief that England must reign supreme in the three kingdoms, and the conflict in Ireland brings home the vital importance of keeping Scotland in its place as second-in-command. Derek Hirst neatly illustrates the extent to which Milton himself was caught up in the complication of interests arising from the competing claims of Scotland and England to ascendancy within the expanding British state: 'the challenge posed by Scottish arguments ensured that even such unlikely bedfellows as John Milton and the Presbyterian lawyer William Prynne could in the middle years of the century make common cause in appropriating "Britain" to England.'[30]

Tom Corns sees the *Observations* as being preoccupied 'much less with Irish affairs than with a crucial phase of English domestic politics', but in my view this underplays the extent to which Milton is juggling with interests that are neither foreign nor domestic in any simple sense.[31] Milton's *Observations* presents an anglocentric British vantage point that is less concerned with confederation than with domination and conquest. Viewed from an English historical perspective, Ireland appears to be a side-show as far as questions of sovereignty are concerned, but the struggle between Crown and parliament in England cannot be seen outside of the interaction between England, Scotland and Ireland. In this expanded 'British' context, Ireland is not simply a convenient alternative power-base for Charles I, or Cromwell, but a crucial site of conflict for competing national identities. More than a scurrilous polemic defaming the Irish nation, the *Observations* is a worrisome meditation on the 'complication of interests' that binds England, Scotland and Ireland. Milton's vision may be anglocentric but it is also distinctively British in a way that many critics have overlooked. Milton's view of Ireland was far more complex than any simple binary model would suggest. Ireland was – and remains – a fulcrum of British identity, and Milton, perhaps more than any other writer, recognised its ambiguous position as a key component of the British state, a bridge between Scotland and England, a focal point of empire, and a crucible of colonial otherness. Like Spenser, Bacon, Shakespeare and Ford, and many other Renaissance writers whose Englishness was by turns consolidated and compromised by the shifting national and political boundaries of the period, Milton was grappling both with a conflict of loyalties and a complication of interests, a struggle within which nationalists, republicans and royalists were at odds in their conception and perception of nation, state and empire, not to mention union and plantation. Theirs was a colonising culture, and colonialism was a process that cut both ways.

Notes

Introduction

1. Roy Foster, 'History and the Irish Question', *Transactions of the Royal Historical Society* 5th series, 33 (1983), pp. 169–92; '"We Are All Revisionists Now"', *Irish Review* 1 (1986), pp. 1–5; 'Varieties of Irishness', in *Modern Ireland, 1600–1972* (London: Allen Lane, 1988), pp. 3–14. My own (doctoral) research was published as *Salvaging Spenser: Colonialism, Culture and Identity* (London: Macmillan, 1997). The present collection of essays may be viewed as a companion volume.

2. See, for example, Brendan Bradshaw, 'Edmund Spenser on Justice and Mercy', *Historical Studies* 16 (1987), pp. 76–89; Ciaran Brady, 'Spenser's Irish Crisis: Humanism and Experience in the 1590s', *Past and Present* 111 (1986), pp. 17–49; Nicholas Canny, 'Edmund Spenser and the Development of an Anglo-Irish Identity', *The Yearbook of English Studies: Colonial and Imperial Themes* 13 (1983), pp. 1–19.

3. I have always regarded myself as a Marxist and viewed my own work as informed by Marxism, even when this has not been evident in my references or bibliography. For work of mine that engages explicitly with Marxism, see for example, 'Brother Tel: the Politics of Eagletonism', in Stephen Regan (ed.), 'Barbarian at the Gate: Essays for Terry Eagleton', *The Year's Work in Critical and Cultural Theory* 1 (1991) (Oxford: Blackwell, 1994), pp. 270–87; 'Spectres of Engels', in Peter Buse and Andrew Stott (eds), *Ghosts: Deconstruction, Psychoanalysis, History* (London: Macmillan; New York: St. Martin's Press, 1999), pp. 23–49; 'Communing with the Church: Revelation and Revolution in Engels' "On the History of Early Christianity" (1894–95)', in John Schad (ed.), *Writing the Bodies of Christ: The Church from Carlyle to Derrida* (London: Ashgate, 2001), pp. 11–23; 'The Collapse of the New International', in *The New International*, a special issue of *Parallax* 20 (2001), guest ed. Martin McQuillan, pp. 73–82; 'À propos of Marx, Attribute to Derrida: A Note on a Note in *Margins of Philosophy*', in Martin McQuillan (ed.), *Deconstruction Reading Politics*, a volume in the series Philosophy, Literature and Culture, general editor Hugh J. Silverman (Evanston, Ill. Northwestern University Press, 2002); 'Do you read me?: Answering the Distress-signal of Deconstruction Reading Politics', in Martin McQuillan (ed.), *Emergencies: Politics, Deconstruction, Cultural Studies*, a volume in the series Leeds Studies in Cultural Analysis, general editors Griselda Pollock and Martin McQuillan (London: Routledge, 2002).

4. See, for example, my 'Varieties of Englishness: Planting a New Culture beyond the Pale', in *Salvaging Spenser*, pp. 48–77, and 'Varieties of Nationalism: Post-revisionist Irish Studies', in Sarah Briggs, Paul Hyland

and Neil Sammells (eds), *Reviewing Ireland: Essays and Interviews from Irish Studies Review* (Bath: Sulis Press, 1998), pp. 265–72.

5. My efforts to insert Scotland into Anglo-Irish history include 'Lost in the Hyphen of History: The Limits of Anglo-Irishness', in Willy Maley, Chris Morash and Shaun Richards, 'The Triple Play of Irish History', *The Irish Review* 20 (Winter/Spring, 1997), pp. 23–46 (pp. 23–9); '*Braveheart*: Raising the Stakes of History', *Irish Review* 22 (Summer 1998) guest editor Frank McGuinness (Cork: Cork University Press, 1998), pp. 67–80; 'Crossing the Hyphen of History: The Scottish Borders of Anglo-Irishness', in Ashok Bery and Patricia Murray (eds), *Comparing Postcolonial Literatures: Dislocations* (London: Macmillan, 2000), pp. 31–42; '"Kilt by kelt shell kithagain with kinagain": Joyce and Scotland', in Derek Attridge and Marjorie Howes (eds), *Semicolonial Joyce* (Cambridge: Cambridge University Press, 2000), pp. 201–18; 'Ireland, Verses, Scotland: Crossing the (English) Language Barrier', in Glenda Norquay and Gerry Smyth (eds), *Across the Margins: Cultural Identity and Change in the Atlantic Archipelago* (Manchester: Manchester University Press, 2002), pp. 13–30. See also Ellen-Raïssa Jackson and Willy Maley, 'Celtic Connections: Colonialism and Culture in Irish-Scottish Modernism', in *Interventions: The International Journal of Postcolonial Studies* 4, 1 (2002), special issue on Postcolonial Studies and Transnational Resistance, eds Elleke Boehmer and Bart Moore-Gilbert, pp. 68–78.

6. Take Marx, for example. He wrote to Engels on 10 December 1869: 'For a long time I believed that it would be possible to overthrow the Irish regime by English working-class ascendancy ... Deeper study has convinced me of the opposite. The English working class *will never accomplish anything* [Marx's emphasis] before it has got rid of Ireland. The lever must be applied in Ireland. That is why the Irish question is so important for the social movement in general'. See Marx and Engels, *Ireland and the Irish Question* (London: Lawrence and Wishart, 1978), pp. 397–8.

7. I take issue with the rhetoric of revisionism in 'Revisionism and Nationalism: Ambiviolences and Dissensus', in Scott Brewster, Virginia Crossman, Fiona Becket and David Alderson (eds), *Ireland in Proximity: History, Gender, Space* (London and New York: Routledge, 1999), pp. 12–27. I should say here that I am by no means one of those unreconstructed nationalist critics who see revisionism as anathema, but I do find postcolonial criticism to be a useful corrective to the more glib and reactionary tendencies of some revisionist scholarship, particularly in an Irish context. On the vexed relationship between Irish studies and postcolonialism, see Colin Graham and Willy Maley (eds), *Irish Studies and Postcolonial Theory*, special issue of *Irish Studies Review* 7, 2 (1999), pp. 149–231. For another perspective, see Steven G. Ellis, 'Writing Irish History: Revisionism, Colonialism and the British Isles', *The Irish Review* 19 (1996), pp. 1–21.

8. The new British history has generated a vast literature over the past fifteen years, but see, for example Steven, G. Ellis and Sarah Barber (eds), *Conquest and Union: Fashioning a British State, 1485–1725*

(London: Longman, 1995); Brendan Bradshaw and John Morrill (eds), *The British Problem, c. 1534–1707* (London: Macmillan, 1996); Alexander Grant and Keith J. Stringer (eds), *Uniting the Kingdom?: The Making of British History* (London: Routledge, 1995); Brendan Bradshaw and Peter Roberts (eds), *British Consciousness and Identity: The Making of Britain, 1533–1707* (Cambridge: Cambridge University Press, 1998). These were the first major collections of essays devoted to a topic whose architect, it is generally agreed, was John Pocock. See J. G. A. Pocock, 'British History: A Plea for a New Subject', *Journal of Modern History* 47 (1975), pp. 601–28. Pocock has gone on to argue for an 'Age of the Three Kingdoms' that would comprise the entire early modern period. See his 'The Atlantic Archipelago and the War of the Three Kingdoms', in Bradshaw and Morrill (eds), *The British Problem*, pp. 172–91. My own acquaintance with the British Problem began, not with Pocock, but with an established English historian who shifted his ground in the late 1980s in a way that I found intriguing. See Conrad Russell, 'The British Problem and the English Civil War', *History* 72 (1987), pp. 395–415, and 'The British Background to the Irish Rebellion of 1641', *Historical Research* 61, 145 (1988), pp. 166–82. No footnote on the British perspective on the early modern period is complete without making reference to Linda Colley's magisterial study, *Britons: Forging the Nation 1701–1837* (New Haven: Yale University Press, 1992), but Colley's comfortable coupling of Britishness and modernity is thrown into question by explorations of the shaky foundations of Britishness in an earlier period, and more specifically by the challenging work of Murray Pittock, most pointedly his *Inventing and Resisting Britain: Cultural Identities in Britain and Ireland, 1685–1789* (London: Macmillan, 1997).

9. See Pocock, 'British History: A Plea for a New Subject'. For some idea of the subsequent development of Pocock's thinking on this matter – the matter of Britain – see 'Limits and Divisions of British History: In Search of the Unknown Subject', *American Historical Review* 87 (1982), pp. 311–36, and 'Contingency, Identity, Sovereignty', in Grant and Stringer (eds), *Uniting the Kingdom? The Making of British History*, pp. 292–302.

10. See, for example, Nicholas Canny, 'The Attempted Anglicization of Ireland in the Seventeenth Century: An Exemplar of "British History"', in Ronald G. Asch (ed.), *Three Nations – a Common History?: England, Scotland, Ireland and British History c. 1600–1920* (Bochum: Universitätsverlag, 1993), pp. 49–82; Steven G. Ellis, '"Not mere English": the British Perspective, 1400–1650', *History Today* 38, 12 (1988), pp. 41–8; Jane H. Ohlmeyer, 'Seventeenth-century Ireland and the New British and Atlantic Histories', *American Historical Review* 104 (1999), pp. 446–62; David Stevenson, 'The Century of the Three Kingdoms', in Jenny Wormald (ed.), *Scotland Revisited* (Collins and Brown: London, 1991), pp. 107–18; Jenny Wormald, 'The Creation of Britain: Multiple Kingdoms or Core and Colonies?', *Transactions of the Royal Historical Society* 6, 2 (1992), pp. 175–94.

11. See, for example, John Morrill, 'The Fashioning of Britain', in Ellis and Barber (eds), *Conquest and Union*, pp. 8–39; Conrad Russell, *The Fall of the British Monarchies 1637–1642* (Oxford: Clarendon Press, 1991).

12. The British Problem is addressed in a sustained fashion from a literary perspective in David J. Baker and Willy Maley (eds), *British Identities and English Renaissance Literature* (Cambridge: Cambridge University Press, 2002).

13. There is evidence to suggest that postcolonialism is backtracking into the Renaissance, and even making inroads into the medieval period. See, for example, Rebecca Ann Bach, *Colonial Transformations: The Cultural Production of the New Atlantic World 1580–1640* (Basingstoke: Palgrave Macmillan, 2000); Jeffrey Jerome Cohen (ed.), *The Postcolonial Middle Ages* (Basingstoke: Palgrave Macmillan, 2001); Ivo Kamps and Jyotsna G. Singh (eds), *Travel Knowledge: European 'Discoveries' in the Early Modern Period* (Basingstoke: Palgrave, 2001). For an incisive introduction to postcolonialism, see Willy Maley, Bart Moore-Gilbert and Gareth Stanton (eds), *A Postcolonial Reader*, Longman Critical Readers (London: Addison, Wesley and Longman, 1997), pp. 1–72.

14. My own interventions into this area interface with the valuable contributions of several scholars who are similarly engaged in charting the shift from Irish to British concerns. See, for example, David J. Baker, *Between Nations: Shakespeare, Spenser, Marvell, and the Question of Britain* (Stanford: Stanford University Press, 1997); Christopher Highley, *Shakespeare, Spenser and the Crisis in Ireland* (Cambridge: Cambridge University Press, 1998); Claire McEachern, *The Poetics of English Nationhood, 1590–1612* (Cambridge: Cambridge University Press, 1996).

15. See David Armitage, 'John Milton: Poet against Empire', in David Armitage, Armand Himy and Quentin Skinner (eds), *Milton and Republicanism* (Cambridge: University of Cambridge Press, 1995), pp. 205–25; Conrad Russell, *Unrevolutionary England, 1603–1642* (London: Hambledon Press, 1989).

Chapter 1

*I would like to record a debt here to Terence Hawkes, whose lively and suggestive treatment of Shakespeare and national identity has informed, at almost every stage, my own work on this topic. John Joughin furnished me with much needed focus during the development of these arguments.

1. George Herbert, *Outlandish Proverbs*, in A. B. Grosart (ed.), *The Complete Works in Verse and Prose of George Herbert* (London, 1874), vol. 3, no. 514.

2. G. Wilson Knight, *Shakespearian Production* (London: Routledge, 1968), p. 313.

3. Cited in Terence Hawkes, *That Shakespeherian Rag: Essays in a Critical Process* (London: Methuen, 1986), p. 68.

4. G. W. Knight, *The Sovereign Flower* (London: Methuen, 1958), pp. 11–91.
5. See my two bibliographies, 'Spenser and Ireland: A Select Bibliography', *Spenser Studies: A Renaissance Poetry Annual* 9 (1991), pp. 227–42, and 'Spenser and Ireland: An Annotated Bibliography, 1986–96', in *Spenser in Ireland: 'The Faerie Queene', 1596–1996, The Irish University Review* 26, 2 (Autumn/Winter, 1996), special issue, ed. Anne Fogarty, pp. 342–53.
6. See Paul Brown, '"This thing of darkness I acknowledge mine": *The Tempest* and the Discourse of Colonialism', in Jonathan Dollimore and Alan Sinfield (eds), *Political Shakespeare: Essays in Cultural Materialism* (Manchester, Manchester University Press, 1985), pp. 48–71.
7. See, for example, Stephen Greenblatt, *Marvelous Possessions: The Wonder of the New World* (Oxford: Clarendon Press, 1991), and Greenblatt (ed.), *New World Encounters* (Berkeley; Oxford: University of California Press, 1993).
8. Dollimore and Sinfield (eds), *Political Shakespeare*, viii; my emphasis.
9. Ibid.
10. J. Dollimore and A. Sinfield, 'History and Ideology: The Instance of *Henry V*', in J. Drakakis (ed.), *Alternative Shakespeares* (London: Methuen, 1986), p. 224.
11. See P. Brown, '"This thing of darkness I acknowledge mine": *The Tempest* and the Discourse of Colonialism', in Dollimore and Sinfield (eds), *Political Shakespeare*, pp. 48–71.
12. Dollimore and Sinfield, 'History and Ideology', p. 226.
13. Alan Sinfield, 'Give an Account of Shakespeare and Education, Showing Why You Think They are Effective and What You Appreciate about Them. Support Your Comments with Precise References', in Dollimore and Sinfield (eds), *Political Shakespeare*, pp. 134–57.
14. G. Parfitt (ed.), *Ben Jonson: The Complete Poems* (London, Penguin, 1975; rpt 1984), p. 264.
15. Cited M. H. Abrams (ed.), *The Norton Anthology of English Literature*, vol. 1, 6th edn (New York and London, Norton, 1993), pp. 2402–3.
16. John Drakakis (ed.), *Alternative Shakespeares* (London, Methuen, 1985), p. 24.
17. Chris Norris, 'Post-structuralist Shakespeare: Text and Ideology', in Drakakis (ed.), *Alternative Shakespeares*, p. 50.
18. Graham Holderness, '"What ish my Nation?": Shakespeare and National Identities', *Textual Practice* 5, 1 (1991), p. 74–93.
19. For a somewhat glib sidelight on Britain, Europe, and the Conservative Party, see my 'Britannia Major: Writing and Unionist Identity', in Tracey Hill and William Hughes (eds), *Contemporary Writing and National Identity* (Bath: Sulis Press Bath College of Higher Education, 1995), pp. 46–53. See also my trenchant take on a contemporary three kingdom depiction, '*Braveheart*: Raising the Stakes of History', *Irish Review* 22 (Summer 1998) guest editor Frank McGuinness (Cork: Cork University Press, 1998), pp. 67–80.
20. For another perspective on Anglocentrism, see Jonathan Scott, *England's Troubles: Seventeenth–Century English Political Instability in European Perspective* (Cambridge; New York: Cambridge University Press, 2000).

21. Geoffrey Bullough (ed.), *Narrative and Dramatic Sources of Shakespeare*, 7 (London, Routledge, 1973), p. 338.
22. Knight, *The Sovereign Flower*, p. 13.
23. D. B. Quinn, *The Elizabethans and the Irish* (Ithaca and New York: Cornell University Press, 1966), my emphasis.
24. Dollimore and Sinfield, 'History and Ideology', 206–7.
25. See C. Z. Weiner, 'The Beleaguered Isle: A Study of Elizabethan and Early Jacobean anti-Catholicism', *Past and Present* 51 (1971), pp. 27–62.
26. B. L. Joseph, *Shakespeare's Eden: The Commonwealth of England* (London: Blandford Press, 1971).
27. A. Palmer and V. Palmer, *Who's Who in Shakespeare England* (Sussex: Harvester, 1981), p. 131, my emphasis.
28. Thomas Churchyard, *The Miserie of Flaunders, Calamitie of Fraunce, Missfortune of Portugall, Unquietness of Irelande, Trowbles of Scotlande: And the blessed State of ENGLANDE* (London, 1579), E³.
29. See K. G. Robbins, 'Insular Outsider?: "British History" and European Integration' (Reading: University of Reading, Stenton Lecture, 1990), pp. 3–16.
30. Raymond Williams, 'Afterword', in Dollimore and Sinfield (eds), *Political Shakespeare*, pp. 231–2.
31. W. F. Bolton, *Shakespeare's English: Language and the History Plays* (Oxford: Blackwell, 1992), p. 244.
32. Bolton, *Shakespeare's English*, p. 246.
33. Hawkes, *That Shakespeherian Rag*, p. 69.
34. Brian P. Levack, *The Formation of the British State: England, Scotland, and the Union, 1603–1707* (Oxford: Clarendon Press, 1987), p. 2.
35. See A. Constable (ed. and trans.), *John Major's History of Greater Britain*, Scottish History Society 10 (Edinburgh, 1892).
36. Robert Devereux, Second Earl of Essex, *Lawes and orders of Warre, established for the good conduct of the service in Ireland* (London, 1599), A².
37. Gary Taylor (ed.), *Henry V* (Oxford: Oxford University Press, 1982; 1984), p. 7.
38. Cited in M. Quinn (ed.), *Henry V: A Selection of Critical Essays* (London, Macmillan, 1983), pp. 37–8.
39. J. A. Froude, *The History of England from the Fall of Wolsey to the Death of Elizabeth*, 12 vols. (London, 1856–70), vol. 10, p. 480.
40. See Levack, *The Formation of the British State*, 169–213.
41. Cited Levack, *The Formation of the British State*, p. 2, n. 4.
42. See Frances Barker and Peter Hulme, 'Nymphs and Reapers Heavily Vanish: The Discursive Con-texts of *The Tempest*', in Drakakis (ed.), *Alternative Shakespeares*, 191–205; Donna B. Hamilton, *Shakespeare and the Politics of Protestant England* (London: Harvester Wheatsheaf, 1992); Terence Hawkes, 'Lear's Maps', in *Meaning by Shakespeare* (London: Routledge, 1992), pp. 121–40; Arthur Kinney, 'Scottish History, the Union of the Crowns and the Issue of Right Rule: The Case of Shakespeare's *Macbeth*', in Jean R. Brink and William F. Gentrup (eds), *Renaissance Culture in Context: Theory and Practice* (Aldershot: Scolar

Press, 1993), pp. 18–53; Jonathan Goldberg, 'Speculations: *Macbeth* and Source', in Jean E. Howard and Marion F. O'Connor (eds), *Shakespeare Reproduced: The Text in History and Ideology* (London: Methuen, 1987), pp. 242–64; Stuart M. Kurland, '*Hamlet* and the Scottish Succession?', *Studies in English Literature* 34, 2 (1994), pp. 279–300; David Norbrook, '*Macbeth* and the Politics of Historiography', in Kevin Sharpe and Steven N. Zwicker (eds), *Politics of Discourse: The Literature and History of Seventeenth Century England* (Berkeley, University of California Press, 1987), 78–116; Alan Sinfield, '*Macbeth*: History, Ideology and Intellectuals', in C. MacCabe (ed.), *Futures for English* (Manchester: Manchester University Press, 1986), 63–77. The Scottish play will be explored further in Willy Maley and Andrew Murphy (eds), *Shakespeare and Scotland* (Manchester: Manchester University Press, forthcoming).

43. Cited Annabel Patterson, 'Censorship and the 1587 "Holinshed's" Chronicles', in Paul Hyland and Neil Sammels (eds), *Writing and Censorship in Britain* (London and New York: Routledge, 1992), pp. 23–35.

Chapter 2

All references to *Cymbeline* are to the Oxford edition by Roger Warren.

1. For recent interventions addressing the multiple national contexts of Shakespeare's drama see for example Roy Battenhouse, '*Measure for Measure* and King James', *Clio* 7 (1978), pp. 193–215; Neville H. Davies, 'Jacobean *Antony and Cleopatra*', *Shakespeare Studies* 17 (1985), pp. 123–58; Barbara Freedman, 'Shakespearean Chronology, Ideological Complicity, and Floating Texts: Something is Rotten in Windsor', *Shakespeare Quarterly* 45, 2 (1994), pp. 190–210; Terence Hawkes, 'Lear's Maps', in *Meaning by Shakespeare* (London: Routledge, 1992), pp. 121–40; Donna B. Hamilton, '*The Winter's Tale* and the Language of Union, 1604–1610'; Graham Holderness, '"What ish my Nation?": Shakespeare and National Identities', *Textual Practice* 5, 1, pp. 74–93; Stuart M. Kurland, '*Hamlet* and the Scottish Succession?', *Studies in English Literature* 34, 2 (1994), pp. 279–300; Richard Levin, 'The King James Version of *Measure for Measure*', *Clio* 3 (1974), pp. 129–63; David Norbrook, '*Macbeth* and the Politics of Historiography', in Kevin Sharpe and Steven N. Zwicker (eds), *Politics of Discourse: The Literature and History of Seventeenth-Century England* (Berkeley: University of California Press, 1987), pp. 78–116; Christopher Wortham, 'Shakespeare, James I and the Matter of Britain', *English* 45, 182 (1996), pp. 97–122. Three new essays promise to enhance the debate. See Matthew Greenfield, '*1 Henry IV*: Metatheatrical Britain', in David J. Baker and Willy Maley (eds), *British Identities and English Renaissance Literature* (Cambridge: Cambridge University Press, 2002), pp. 71–80; Patricia Parker, 'Uncertain Unions: Welsh Leeks in *Henry V*', in Baker and Maley (eds), *British Identities*, pp. 81–100; Mary Floyd-Wilson, 'Delving to the Root:

    Cymbeline, Scotland, and the English Race', in Baker and Maley (eds), *British Identities*, pp. 101–15.

2. On the British Problem see, for example, Conrad Russell, *The Fall of the British Monarchies 1637–1642* (Oxford:Clarendon Press, 1992). For a compelling and profound literary perspective see David J. Baker, *Between Nations: Shakespeare, Spenser, Marvell, and the Question of Britain* (Stanford: Stanford University Press, 1997). Equally impressive is Christopher Highley, *Shakespeare, Spenser, and the Crisis in Ireland* (Cambridge: Cambridge University Press, 1997). On postcolonialism, see the introduction to Bart Moore-Gilbert, Gareth Stanton and Willy Maley (eds.) (1997), *Postcolonial Criticism* (London: Addison, Wesley and Longman, 1997), pp. 1–72.

3. Brian P. Levack, *The Formation of the British State: England, Scotland, and the Union, 1603–1707* (Oxford: Clarendon Press, 1987), p. 2.

4. Claire McEachern, *The Poetics of English Nationhood, 1590–1612* (New York and London: Cambridge University Press, 1996), p. 1.

5. McEachern, *The Poetics of English Nationhood*, p. 2.

6. See Patricia Parker, 'Preposterous Estates, Preposterous Events: From Late to Early Shakespeare', in *Shakespeare from the Margins: Language, Culture, Context* (Chicago: The University of Chicago Press, 1996), pp. 20–55. See also Patricia Parker, 'Romance and Empire: Anachronistic *Cymbeline*', in George M. Logan and Gordon Teskey (eds), *Unfolded Tales: Essays on Renaissance Romance* (Ithaca, New York: Cornell University Press, 1989), pp. 189–207. If this chapter owes much to Pat Parker's concept of 'preposterousness', then I am equally indebted to Claire MacEachern's notion of 'anachronism' as 'a habit for which the national narrative is notorious'. See McEachern, *The Poetics of English Nationhood*, p. 7.

7. Richard Hosley (ed.), *Cymbeline* (New York: NEL, 1968), p. xxxv.

8. Frances Yates, 'The Elizabethan Revival in the Jacobean Age', in *Shakespeare's Last Plays: A New Approach* (London: Routledge, 1975), p. 17.

9. Philippa Berry, 'Reversing History: Time, Fortune and the Doubling of Sovereignty in *Macbeth*', *European Journal of English Studies* 1, 3 (1997), p. 373.

10. Ibid., p. 387.

11. Ibid., p. 385.

12. Warren, 'Introduction', *Cymbeline* (Oxford: Clarendon Press, 1998), p. 37.

13. Emrys Jones, 'Stuart *Cymbeline*', *Essays in Criticism* 11 (1961), pp. 84–99.

14. Warren, 'Introduction', *Cymbeline*, p. 63.

15. Christopher Wortham, 'Shakespeare, James I and the Matter of Britain'.

16. On England's Roman reflection, see Andrew Barnaby, '"Another Rome in the West?" Milton and the Imperial Republic, 1654–1670', *Milton Studies* 30, ed. Albert C. Labriola (Pittsburgh, PA: University of Pennsylvania, 1993).

17. Eleanor Davies, 'Her Blessing' (1644), in Esther S. Cope (ed.), *Prophetic Writings of Eleanor Davies, Women Writers in English 1350–1850* (New

York and Oxford: Oxford University Press, 1995), p. 123. On prophecy as a vehicle for women writers in the Renaissance, see Kate Chedgzoy, 'Female Prophecy in the Seventeenth Century: The Instance of Anna Trapnel', in William Zunder and Suzanne Trill (eds), *Writing and the English Renaissance* (London and New York: Longman, 1996), pp. 238–54. See also Marjorie Garber, '"What's Past is Prologue": Temporality and Prophecy in Shakespeare's History Plays', in Barbara Kiefer Lewalski (ed.), *Renaissance Genres: Essays on Theory, History, and Interpretation* (Cambridge, Mass.: Harvard University Press, 1986), pp. 301–31; Phyllis Mack, Women as Prophets during the English Civil War', in Margaret C. Jacob and James Jacob (eds), *The Origins of Anglo-American Radicalism* (London: Allen & Unwin, 1984), pp. 214–30. In a postcolonial context prophecy is also a vital force for change and plays a part in numerous national liberation struggles. See Cornel West, *Prophesy Deliverance!: An Afro-American Revolutionary Christianity* (Philadelphia: Mentor, 1982).

18. Sir John Davies, *A Discovery of the True Causes why Ireland was never entirely Subdued, nor brought under Obedience of the Crowne of ENGLAND, untill the Beginning of his Majesties happie Raigne* (London, 1612).

19. Homi K. Bhabha, ''The Other Question: Difference, Discrimination and the Discourse of Colonialism', in Francis Barker, Peter Hulme, Margaret Iversen and Diana Loxley (eds), *Literature, Politics and Theory: Papers from the Essex Conference, 1976–84* (London: Methuen, 1986), p. 171.

20. George Watson remarks of these lines: 'In fact, Joyce is most vitriolic about the Church precisely at those moments where he senses its identity and common cause with that other imperial tyranny; behind much of the Parnellite anti-clericalism he inherited from his father can be glimpsed a sense of thwarted nationalism raging before an unshakeable combination of forces.' See Watson, *Irish Identity and the Literary Revival: Synge, Yeats, O'Casey* (Washington, D.C.: The Catholic University of America Press, 1994), pp. 154–5.

21. Linda Colley, *Britons: Forging the Nation, 1707–1837* (New Haven and London: Yale University Press, 1992).

22. Murray Pittock, *Inventing and Resisting Britain: Cultural Identities in Britain and Ireland, 1685–1789* (London: Macmillan, 1997).

23. This chapter works in the wake of some excellent material on *Cymbeline*. See, for example, Bernard Harris, '"What's Past is Prologue": *Cymbeline* and *Henry VIII'*, in John Russell Brown and Bernard Harris (eds), *Later Shakespeare* (London: Edward Arnold, 1966), pp. 203–34; Jodi Mikalachki, 'The Masculine Romance of Roman Britain: *Cymbeline* and Early Modern Nationalism', *Shakespeare Quarterly* 3 (1995), pp. 301–22. For a much more nimble and nuanced reading of the play than I have been able to execute here, see Alison Thorne, '"To write and read / Be henceforth treacherous": *Cymbeline* and the Problem of Interpretation', in Jennifer Richards and James Knowles (eds),

Shakespeare's Late Plays: New Readings (Edinburgh: Edinburgh University Press, 1999), pp. 176–90.

Chapter 3

I wish to thank my colleague, Dr David Pascoe, and Mark Thornton Burnett and Ramona Wray, both of Queen's University, Belfast, for assiduous readings of this chapter in typescript which made me think a lot harder about the topic.

1. The phrases appear in Vijay Mishra, 'The Centre Cannot Hold: Bailey, Indian Culture and the Sublime', *South Asia*, 12 (1989), pp. 103–14, and in Paul Brown, '"This thing of darkness I acknowledge mine": *The Tempest* and the Discourse of Colonialism', in Jonathan Dollimore and Alan Sinfield (eds), *Political Shakespeare: Essays in Cultural Materialism* (Manchester: Manchester University Press, 1985), pp. 48–71. See also Kim F. Hall, *Things of Darkness: Economies of Race and Gender in Early Modern England* (Ithaca and London: Cornell University Press, 1995).

2. See Homi K. Bhabha, 'The Other Question: Difference, Discrimination and the Discourse of Colonialism', in Francis Barker, Peter Hulme, Margaret Iversen and Diana Loxley (eds), *Literature, Politics and Theory: Papers from the Essex Conference 1976–84* (London and New York: Methuen, 1986), pp. 148–72; Abdul R. JanMohamed, 'The Economy of Manichean Allegory: The Function of Racial Difference in Colonialist Literature', in Henry Louis Gates, Jr. (ed.), *'Race', Writing, and Difference* (Chicago and London: University of Chicago Press, 1986), pp. 79–106.

3. On Shakespeare and Holinshed see, for example, Elizabeth Story Donno, 'Some Aspects of Shakespeare's Holinshed', *Huntington Library Quarterly* 50 (1987), pp. 229–48; R. A. Law, 'Holinshed as a Source of *Henry V* and *King Lear*', *The University of Texas Bulletin* 14 (1934), pp. 38–44. Evidence for Holinshed's presence in Ireland is contained in William Pinkerton, 'Barnaby Googe', *Notes and Queries* 3 (1863), p. 182. On Shakespeare's sources more generally, see Geoffrey Bullough, *Narrative and Dramatic Sources of Shakespeare*, 8 vols. (London: Routledge, 1957–75). For a crucial new account of Holinshed, see Annabel M. Patterson, *Reading Holinshed's Chronicles* (Chicago and London: University of Chicago Press, 1994).

4. See Stephen Booth, *The Book Called Holinshed's Chronicles* (San Francisco: The Book Club of California, 1968), p. 72, cited in Annabel Patterson, 'Censorship and the 1587 "Holinshed's" Chronicles', in Paul Hyland and Neil Sammells (eds), *Writing and Censorship in Britain* (London and New York: Routledge, 1992), p. 23. The irony is that we don't read Holinshed, at least not with the care it demands.

5. Francis Barker and Peter Hulme, 'Nymphs and Reapers Heavily Vanish: The Discursive Con-texts of *The Tempest*', in John Drakakis (ed.), *Alternative Shakespeares* (London; Methuen, 1985), p. 236, n. 7. I also

have in mind Derrida's provocative reformulation of the notorious claim that there is nothing outside the text: 'An "internal" reading will always be insufficient. And moreover impossible. Question of context, as everyone knows, there is nothing but context, and therefore: there is no outside-the-text'. See Jacques Derrida, 'Biodegradables: Seven Diary Fragments', trans. Peggy Kamuf, *Critical Inquiry* 15 (1989), p. 873. The *OED* includes in its definition of 'resource' and 'resources': 'means of supplying what is needed, stock that can be drawn on', 'available assets', 'country's collective means for support and defence', and 'expedient, device, shift'. See J. B. Sykes (ed.), *The Concise Oxford Dictionary* (Oxford: Clarendon, 1982), p. 887. In place of the originary claims of 'sources', I offer here a mobile and multiple resourcefulness.

6. See Michael Cronin, *Translating Ireland: Translation, Languages, Cultures* (Cork: Cork University Press, 1996), p. 78. There are several important new essays on this topic that have opened up the whole question of Holinshed as much more than mere source for Shakespeare. See, for example, Christopher Ivic, 'Incorporating Ireland: Cultural Conflict in Holinshed's Irish *Chronicles*', *Journal of Medieval and Early Modern Studies* 29 (1999), pp. 437–98; Richard McCabe, 'Making History: Holinshed's Irish *Chronicles*, 1577 and 1587', in David J. Baker and Willy Maley (eds), *British Identities and English Renaissance Literature* (Cambridge: Cambridge University Press, 2002), pp. 51–67.

7. For earlier work that comprehended the portrayal of the Celtic peoples see, for example, J. O. Bartley, *Teague, Shenkin, and Sawney: Being an Historical Study of the Earliest Irish, Welsh and Scottish Characters in English Plays* (Cork: Cork University Press, 1954); Edward D. Snyder, 'The Wild Irish: A Study of Some English Satires against the Irish, Scots, and Welsh', *Modern Philology* 17 (1920), pp. 147–85. Jonson's 'Irish masque' is a key text in such criticism since it is the most sustained treatment of the Celtic other by a canonical author. See 'The Irish Masque at Court', in Stephen Orgel (ed.), *Ben Jonson: The Complete Masques* (New Haven: Yale University Press, 1969), pp. 206–12.

8. For excellent examples of such work, see David J. Baker, '"Wildehirissheman": Colonialist Representation in Shakespeare's *Henry V*', *English Literary Renaissance* 22 (1993), pp. 37–61; Brown, '"This thing of darkness"', pp. 48–71; Ann Rosalind Jones, 'Italians and Others: Venice and the Irish in *Coryat's Crudities* and *The White Devil*', *Renaissance Drama*, 18 (1987), pp. 101–20; Michael Neill, 'Broken English and Broken Irish: Nation, language, and the Optic of Power in Shakespeare's Histories', *Shakespeare Quarterly*, 45 (1994), pp. 1–32.

9. See also Donna B. Hamilton, *Shakespeare and the Politics of Protestant England* (Lexington: University Press of Kentucky, 1992); Terence Hawkes, 'Lear's Maps', in *Meaning by Shakespeare* (London and New York: Routledge, 1992), pp. 121–40; Christopher Highley, 'Wales, Ireland, and *1 Henry IV*', *Renaissance Drama* 21 (1990), pp. 91–114; Graham Holderness, '"What ish my Nation?": Shakespeare and National Identities', *Textual Practice*, 5 (1991), pp. 74–93; Stuart

Kurland, '*Hamlet* and the Scottish Succession?', *Studies in English Literature* 34 (1994), pp. 279–300; David Norbrook, '*Macbeth* and the Politics of Historiography', in Kevin Sharpe and Steve N. Zwicker (eds), *Politics of Discourse: The Literature and History of Seventeenth-Century England* (Berkeley: University of California Press, 1987), pp. 78–116; Alan Sinfield, '*Macbeth*: History, Ideology and Intellectuals', in Colin MacCabe (ed.), *Futures for English* (Manchester: Manchester University Press, 1986), pp. 63–77; Christopher Wortham, 'Shakespeare, James I and the Matter of Britain', *English* 45 (1996), pp. 97–122.

10. See Roy Foster, 'Varieties of Irishness', in *Modern Ireland, 1600–1972* (London: Allen Lane, 1988), pp. 3–14; Willy Maley, 'Varieties of Englishness: Planting a New Culture beyond the Pale', in *Salvaging Spenser: Colonialism, Culture and Identity* (London: Macmillan, 1997), pp. 48–77, and 'Varieties of Nationalism: Post-revisionist Irish Studies', in Sarah Briggs, Paul Hyland and Neil Sammells (eds), *Reviewing Ireland: Essays and Interviews from Irish Studies Review* (Bath: Sulis Press, 1998), pp. 265–72.

11. Stephen Greenblatt, 'Invisible Bullets: Renaissance Authority and its Subversion, *Henry IV* and *Henry V*', in Jonathan Dollimore and Alan Sinfield (eds), *Political Shakespeare: Essays in Cultural Materialism* (Manchester, Manchester University Press, 1985), p. 42. David Baker's *Between Nations* takes the New Historicists to task for their anglocentrism, however well intentioned. Baker cites numerous instances of insensitivity to the non-English constituents of the emerging British state, including Greenblatt's glib characterisation of Shakespeare's Fluellen, Jamy and Macmorris as 'humorous grotesques ... puppets jerked on the strings of their own absurd accents'. But within a page or two Baker himself presents us with a Fluellen endowed with an 'amiably accented English', and, more tellingly, offers a Macmorris who, speaking 'in an often overwrought dialect, is finally reduced to outraged and stammering questions'. This is an odd way of depicting the querulous Irish captain given the weight Baker attaches to the process of questioning and his central thesis that Britain is itself 'a question'. See David J. Baker, *Between Nations: Shakespeare, Spenser, Marvell, and the Question of Britain* (Stanford: Stanford University Press, 1997), pp. 23, 29. Baker is one of a number of literary critics whose company I'm honoured to keep, critics who, having begun their careers by working on the representation of Ireland in English Renaissance texts, are now turning their attention to what historians term the 'British Problem', and in the process are interrogating the other national identities that have been let off the hook by a preoccupation with Ireland, most notably Englishness. Baker contends that most new historicists have 'either taken English nationalism as a given or charted its autonomous emergence' (p. 15). By contrast, *Between Nations* painstakingly reveals the extent to which, even before the Union of Crowns, England is defined in relation to its neighbours.

12. *King Henry V*, ed. John Walter (London: Methuen, 1965), III.ii.123–7.

13. See 'Giraldus as Historian', in Giraldus Cambrensis, *Expugnatio Hibernica: The Conquest of Ireland*, edited with translation and notes by A. B. Scott and F. X. Martin (Dublin: Royal Irish Academy, 1978), pp. 267–84. The authoritative biography is Thomas Bartlett, *Gerald of Wales, 1146–1223* (Oxford: Clarendon Press, 1982).

14. See C. Litton Falkiner, *Essays Relating to Ireland: Biographical, Historical, and Topographical* (London: Longman, 1909), pp. 237–40; Edward M. Hinton, *Ireland Through Tudor Eyes* (Philadelphia: University of Pennsylvania Press, 1935), p. 203.

15. Raphael Holinshed, *Chronicles of England, Scotland, and Ireland*, 6 vols. (London: printed for J. Johnson, 1807–8; repr. with an introduction by Vernon Snow, ed. Henry Ellis (New York: AMS Press, 1965, 1976), VI, p. 321.

16. *The Conquest of Ireland*, in *Holinshed's Chronicles*, VI, p. 152. The modern translation reads: 'Surely we do not look to our own people for succour? We are now constrained in our actions by this circumstance, that just as we are English as far as the Irish are concerned, likewise to the English we are Irish, and the inhabitants of this island and the other assail us with an equal degree of hatred.' See A. B. Scott and F. X. Martin (eds), *Expugnatio Hibernica*, p. 81.

17. See also Sir D. Plunket Barton, *Links between Ireland and Shakespeare* (Dublin and London: Maunsel and Company, 1919), where it is noted that: 'The Anglo-Norman families ... often assumed Irish prefixes ... they never took the prefix O, but they frequently dropped the Norman prefix Fitz and assumed the Irish equivalent Mac' (p. 121).

18. Andrew Murphy, '"Tish ill done": *Henry the Fift* and the Politics of Editing', in Mark Thornton Burnett and Ramona Wray (eds), *Shakespeare and Ireland: History, Politics, Culture* (London: Macmillan, 1997), pp. 213–34.

19. On Macmorris, see Bartley, *Teague, Shenkin, and Sawney*, pp. 16–17; Barton, *Links between Ireland and Shakespeare*, pp. 114–36; R. A. Law, 'Holinshed as a Source of *Henry V* and *King Lear*', p. 39; W. J. Lawrence, 'Was Shakespeare ever in Ireland?', *Shakespeare Jahrbuch* 42 (1906), p. 70.

20. See Philip Edwards, *Threshold of a Nation: A Study in English and Irish Drama* (Cambridge: Cambridge University Press, 1979), pp. 75–8. See also Jonathan Dollimore and Alan Sinfield, 'History and Ideology: The Instance of *Henry V*', in Drakakis (ed.), *Alternative Shakespeares*, p. 224; Stephen Greenblatt, 'Invisible Bullets: Renaissance Authority and its Subversion, *Henry IV* and *Henry V*', in Dollimore and Sinfield (eds), *Political Shakespeare*, p. 42; Gary Taylor (ed.), *Henry V* (Oxford: Oxford University Press, 1984), p. 169.

21. See Ciarán Brady, 'Conservative Subversives: The Community of the Pale and the Dublin Administration', in P. J. Corish (ed.), *Radicals, Rebels and Establishments, Historical Studies*, 15 (Belfast: Appletree Press, 1985), p. 32, n. 46.

22. See D. G. White, 'Henry VIII's Irish kerne in France and Scotland', *The Irish Sword*, 3 (1957–58), pp. 213–25. For the danger posed to England by the threat of a Franco-Irish alliance, see P. J. Piveronus, 'The

Desmond Imperial Alliance of 1529: Its Effect on Henry VIII's Policy toward Ireland', *Éire-Ireland*, 10, 2 (1975), pp. 19–31; D. Potter, 'French Intrigue in Ireland during the Reign of Henri II, 1547–1559', *International History Review*, 5 (1983), pp. 159–80.

23. For the story behind the publication of this text, see D. B. Quinn, 'Edward Walshe's *The office and duety in fightyng for our country* (1545)', *Irish Book Lore* 3, 1 (1976), pp. 28–31.
24. D. B. Quinn, 'Edward Walshe's "Conjectures" concerning the State of Ireland', *Irish Historical Studies*, 5 (1947), pp. 303–22.
25. Stanyhurst, 'A Plaine and Perfect Description of Ireland', in *Holinshed's Chronicles*, VI (London, 1807–8), p. 66.
26. Edward Walshe, *The office and duety in fightyng for our countrey. Set forth with dyverse stronge argumentes gathered out of the holy scripture provynge that the affection to the native countrey shulde moch more rule in us then in the Turkes and infidels, who were therein so fervent, as by the historiis doth appere* (London, 1545, p. A⁴C.
27. Richard Stanyhurst, 'The Chronicle of Ireland', in *Holinshed's Chronicles*, VI (1807–8), p. 314.
28. Stanyhurst, 'The Chronicle of Ireland', p. 315.
29. Steven G. Ellis, *Tudor Ireland: Crown, Community and the Conflict of Cultures, 1470–1603* (London: Longman, 1985), p. 268.
30. See Nicholas P. Canny, *The Formation of the Old English Élite in Ireland*, 18th O'Donnell Lecture (Dublin: National University of Ireland, 1975), p. 31.
31. *King Richard II*, ed. Peter Ure (London: Methuen, 1978), II.i.155–8.
32. Stanyhurst, 'A Plaine and Perfect Description of Ireland', p. 13.
33. Ibid., p. 17.
34. Ibid., p.13.
35. Ibid.
36. John Derricke, *The Image of Irelande, with A Discoverie of Woodkarne* (1581), ed. John Small (Edinburgh: Adam and Charles Black, 1883), pp. 42–3.
37. On Stanyhurst's connections, see Vincent P. Carey, 'Collaborator *and* Survivor? Gerald the eleventh Earl of Kildare and Tudor Rule in Ireland', *History Ireland* 2 (1994), pp. 13–17; Willy Maley, 'Spenser's *View* and Stanyhurst's *Description*', *Notes and Queries*, 43 (1996), pp. 140–2.
38. Barnaby Rich, *A New Description of Ireland* (London, 1610), p. 43.
39. Canny, *The Formation of the Old English Élite in Ireland*, p. 26.
40. Ibid.
41. John Arden, 'Rug-headed Irish Kerns and British Poets', *New Statesman* (13 July 1979), pp. 56–7.
42. Ibid., p. 56.
43. John Bale, *The Vocacyon of John Bale to the bishoprick of Ossorie in Irela[n]de his persecucio[n]s in yᵉ same & finall delyveraunce* ('Rome' [Wesel], 1553).
44. Conor Cruise O'Brien, 'Shakespeare: Not Guilty', *New Statesman* (27 July 1979), p. 130.
45. John Arden, 'Shakespeare Guilty', *New Statesman* (10 August 1979), p. 199.

46. *King Henry IV Part One*, ed. A. R. Humphreys (London: Methuen, 1985), I.iii.149–50.
47. See Taylor (ed.), *Henry V*, p. 7. It goes without saying that I do not accept such a stultifying definition of 'contemporary reference', preferring to think in terms of open and multiple 'con-texts'.
48. In a second reply, this time to Arden's side-swipe at Spenser, Helen Watanabe-O'Kelly produced a defence of the poet which is every bit as excessive as Arden's attack. Without bothering to quote from the text in question, this critic informs us that 'The *View*, written at a time when Spenser's affairs in Ireland were prospering, is a calm and reasoned piece of writing', advocating a 'comparatively benevolent scheme'. See Helen Watanabe-O'Kelly, 'Edmund Spenser and Ireland: A Defence', *Poetry Nation Review*, 6.6 (1980), p. 18.
49. Colm Lennon, *Richard Stanyhurst: The Dubliner, 1547–1618* (Dublin: Irish Academic Press, 1981), pp. 72–3, 97, 118, 121, 125.
50. *DNB*; Stanyhurst, *Description*, p. 15; L. E. Whatmore (ed.), *Archdeacon Harpsfield's Canterbury Visitations, 1556–1558*, Publications of the Catholic Record Society, 45 (1950).
51. Gayatri Chakravorty Spivak, *Outside in the Teaching Machine* (New York and London: Routledge, 1993), p. 217.
52. For a far fuller account of the part played by Ireland in Shakespeare's 'domestic' drama than the furtive following of fragments enacted in this chapter, see my 'The Irish text and subtext of Shakespeare's English histories', in Richard Dutton and Jean Howard (eds), *A Companion to Shakespeare, Volume II: The Histories* (Oxford: Blackwell, 2003). In that essay I can say with Falstaff: 'I am a rogue if I were not at half-sword with a dozen/ of them, two hours together'. (*1 Henry IV* 2.v.150–1)

Chapter 4

1. John Breen, 'Imagining Voices in *A View of the Present State of Ireland*: A Discussion of Recent Studies Concerning Edmund Spenser's Dialogue', *Connotations* 4, 1–2 (1994/95) pp. 119–30; Andrew Hadfield, 'Who is Speaking in Spenser's *A View of the Present State of Ireland*? A Response to John Breen', *Connotations* 4, 3 (1994/95), pp. 233–41; Patricia Coughlan, '"Some secret scourge which shall by her come unto England": Ireland and Incivility in Spenser', in Patricia Coughlan (ed.), *Spenser and Ireland: An Interdisciplinary Perspective* (Cork: Cork University Press, 1989), p. 47.
2. Arguably the earliest dialogue on Ireland, certainly the earliest to draw on classical precedents for Renaissance recolonisation, was 'The conjectures of Edwarde Walshe tochinge the state of yrlande' (1552). See David Beers Quinn (ed.), 'Edward Walshe's "Conjectures" Concerning the State of Ireland', *Irish Historical Studies* 5, 20 (1947), pp. 303–22. Other examples of the genre are the 'Dialogue between Peregryne and

Sylvanus, c.1598', *State Papers, Ireland*, 63/203/119, ff. 283–357,
London: Public Record Office; Richard Beacon, *Solon his follie, or A
Politique Discourse, touching the Reformation of common-weales conquered,
declined or corrupted* (Oxford, 1594). There is now an authoritative
edition of Beacon's text, edited by Clare Carroll and Vincent Carey
(SUNY at Binghamton: Center for Medieval and Early Renaissance
Studies, 1996); Barnaby Rich, *A Right Exelent and pleasaunt Dialogue,
betwene Mercury and an English Souldier: Contayning his Supplication to
Mars: Bewtified with sundry worthy Histories, rare inventions and politike
devises* (London, 1574); E. M. Hinton (ed.), 'Rych's "Anothomy of
Ireland" [1615], with an Account of the Author', *Publications of the
Modern Language Association of America*, vol. 55, no. 1 (1940), pp.
73–101; *A Catholicke Conference betweene Syr Tady Mac Mareall a popish
priest of Waterforde, and Patricke Plaine a young student of Trinity Colledge
by Dublin in Ireland* (London, 1612); Aidan Clarke (ed.), 'A Discourse
between Two Councillors of State, the One of England, and the Other
of Ireland (1642)', *Analecta Hibernica* 26 (1970), pp. 159–75. The ques-
tion-and-answer format is a variation on the dialogue. See, for example,
Norah Carlin (ed.), *Certain Queries Propounded to the Consideration of such
as were Intended for the Service in Ireland (1649)* (London: Aporia Press,
1992); Hiram Morgan (ed.), 'A Booke of Questions and Answars concerning the Warrs or Rebellions of the Kingdome of Irelande (1597)',
Analecta Hibernica 36 (1994), pp. 93–153. One could also consider
Lodowick Bryskett's *The Discourse of Civill Life*, in H. R. Plomer and T. P.
Cross (eds), *The Life and Correspondence of Lodowick Bryskett* (Chicago:
Chicago University Press, 1927), pp. 1–279. Richard Stanyhurst, in his
contribution to the Irish section of Holinshed's *Chronicles*, referred to
the dialogue form as 'a kind of writing as it is used, so commended of
the learned.' Cited in Edwin A. Greenlaw, 'Spenser and British imperialism', *Modern Philology* 9, 3 (1912), p. 12.
3. Cited in Roger Fowler (ed.), *A Dictionary of Modern Critical Terms*
(London: Routledge, 1991), p. 59. Patricia Coughlan complicates the
'dialogism' of the *View*: 'It is true that the *View* lacks dialogicality in the
sense of making two different registers of language confront each other.
Both voices are, linguistically speaking, equally authoritative; both are
standard users of official English; neither is lexically or syntactically a
less adequate formulator of judgement or description. But this should
not warrant any rash decision to write off the dialogue form, or assume
it merely a decoy or mantle to conceal an absolute decisiveness.' See
Coughlan, '"Some secret scourge which shall by her come unto
England"', pp. 65–6. For Derek Hirst, 'multiplicity of voice is inherent
in the dialogue form.' See Derek Hirst, 'Text, Time, and the pursuit of
"British Histories"', in David J. Baker and Willy Maley (eds), *British
Identities and English Renaissance Literature* (Cambridge: Cambridge
University Press, 2002), p. 256.
4. Bruce Avery, 'Mapping the Irish Other: Spenser's *A View of the Present
State of Ireland*', *ELH* 57, 2 (1990), p. 264.

5. Avery, 'Mapping the Irish Other', p. 264.
6. Breen, 'Imagining Voices', p. 124.
7. Ibid., p. 126.
8. Kenneth Gross, 'Mythmaking in Hibernia (*A View of the Present State of Ireland*)', in *Spenserian Poetics: Idolatry, Iconoclasm, and Magic* (Ithaca: Cornell University Press, 1985), p. 81.
9. Ciarán Brady, 'The Road to the *View*: On the Decline of Reform Thought in Tudor Ireland', in Coughlan (ed.), *Spenser and Ireland*, p. 41. Compare Andrew Hadfield, who writes: 'The implied reader of the *View* is manipulated into accepting Irenius's arguments, which is why, I would argue, it was written as a dialogue.' See Andrew Hadfield, 'Spenser, Ireland, and Sixteenth-century Political Theory', *Modern Language Review* 9, 1 (1994), p. 7.
10. Helena Shire, *A Preface to Spenser* (London: Longman, 1978; 1981), pp. 49–51.
11. Coughlan, '"Some secret scourge which shall by her come unto England"', p. 67.
12. Ibid., p. 71.
13. Roland M. Smith, 'Spenser's tale of the two sons of Milesio', *Modern Language Quarterly* 3, 4 (1942), p. 554.
14. Anne Fogarty, 'The Colonization of Language: Narrative Strategy in *A View of the Present State of Ireland* and *The Faerie Queene*, Book VI', in Coughlan (ed.), *Spenser and Ireland*, p. 83.
15. Fogarty, 'The Colonization of Language', p. 104.
16. Donald Bruce, 'Edmund Spenser and the Irish Wars', *Contemporary Review* 266 (1995), pp. 135–6.
17. The arguments surrounding the apparent suppression of the *View* are incisively rehearsed in Andrew Hadfield, 'Was Spenser's *View of the Present State of Ireland* Censored? A Review of the Evidence', *Notes and Queries* 240, 4 (1994) 459–63.
18. Donald Bruce, 'Spenser's Irenius and the Nature of Dialogue', *Notes and Queries* n.s. 39, 3 (1992), p. 355.
19. John T. Day, 'Dialogue, Prose', in A. C. Hamilton (ed.), *The Spenser Encyclopedia* (London and Toronto: Routledge, 1990), p. 217.
20. Thomas E. Wright, 'Bryskett, Lodowick', in Hamilton (ed.), *The Spenser Encyclopedia*, p. 119.
21. Day, 'Dialogue, Prose', p. 217.
22. Beverley Sherry, 'Dialogue, Poetic', in Hamilton (ed.), *The Spenser Encyclopedia*, p. 216.
23. Fogarty, 'The Colonization of Language', p. 76.
24. Ciarán Brady, 'Spenser's Irish Crisis: Humanism and Experience in the 1590s', *Past and Present* 111 (1986), p. 18.
25. David J. Baker, '"Some quirk, some subtle evasion": Legal Subversion in Spenser's *A View of the Present State of Ireland*', *Spenser Studies* 6 (1986), p. 163.
26. Brady, 'Spenser's Irish Crisis', p. 40.
27. See Hinton (ed.), 'Rych's "Anothomy of Ireland"', p. 91.

28. R. B. Gottfried, 'Spenser's *View* and Essex', *PMLA* 52, 3 (1937), p. 647.
29. Eva Gold, 'Spenser the Borderer: Boundary, Property, Identity in *A View of the Present State of Ireland* and Book 6 of *The Faerie Queene*', *Journal of the Rocky Mountain Medieval and Renaissance Association* 14 (1993), pp. 105–6.
30. On self-fashioning and the construction of identity over and against an excluded Other, see Stephen Greenblatt, 'To Fashion a Gentleman: Spenser and the Destruction of the Bower of Bliss', in *Renaissance Self-Fashioning: From More to Shakespeare* (Chicago: Chicago University Press, 1980), pp. 157–92.
31. See Lynda E. Boose, '"The getting of a lawful race": Racial Discourse in Early Modern England and the Unrepresentable Black Woman', in Margo Hendricks and Patricia Parker (eds), *Race, Women and Writing in Early Modern Europe* (London: Routledge, 1994), p. 36. For a subtle and searching account of Spenser's racial politics from a different perspective than that offered in this chapter, see Christopher Ivic, 'Spenser and the Bounds of Race', *Genre* 32 (1999), pp. 141–74. Maryclaire Moroney instructively compares Spenser's approach to that of a less well-known contemporary, in 'Apocalypse, Ethnography, and Empire in John Derricke's *Image of Ireland* (1581) and Spenser's *View of the Present State of Ireland* (1596)', *English Literary Renaissance* 29, 3 (1999), pp. 355–74. A persuasive essay that appeared too late for me to draw on for this chapter is Jean Feerick, 'Spenser, Race, and Ire-land', *English Literary Renaissance* 32, 1 (2002), pp. 85–117. Feerick's conclusion – that 'homogenizing colonialist discourses erases the historically variable languages and tools deployed for the purpose of conquest' (p. 117) – is one to which I can comfortably subscribe. I was equally impressed by the thoroughness and precision of an essay by Bart Van Es in the same journal. See 'Discourses of Conquest: *The Faerie Queene*, the Society of Antiquaries, and *A View of the Present State of Ireland*', *English Literary Renaissance* 32, 1 (2002), pp. 118–51. This essay is clearly crucial to any discussion of Sir James Ware's edition of the *View*, and especially pertinent for an approach like my own, which engages with the uses of antiquity, but again it appeared too late for me to do more than acknowledge the force of its arguments. I am grateful to David J. Baker for providing me with a typescript of his excellent essay, '"Men to Monsters": Civility, Barbarism, and "Race" in Early Modern Ireland', forthcoming in Philip Beidler and Gary Taylor (eds), *Writing Race Across the Atlantic World, 1492–1763* (London and New York: Palgrave Macmillan, 2003). Again, I encountered Baker's compelling account of cultural and racial difference after my own reading was completed, but his essay marks a decisive intervention into an ongoing debate, and I am convinced by its argument and grateful for the evidence.
32. Brendan Bradshaw, 'Robe and Sword in the Conquest of Ireland', in C. Cross, D. Loades and J. J. Scarisbrick (eds), *Law and Government under the Tudors: Essays presented to Sir Geoffrey Elton on his Retirement* (Cambridge: Cambridge University Press, 1988), p. 153.
33. Margaret MacCurtain, 'The Roots of Irish Nationalism', in Robert Driscoll (ed.), *The Celtic Consciousness* (Edinburgh: Canongate, 1982), p. 373.

34. Rudolf B. Gottfried, 'Spenser as an Historian in Prose', *Transactions of the Wisconsin Academy of Sciences, Arts and Letters* 30 (1937), p. 328.
35. Brady, 'Spenser's Irish Crisis', p. 38.
36. Tracey Hill, 'Humanism and Homicide: Spenser's *A View of the Present State of Ireland*', *Irish Studies Review* 4 (1993), p. 4.
37. Andrew Hadfield and Willy Maley (eds), *Edmund Spenser, A View of the State of Ireland (1633): From the First Printed Edition* (Blackwell: Oxford and Malden, Mass., 1997), p. 6. All further references to the *View* are to this edition, given by page number in the text.
38. Edward W. Said, *Culture and Imperialism* (London: Vintage, 1994), pp. 284–5.
39. See Andrew Hadfield, '"Who knowes not Colin Clout?": The Permanent Exile of Edmund Spenser', in *Literature, Politics and National Identity: Reformation to Renaissance* (Cambridge: Cambridge University Press, 1994), pp. 193–4.
40. Judith H. Anderson, 'The Antiquities of Fairyland and Ireland', *JEGP* 86, 2 (1987), pp. 202–3.
41. Breen, 'Imagining Voices', p. 126.
42. Kim F. Hall, *Things of Darkness: Economies of Race and Gender in Early Modern England* (Ithaca and London: Cornell University Press, 1995), p. 145.
43. Ibid., p. 146.
44. Thomas Healy, 'Civilisation and its Discontents: The Case of Edmund Spenser', in *New Latitudes: Theory and English Renaissance Literature* (London: Edward Arnold, 1992), p. 89.
45. I have mapped out in some detail the neglected Scottish dimension of the *View* in chapter 7 of *Salvaging Spenser: Colonialism, Culture and Identity* (London: Macmillan, 1997), pp. 136–62.
46. Brady, 'Spenser's Irish Crisis', p. 30.
47. Roland M. Smith, 'More Irish Words in Spenser', *Modern Language Notes* 59, 7 (1944), p. 473.
48. Ibid., p. 476.
49. In another place I have expounded at length upon the varieties of Englishness found in early modern Ireland. See chapter 3 of *Salvaging Spenser*, pp. 48–77.
50. For an early attack on Spenser's alleged imbrication in Error's train, see J. O'Donovan, 'Errors of Edmund Spenser: Irish Surnames', *Ulster Journal of Archaeology*, 6 (1858), pp. 135–44.
51. See Deborah Shuger, 'White Barbarians: Irishmen, Indians and Others in Spenser's *View*', *Renaissance Quarterly* 50, 2 (1997), pp. 494–525.
52. Ibid., p. 519.
53. Coughlan, '"Some secret scourge which shall by her come unto England"', p. 70.
54. See Patricia Fumerton, 'Exchanging Gifts: the Elizabethan Currency of Children and Poetry', *ELH* 53 (1986), p. 256.
55. Clare Carroll, 'The Construction of Gender and the Cultural and Political Other in *The Faerie Queene* 5 and *A View of the Present State of*

Ireland: The Critics, the Context, and the Case of Radigund', *Criticism* 32, 2 (1990), p. 167.

56. 'For there to be a critical discourse which is more than a superficial and futile *reprise* of the work, the speech stored in the book must be incomplete; because it has not said everything, there remains the possibility of saying something else, *after another fashion* ... What is important in the work is what it does not say. This is not the same as the careless notation "what it refuses to say", although that would in itself be interesting: a method might be built on it, with the task of *measuring silences*, whether acknowledged or unacknowledged. But rather than this, what the work *cannot say* is important, because there the elaboration of the utterance is acted out, in a sort of journey to silence ... the work has its *margins*, an area of incompleteness from which we can observe its birth and its production' (Pierre Macherey, 'The Text Says What it Does not Say", in Dennis Walder (ed.), *Literature in the Modern World* (Oxford University Press, 1990), pp. 215–16, 220).

57. I have taken issue on another occasion with the critical tendency that allows Ireland to overrun Spenser's work. See my '"To weet to work *Irenaes* franchisement": Ireland in *The Faerie Queene*', in *Spenser in Ireland: 'The Faerie Queene', 1596–1996*, The Irish University Review 26, 2 (Autumn/Winter, 1996), special issue, ed. Anne Fogarty, pp. 303–19.

58. Michael Neill, 'Broken English and Broken Irish: Nation, Language, and the Optic of Power in Shakespeare's Histories', *Shakespeare Quarterly* 45 (1994), p. 5.

59. Hitherto, the 'British Problem' has been dealt with almost exclusively by historians. See, for instance, Brendan Bradshaw and John Morrill (eds), *The British Problem, c. 1534–1707* (London: Macmillan, 1996). The literary critics have their say in David J. Baker and Willy Maley (eds), *British Identities and English Renaissance Literature* (Cambridge: Cambridge University Press, 2002).

60. If the strategic separation of the Irish from Ireland in Spenser's *View* seems like a particularly perverse instance of colonial discourse, consider its use as a native reaction to national stereotyping, as discussed in the work of a key contemporary. Richard Stanyhurst raised and rehearsed the vexed nature of English, Irish, and Anglo-Irish identities in his 'Plaine and Perfect Description of Ireland', published in Holinshed's *Chronicles*. This is a text to which Spenser had access, so it is worth attending to what Stanyhurst has to say right at the outset: 'There are some of the ruder sort so quaint in seuering the name Irish and Ireland, as that they would be named Ireland men, but in no wise Irishmen. But certes, in my fantasie such curious distinctors may be verie aptlie resembled to the foolish butcher, that offred to have sold his mutton for fifteene grots, and yet would not take a crowne. Who so will grate upon such nice diversities, in respect that he is ashamed of his countrie; trulie (in mine opinion) his countrie maie be ashamed of him' (Richard Stanyhurst, 'A plaine and perfect description of Ireland', in *Holinshed's Chronicles*, VI (London, 1807–8), p. 2). On the relationship between

Spenser and Stanyhurst, see my 'Spenser's *View* and Stanyhurst's *Description*', *Notes and Queries* 241, 2 (1996), pp. 140–2. For a trenchant reading of discourses of discrimination in Irish history that covers a later period, and from a different angle, see Luke Gibbons, 'Race against Time: Racial Discourse and Irish History', *Oxford Literary Review* 13 (1991), special issue on *Neocolonialism*, ed. Robert Young, pp. 95–117.

Chapter 5

1. On the 'British Problem', see Conrad Russell, 'The British Problem and the English Civil War', *History* 72, 236 (1987), pp. 395–415; 'The British Background to the Irish Rebellion of 1641', *Historical Research* 61, 145 (1988), pp. 166–82; David Stevenson, 'The Century of the Three Kingdoms', in *Scotland Revisited*, ed. Jenny Wormald (London: Collins & Brown, 1991), pp. 107–18.
2. All references to Bacon are by volume and page number from James Spedding, Robert Leslie Ellis, and Douglas Denon Heath (eds), *The Works of Francis Bacon*, 15 vols. (London, 1857–74); and Spedding (ed.), *The Life and Letters of Francis Bacon*, 7 vols. (London, 1861–74).
3. See, for example, Clare Carroll, 'The Construction of Gender and the Cultural and Political Other in *The Faerie Queene* and *A View of the Present State of Ireland*: The Critics, the Context, and the Case of Radigund', *Criticism* 32, 2 (1990), pp. 163–92; Andrew Hadfield, 'The Course of Justice: Spenser, Ireland and Political Discourse', *Studia Neophilologica* 65 (1993), pp. 187–96; Thomas N. Corns, 'Milton's *Observations upon the Articles of Peace*: Ireland under English Eyes', in David Loewenstein and James Grantham Turner (eds), *Politics, Poetics, and Hermeneutics in Milton's Prose* (Cambridge University Press: Cambridge, 1990), pp. 123–34; Jim Daems, 'Dividing Conjunctions: Milton's *Observations Upon the Articles of Peace*', *Milton Quarterly* 33,2 (May 1999), pp. 51–5; Christopher Hill, 'Seventeenth-century English Radicals and Ireland', in Patrick J. Corish (ed.), *Radicals Rebels and Establishments: Historical Studies* 15 (Appletree Press: Belfast, 1985), pp. 33–49; David Loewenstein, '"An Ambiguous Monster": Representing Rebellion in Milton's Polemics and *Paradise Lost*', *Huntington Library Quarterly* 55 (1992), pp. 295–315; Paul Stevens, 'Spenser and Milton on Ireland: Civility, Exclusion, and the Politics of Wisdom', *Ariel* 26, 4 (1995), pp. 151–67; Denise Albanese, '*The New Atlantis* and the Uses of Utopia', *ELH* 57 (1990), pp. 503–28.
4. F. J. Levy, 'Francis Bacon and the Style of Politics', *ELR* 16 (1986); p. 117.
5. Willy Maley, 'How Milton and Some Contemporaries Read Spenser's *View*', in *Representing Ireland: Literature and the Origins of Conflict, 1534–1660*, eds. Brendan Bradshaw, Andrew Hadfield and Willy Maley (Cambridge: Cambridge University Press), pp. 191–208.
6. Sir John Davies, *A Discoverie of the True Causes why Ireland was never entirely Subdued, nor brought under Obedience of the Crowne of England,*

untill the Beginning of his Majesties happie Raigne (London, 1612); William Petty, 'A Treatise of Ireland', 1687', in *Economic Writings of Sir William Petty*, ed. C. H. Hull, 2 vols. (Cambridge, 1899), 2, pp. 545–621.

7.　Bacon, *Works* 5: 36

8.　Bacon, *Works* 4: 16.

9.　*Ben Jonson: The Complete Poems*, ed. George Parfitt (Harmondsworth: Penguin, 1975; rept. 1984), p. 36.

10.　Michael Perceval-Maxwell, *The Scottish Migration to Ulster in the reign of James I* (London: Routledge, 1973), p. 22.

11.　Perceval-Maxwell, *The Scottish Migration to Ulster*, p. 64.

12.　J. Michael Hill, 'The origins of the Scottish plantations in Ulster to 1625: a reinterpretation', *Journal of British Studies* 32 (January 1993), p. 25.

13.　Edmund Campion, *Two Bokes of the Histories of Ireland* (1571), ed. A. F. Vossen (Assen, Netherlands: Van Gorcum, 1963), p. 149.

14.　Campion, *Two Bokes of the Histories of Ireland*, pp. 149–50.

15.　Robert Dunlop, 'Sixteenth-century Schemes for the Plantation of Ulster', *Scottish Historical Review* 22, 87 (1925), p. 211.

16.　Toby Barnard, 'Planters and Policies in Cromwellian Ireland', *Past and Present* 61 (1973), p. 33.

17.　Michael MacCarthy-Morrogh, *The Munster Plantation: English Migration to Southern Ireland, 1583–1641* (Oxford: Clarendon Press, 1986), pp. 130–5; Anthony J. Sheehan, 'The Overthrow of the Plantation of Munster in October 1598', *The Irish Sword* 15, 58 (1982), pp. 11–22.

18.　Cited Perceval-Maxwell, *The Scottish Migration to Ulster*, p. 11.

19.　David Stevenson, 'Ulster 1641 in the Context of Political Developments in the Three Kingdoms', in *Ulster 1641: Aspects of the Rising*, ed. Brian Mac Cuarta (Belfast: Institute of Irish Studies, The Queen's University of Belfast, 1993), p. 94.

20.　Cited Perceval-Maxwell, *The Scottish Migration to Ulster*, p. 11.

21.　*Conditions to be observed by the Brittish Undertakers of the Escheated Lands in Ulster* (London, 1610), 5; Perceval-Maxwell, p. 64.

22.　Hiram Morgan, 'The End of Gaelic Ulster: A Thematic Interpretation of Events between 1534 and 1610', *Irish Historical Studies* 26, 101 (1988), p. 31.

23.　Morgan, 'The End of Gaelic Ulster', p. 32.

24.　Bacon, *Works* 7: 660.

25.　Bacon, *Works* 11: 4, 114. Further references to the 'Considerations' will be cited by page number in the text. Elsewhere, Bacon alludes to Ireland as a 'younger sister to Great Britain'. See Constantia Maxwell, *Irish History from Contemporary Sources (1509–1610)* (London: Allen and Unwin, 1923), p. 215, cited in Christopher Highley, *Shakespeare, Spenser, and the Crisis in Ireland* (Cambridge: Cambridge University Press, 1997), p. 163.

26.　Hans S. Pawlisch, *Sir John Davies and the Conquest of Ireland: A Study in Legal Imperialism* (Cambridge: Cambridge University Press, 1985), p. 30.

27.　Bacon, *Works* 6: 531.

28.　Charles Whitney, *Francis Bacon and Modernity* (New Haven and London: Yale University Press, 1986), p. 225, n.20.

29. Judith Anderson, '"But we shall teach the lad another language": History and Rhetoric in Bacon, Ford, and Donne', *Renaissance Drama* n.s. 20, ed. Mary Beth Rose (Evanston, Ill.: Northwestern University Press and The Turnberry Library Center for Renaissance Studies, 1989), p. 171.
30. Clark Hulse, 'Spenser, Bacon, and the Myth of Power', in *The Historical Renaissance: New Essays on Tudor and Stuart Literature and Culture*, eds Heather Dubrow and Richard Strier (Chicago: University of Chicago Press, 1988), p. 338.
31. Bacon, *Life and Letters* 10:3, 313.
32. Ibid., 321.
33. Ibid., 92.
34. Ibid., 218.
35. Ibid., 96; 97.
36. Ibid., 10:3, 99.
37. Bacon, *Works* 6, 216.
38. Bacon, *Life and Letters* 10:3, 222.
39. Keith G. Robbins, *Insular Outsider? 'British History' and European Integration: The Stenton Lecture 1989* (Reading: University of Reading, 1990), p. 15.
40. Bacon, *Life and Letters* 10:3, 228.
41. Ibid., 322–3.
42. Ibid., 325.
43. Ibid., 310.
44. Ibid., 312.
45. Ibid., 313.
46. Cited in Brian P. Levack, *The Formation of the British State: England, Scotland and the Union, 1603–1707* (Oxford: Clarendon, 1987), p. 195.
47. Lisa Jardine, *Francis Bacon: Discovery and the Art of Discourse* (Cambridge: Cambridge University Press, 1974), pp. 166–7.
48. Ian Box, 'Politics and Philosophy: Bacon on the Values of War and Peace', *The Seventeenth Century* 7, 2 (1992), p. 116.
49. Robert K. Faulkner, 'The Empire of Progress: Bacon's Improvement upon Machiavelli', *Interpretation* 20, 1 (1992), pp. 54–60.
50. Cited Perceval-Maxwell, *The Scottish Migration to Ulster*, p. 27.
51. Ibid., p. 26.
52. Bacon, *Works* 9, 131.
53. See Achsah Guibbory, 'Imitation and Originality: Cowley and Bacon's Vision of Progress', *Studies in English Literature, 1500–1900* 29, 1 (1989), pp. 99–120.
54. David Stevenson, 'The Century of the Three Kingdoms', in Jenny Wormald (ed.), *Scotland Revisited* (London: Collins & Brown, 1991), p. 107.
55. Denise Albanese, 'The *New Atlantis* and the Uses of Utopia', *ELH* 57 (1990), p. 503.
56. Albanese, 'The *New Atlantis* and the Uses of Utopia', p. 524; my emphasis.
57. *Sir William Herbert: Croftus Sive de Hibernia Liber*, eds Arthur Keaveney and John A. Madden (Dublin: Irish Manuscripts Commission, 1992), pp. 93, 95.

58. D. B. Quinn, '"A discourse on Ireland (circa 1599)": A Sidelight on English Colonial Policy', *Proceedings of the Royal Irish Academy* 47, Sec. C, No. 3 (1942), p. 166.
59. Davies, *Discoverie*, p. 281.
60. Ibid., p. 286.
61. Ibid., p. 280.
62. John Davies, 'Letter to Salisbury', Coleraine, 28 August 1609, Public Record Office, London, SP 63/227/122.
63. Jenny Wormald, 'The Creation of Britain: Multiple Kingdoms or Core and Colonies?', *Transactions of the Royal Historical Society* 6, 2 (1992), p. 180.

Chapter 6

I am grateful to Andrew Murphy and Ellen-Raïssa Jackson for reading and commenting on an earlier draft of this chapter, and for making a number of helpful suggestions.

1. One could ask whether Shakespeare ever stopped writing histories, as Anne Barton does when she remarks that '*Macbeth* (1606) is surely as much a history play as *Richard II*'. See Anne Barton, 'He that Plays the King: Ford's *Perkin Warbeck* and the Stuart History Play', in Marie Axton and Raymond Williams (eds), *English Drama: Forms and Development* (Cambridge: Cambridge University Press, 1977), p. 70.
2. See L. E. Stock (ed.), *Fames Memoriall, or The Earle of Devonshire Deceased*, in L. E. Stock, Gilles D. Monsarrat, Judith M. Kennedy and Dennis Danielson (eds), *The Nondramatic Works of John Ford* (Binghamton, New York: Medieval and Renaissance Texts and Studies, 1991), Medieval & Renaissance Texts & Studies, vol. 85. Renaissance English Text Society. Seventh series vol. 15, p. 111. I am grateful to Andrew Murphy for directing my attention to this text.
3. See Mildred Clara Struble, *Perkin Warbeck. A Critical Edition of Ford's Perkin Warbeck*, University of Washington Publications in Language and Literature 3 (Seattle: University of Washington Press, 1926), p. 21.
4. All references to *Perkin Warbeck* are to Keith Sturgess (ed.), *John Ford: Three Plays* (London: Penguin, 1970). Ford's revisionist history play has attracted serious critical attention, but its engagement with history is not always viewed in a positive light. See, for example, Joseph Candido, 'The "Strange Truth" of *Perkin Warbeck*', *Philological Quarterly* 59, 3 (1980), pp. 300–16; Ellen Ryan Dubinski, 'The Chronicling of Majesty in *Perkin Warbeck* ', *Iowa State Journal of Research* 59, 3 (1985), pp. 233–40; Dorothy M. Farr, 'Revival of Chronicle History at the Phoenix in *Perkin Warbeck*,' in *John Ford and the Caroline Theatre* (London: Macmillan, 1979), pp. 105–24; Lisa Hopkins, '*Perkin Warbeck*: a Stuart Succession Play?', in *John Ford's Political Theatre* (Manchester: Manchester University Press, 1994), pp. 39–71; Dale B. J. Randall, '*Theatres of Greatness': A Revisionary View of Ford's* Perkin Warbeck

(English Literary Studies: University of Victoria, 1986). For a popular account of the pretender's progress, see Ian Arthurson, *The Perkin Warbeck Conspiracy 1491–1499* (Stroud: Sutton, 1994). See also James Gairdner, *History of the Life and Reign of Richard the Third; to which is added the story of Perkin Warbeck from original documents* (Cambridge: Cambridge University Press, 1898).

5. See Jane Ohlmeyer, *Civil War and Restoration in the Three Stuart Kingdoms: The Career of Randall MacDonnell, Marquis of Antrim, 1609–1683* (Cambridge: Cambridge University Press, 1993), pp. 119, 130.

6. See Stanley Bertram Chrimes, *Henry VII* (London: Eyre Methuen, 1972), p. 81.

7. W. Moelwyn Merchant (ed.), *Christopher Marlowe: Edward the Second* (London: Ernest Benn, 1967), p. 44, II.ii.161–7. Marlowe's play is riddled with references to Ireland. Mortimer Junior warns against Gaveston's Irish exile on the grounds that it will empower rather than disempower him:

> Know you not Gaveston hath store of gold
> Which may in Ireland purchase him such friends
> As he will front the mightiest of us all.

(1.4.258–60)

Later, a supporter of the King urges: 'Shape we our course to Ireland there to breathe' (4.5.3). Even when state censorship denied it the oxygen of publicity, Ireland remained a vital breathing-space for English exiles, royal, recusant, or republican.

8. P. H. Davidson (ed.), *Shakespeare: Henry IV Part One* (Harmondsworth: Penguin, 1968), p. 47, I.i.1–9. Anne Barton has pointed out this common comparison. See Barton, 'He that plays the king', p. 83.

9. Warbeck's followers include John a-Water, 'sometimes Mayor of Cork'. For a discussion of Perkin Warbeck's bases of support in Ireland, see Steven G. Ellis, *Tudor Ireland: Crown, Community and the Conflict of Cultures, 1470–1603* (London: Longman, 1985), pp. 72–83. See also Agnes Conway, *Henry VII's Relations with Scotland and Ireland, 1585–1498* (Cambridge: Cambridge University Press, 1932), especially Chapter VI, 'Anglo-Scottish and Anglo-Irish Relations, 1496–98', pp. 99–117; Steven G. Ellis, 'Henry VII and Ireland, 1491–1496', in James F. Lydon, *England and Ireland in the Later Middle Ages* (Dublin: Royal Irish Academy, 1981), pp. 237–54. For a useful sidelight on Yorkist activity in Ireland, and on Ireland as a haven for claimants to the English throne, see Art Cosgrove, 'Parliament and the Anglo-Irish Community: The Declaration of 1460', in Art Cosgrove and J. I. McGuire (eds), *Parliament and Community*, *Historical Studies* 14 (Belfast, 1983), pp. 25–41. Cosgrove maintains that: 'By the opening of 1460 it had become clear that, while Henry VI ruled in England, his authority was no longer effective in the two English "Pales" – in France and in Ireland' (p. 25).

10. Struble, *Perkin Warbeck. A Critical Edition of Ford's Perkin Warbeck*, pp. 33–4.
11. See Gary Taylor (ed.), *Henry V*, The Oxford Shakespeare (Oxford: Oxford University Press, 1982), I.ii.136–53. Taylor conjectures that the scene with Jamy was cut from Henry V to placate James. See Taylor (ed.), *Henry V*, Appendix F, p. 313. My own impression is that negative images of Scots were arguably more of an issue immediately before the Union than after it, when the Stuart succession was secure. That is, anti-Scottish sentiment was more of an issue for James VI than James I. One thinks here of the Scottish king's objections, voiced in 1596, to Spenser's representation of his mother as Duessa in V.ix of *The Faerie Queene* (1596), an objection that can hardly have been sustained given the publication of the poet's complete works in 1613, complete with the offending passage. The matter is discussed in my *Salvaging Spenser: Colonialism, Culture and Identity* (London: Macmillan, 1997), pp. 156–60. See also Richard McCabe's exemplary essay, 'The Masks of Duessa: Spenser, Mary Queen of Scots, and James VI', *English Literary Renaissance* 17, 2 (1987), pp. 224–42.
12. One historian has observed that sixteenth-century Scotland 'was imperial in the sense of its unassailable sovereignty', but 'in no way constituted a multiple state', despite its claims to the Isle of Man, to Ulster, and to the northern counties of England. See Arthur H. Williamson, 'Scots, Indians and Empire: The Scottish Politics of Civilization, 1519–1609', *Past and Present* 150 (1996), pp. 75–6.
13. See Patricia Parker, *Shakespeare from the Margins: Language, Culture, Context* (Chicago: The University of Chicago Press, 1996), pp. 168–9.
14. G. K. Hunter (ed.), *Shakespeare: Macbeth* (Harmondsworth: Penguin, 1967; 1984), II.iii.3–4.
15. See Glanmor Williams, *Henry Tudor and Wales* (Cardiff: University of Wales Press, 1985), p. 73.
16. On Henry VII's relations with Wales, see Williams, *Henry Tudor and Wales*. See also Brendan Bradshaw, 'The Tudor Reformation and Revolution in Wales and Ireland: The Origins of the British Problem', in Brendan Bradshaw and John Morrill (eds), *The British Problem, c.1534–1707: State Formation in the Atlantic Archipelago* (London: Macmillan, 1996), pp. 39–65. For another perspective, see Ciarán Brady, 'Comparable Histories?: Tudor Reform in Wales and Ireland', in Steven G. Ellis and Sarah Barber (eds), *Conquest and Union: Fashioning a British State, 1485–1725* (London: Longman, 1995), pp. 64–86.
17. See Chrimes, *Henry VII*, p. 245.
18. See Gráinne Henry, 'Ulster Exiles in Europe, 1605–1641', in Brian Mac Cuarta (ed.), *Ulster 1641: Aspects of the Rising* (Belfast: Institute of Irish Studies, Queen's University, 1993), pp. 37–60, p. 39.
19. See Stephen Orgel (ed.), *Ben Jonson: The Complete Masques* (New Haven and London: Yale University Press, 1969), pp. 206–12.
20. Jonas A. Barish, '*Perkin Warbeck* as Anti-history', *Essays in Criticism* 20, 2 (1970), p. 161.
21. See Ohlmeyer, *Civil War and Restoration in the Three Stuart Kingdoms*, pp. 14–17.

22. Philip Edwards, 'The royal pretenders: Ford's *Perkin Warbeck* and Massinger's *Believe as You List* ', in *Threshold of a Nation: A Study in English and Irish Drama* (Cambridge: Cambridge University Press, 1979), p. 185.
23. Alexander Leggatt, 'A Double Reign: *Richard II* and *Perkin Warbeck*', in E. A. J. Honigmann (ed.), *Shakespeare and his Contemporaries* (Manchester: Manchester University Press, 1986), p. 129.
24. See Leggatt, 'A Double Reign'.
25. Mark Thornton Burnett, 'Marlovian Echoes in Ford's *Perkin Warbeck*', *Notes and Queries* 234 (1989), pp. 347–9.
26. See H. J. Oliver, 'The Chronicle Historie of Perkin Warbeck', in *The Problem of John Ford* (London and New York: Cambridge University Press, 1955), p. 106; Joanne Sargeaunt, *John Ford* (Oxford, 1935), cited in Peter Ure, 'Introduction', *The Chronicle History of Perkin Warbeck: A Strange Truth*, The Revels Plays (London: Methuen, 1968), p. 69. Mildred Struble compares *Perkin Warbeck* with *Henry VI Part One*, with the pretender's rebellion mirroring the popular revolt of Jack Cade. See Struble, *Perkin Warbeck. A Critical Edition of Ford's Perkin Warbeck*, p. 16.
27. See J. H. Elliott, 'A Europe of Composite Monarchies', *Past and Present* 137 (1992), p. 51.
28. See Parker, *Shakespeare from the Margins*, p. 1.
29. See Graham Holderness, Bryan Loughrey and Andrew Murphy, 'Busy Doing Nothing: A Response to Edward Pechter', *Textual Practice* 11, 1 (1997), p. 85. For two recent interventions that resonate with the present chapter, see David Armitage, 'Making the Empire British: Scotland in the Atlantic World, 1542–1717', *Past and Present* 155 (1997), pp. 34–63, and Martin Butler, 'The Invention of Britain and the Early Stuart Masque', in R. Malcolm Smuts (ed.), *The Stuart Court and Europe: Essays in Politics and Political Culture* (Cambridge: Cambridge University Press, 1996), pp. 65–85.

Chapter 7

An earlier version of this chapter was read at a seminar at the University of Michigan on 24 February 1997 entitled 'Colonial Contexts: Indians, Irish, and Others.' I would like to thank Linda Gregerson, Steven Mullaney and other participants for comments and criticism. I am also grateful to Tom Luxon, Don Pease and Peter Cosgrove of Dartmouth College, who discussed some of the issues of sovereignty and representation with me and made some valuable suggestions.

1. *Public Record Office, State Papers Domestic Series* 25/62/125.
2. John Milton, 'Observations upon the Articles of Peace', in *John Milton: Complete Prose Works*, ed. M. Y. Hughes (Yale University Press: New Haven, 1962), vol. III, pp. 259–334. All further references to this work will be by page number in the text.
3. See Thomas N. Corns, 'Milton's *Observations upon the Articles of Peace*: Ireland under English Eyes', in David Loewenstein and James Grantham

Turner (eds), *Politics, Poetics, and Hermeneutics in Milton's Prose* (Cambridge University Press: Cambridge, 1990), pp. 123–34; Merritt Y. Hughes, 'The Historical Setting of Milton's *Observations on the Articles of Peace*', *PMLA* 64, 5 (1949), pp. 1049–73; 'The Background of the *Observations upon the Articles of Peace*', *John Milton: Complete Prose Works*, ed. Don Wolfe (Yale University Press: New Haven, 1962), pp. 168–89; Paul Stevens, '"Leviticus thinking" and the Rhetoric of Early Modern Colonialism', *Criticism* 35, 3 (1993), pp. 441–61.

4. Marx and Engels, *Ireland and the Irish Question* (London: Lawrence and Wishart, 1978), p. 395. Marx and Engels recommended raising the issue of Poland when in Russia and Ireland when in England. Politics begins at home. But what exactly were Marx's views on Ireland? Engels wrote to Marx on 24 October 1869: 'Irish history shows one what a misfortune it is for a nation to have subjugated another nation. All the abominations of the English have their origin in the Irish Pale. I have still to plough my way through the Cromwellian period, but this much seems certain to me, that things would have taken another turn in England too, but for the necessity for military rule in Ireland and the creation of a new aristocracy there' (Marx and Engels, *Ireland and the Irish Question*, p. 387). Marx addressed Ludwig Kugelmann on 4 December 1869: 'I have become more and more convinced – and the only question is to drive this conviction home to the English working-class – that it can never do anything decisive here in England until it separates its policy with regard to Ireland most definitely from the policy of the ruling classes, until it not only makes common cause with the Irish but actually takes the initiative in dissolving the Union established in 1801 and replacing it with a free federal relationship. And this must be done, not as a matter of sympathy with Ireland but as a demand made in the interests of the English proletariat. If not, the English people will remain tied to the leading-strings of the ruling classes, because *it* will have to join them in a common front against Ireland. Every one of its movements in England herself is crippled by the strife with the Irish, who form a very important section of the working class in England ... But since the English working class undoubtedly throws the decisive weight into the scale of social emancipation generally, the lever has to be applied here. As a matter of fact, the English republic under Cromwell met shipwreck in Ireland. *Non bis in idem!* [Not twice for the same thing!]' (pp. 394–5). Marx wrote to Engels on 10 December 1869: 'For a long time I believed that it would be possible to overthrow the Irish regime by English working-class ascendancy ... Deeper study has convinced me of the opposite. The English working class *will never accomplish anything* [Marx's emphasis] before it has got rid of Ireland. The lever must be applied in Ireland. That is why the Irish question is so important for the social movement in general. [Referring to parallels between the Elizabethan period and the United Irishmen of the 1790s, Marx adds something that he knows will be] very irksome to the English gentlemen ... that Ireland came to grief because, in fact, from a

revolutionary standpoint, *the Irish were too far advanced for the English King and Church mob*, while on the other hand the English reaction in England had its roots (as in Cromwell's time) in the subjugation of Ireland [Marx's emphasis]' (pp. 397–8). Engels wrote to Jenny Longuet on 24 February 1881: 'The Versailles massacred 30,000 Communards and called that the horrors of the Commune. The English Protestants under Cromwell massacred at least 30,000 Irish and to cover their brutality, *invented* the tale that this was to avenge 30,000 Protestants murdered by the Irish Catholics' (p. 443). Milton was complicit with the atrocity literature of the period, which was used to justify subsequent atrocities. For a Marxist reading of the 1640s that overlooks Ireland, see Norah Carlin, 'Marxism and the English Civil War', *International Socialism*, 2nd series, 10 (1980–81), pp. 106–28. Paradoxically, advocates of the new British history are more in line with Marx's views on the English Revolution than are self-professed English Marxists. Conrad Russell's *Unrevolutionary England, 1603–1642*, is a book that could be read as a vindication of Marx's irksome opinion that 'from a revolutionary standpoint, *the Irish were too far advanced for the English King and Church mob*.' Which is why I was heartened by John Pocock's pronouncement on keeping open lines of communication between the new historiography and apparently outmoded schools of thought: 'I accept all that is said about the need to escape from Whig constitutionalist and Marxist socialist explanations, though when we have escaped from them I want to go back and look at both, and see what may be left of them.' See J. G. A. Pocock, 'The Atlantic Archipelago and the War of the Three Kingdoms', in Bradshaw and Morrill (eds), *The British Problem, c. 1534–1707*, p. 177. I hope I have done enough in this footnote to suggest that Marx's own interpretation of the failure of the English Revolution is not so far removed from the conclusions of the new British history. Indeed, the whole thrust of Marxist-Leninist thought on empire points to the colonial periphery, rather than the putative centre, as the likely site of revolution.

5. Christopher Hill, 'Seventeenth-century English Radicals and Ireland', in Patrick J. Corish (ed.), *Radicals Rebels and Establishments: Historical Studies* 15 (Belfast: Appletree Press, 1985), p. 35. For another perspective, see Norah Carlin, 'Extreme or Mainstream?: the English Independents and the Cromwellian Reconquest of Ireland, 1649–1651', in Bradshaw, Hadfield and Maley (eds), *Representing Ireland*, pp. 209–26.

6. Stevens, '"Leviticus thinking"', p. 456. Although I find the arguments of Tom Corns on the *Observations* generally compelling, he too is of the opinion that Ireland qualified Milton's radicalism: 'Milton's complicity in this dark chapter of Anglo-Irish relations defines the complexities and limitations of his political radicalism.' See Corns, 'Milton's *Observations upon the Articles of Peace*: Ireland under English Eyes', p. 123. My argument is that Milton's radical conception of an expansive Britishness forged in Ireland but fuelled from England is quite in keeping with his status as a colonial republican.

7. See, for example, Paul Stevens, 'Spenser and Milton on Ireland: Civility, Exclusion, and the Politics of Wisdom', *Ariel* 26, 4 (1995), pp. 151–67.

8. See Willy Maley, 'How Milton and Some Contemporaries Read Spenser's *View*', in Brendan Bradshaw, Andrew Hadfield and Willy Maley (eds), *Representing Ireland: Literature and the Origins of Conflict, 1534–1660* (Cambridge: Cambridge University Press, 1993), pp. 191–208.

9. For an example of such an historically undifferentiated account, see Liz Curtis, *Nothing But The Same Old Story: The Roots of Anti-Irish Racism* (London: Information on Ireland, 1984).

10. See Don Wolfe, 'Introduction', *John Milton: Collected Prose Works* vol. I, ed. D. M. Wolfe (Yale University Press: New Haven, 1960), p. 169.

11. See Norah Carlin, 'Extreme or Mainstream?: The English Independents and the Cromwellian Reconquest of Ireland, 1649–1651', in Bradshaw, Hadfield and Maley (eds), *Representing Ireland*, p. 210. For another view that insists on the centrality of religion, see Paul Stevens, '"Leviticus thinking".'

12. See David Armitage, 'John Milton: Poet against Empire', in David Armitage, Armand Himy and Quentin Skinner (eds), *Milton and Republicanism* (Cambridge: University of Cambridge Press, 1995), pp. 205–25. Linda Gregerson takes a similar line: 'Milton's analysis of empire more readily accords with our own than does Spenser's, and that analysis is devastating.' See Linda Gregerson, *The Reformation of the Subject: Spenser, Milton and the English Protestant Epic* (Cambridge: Cambridge University Press, 1995), p. 230. My own feeling is that the difference between the two writers is far less distinct, and Spenser is not the royalist imperialist we have inherited, but the English colonial republican that Milton admired.

13. Andrew Hadfield argues forcefully against the conventional perception of Spenser as an arch-royalist in a compelling essay entitled 'Was Spenser a Republican?', *English* 47 (1998), pp. 169–82.

14. Hughes, 'The Background of the *Observations upon the Articles of Peace*', p. 170.

15. Ibid., p. 171.

16. Hughes, 'The Historical Setting of Milton's *Observations on the Articles of Peace*', p. 1051.

17. David Underdown, 'Civil War in Ireland: Commentary', *Emory University Quarterly* 22, 1 (1966), p. 78.

18. Underdown, 'Civil War in Ireland', p. 79.

19. Ibid.

20. Aidan Clarke, 'The Genesis of the Ulster Rising of 1641', in Peter Roebuck (ed.), *Plantation and Partition: Essays in Honour of J. L. McCracken* (Belfast: Blackstaff Press 1981), p. 33.

21. Ibid.

22. Ibid.

23. Ibid., p. 43.

24. Ibid., p. 44.

25. Cited in J. R. MacCormack, 'The Irish Adventurers and the English Civil War', *Irish Historical Studies* 10 (1956), p. 24.

26. See Lawrence Stone, *The Causes of the English Revolution, 1529–1642* (London: Routledge, 1972), p. 138; my emphasis. If Ireland gets short shrift as a cause of the 'English Revolution', Stone's treatment of Scotland is no less dismissive. Here is how the first British monarch is presented: 'As a hated Scot, James was suspect to the English from the beginning, and his ungainly presence, mumbling speech and dirty ways did not inspire respect. Reports of his blatantly homosexual attachments and his alcoholic excesses were diligently spread back to a horrified countryside.' So much for diligence. Presumably the 'horrified countryside' that James was spoiling with his 'dirty ways' was English. This type of history, however radical it styled itself, was always embarrassingly English-oriented, and thus inclined to yield to other kinds of chauvinism.

27. Milton, *Eikonoklastes* (1649), in M. Y. Hughes (ed.), *Complete Prose Works* III, pp. 470–1.

28. *Eikonoklastes*, p. 478.

29. Milton, *Eikonoklastes*, pp. 595–6.

30. Derek Hirst, 'The English Republic and the Meaning of Britain', in Brendan Bradshaw and John Morrill (eds), *The British Problem, c. 1534–1707* (London: Macmillan, 1996), p. 209.

31. Corns, 'Milton's *Observations upon the Articles of Peace*: Ireland under English Eyes', p. 125. See also Robert Fallon's allusion to 'England's domestic conflicts' in *Captain or Colonel: The Soldier in Milton's Life and Art* (Columbia: University of Missouri Press, 1984), p. 58.

Index